HENRY MINTZBERG
MANAGING

**Financial Times
Prentice Hall
is an imprint of**

Harlow, England • London • New York • Boston • San Francisco • Toronto
Sydney • Tokyo • Singapore • Hong Kong • Seoul • Taipei • New Delhi
Cape Town • Madrid • Mexico City • Amsterdam • Munich • Paris • Milan

PEARSON EDUCATION LIMITED

Edinburgh Gate
Harlow CM20 2JE
Tel: +44 (0)1279 623623
Fax: +44 (0)1279 431059
Website: www.pearsoned.co.uk

First published in North America by Berrett-Koehler Publishers Inc., San Francisco 2009

First published in hardback in Great Britain 2009
First published in paperback in Great Britain 2011

ISBN: 978-0-273-74562-4

British Library Cataloguing-in-Publication Data
A catalogue record for this book is available from the British Library

10 9 8 7 6 5 4 3 2
14 13 12 11

Typeset in 10.5pt Plantin Light by 3
Printed by Ashford Colour Press Ltd., Gosport

MANAGING

FT Prentice Hall
FINANCIAL TIMES

In an increasingly competitive world, we believe it's quality of thinking that gives you the edge – an idea that opens new doors, a technique that solves a problem, or an insight that simply makes sense of it all. The more you know, the smarter and faster you can go.

That's why we work with the best minds in business and finance to bring cutting-edge thinking and best learning practice to a global market.

Under a range of leading imprints, including *Financial Times Prentice Hall*, we create world-class print publications and electronic products bringing our readers knowledge, skills and understanding, which can be applied whether studying or at work.

To find out more about Pearson Education publications, or tell us about the books you'd like to find, you can visit us at **www.pearsoned.co.uk**

PEARSON

To all those
—Saša first of all—
who manage with wisdom and respect.

Contents

About the Author

After studying mechanical engineering at McGill University, Henry Mintzberg worked in Operational Research at the Canadian National Railways before receiving his Master of Science and Ph.D. degrees from the Sloan School of Management at MIT. He has been at the McGill University Faculty of Management ever since—in recent years as Cleghorn Professor of Management Studies—aside from visiting professorships at Carnegie Mellon University, Université d'Aix-Marseille, École des hautes études commerciales of Montreal, London Business School, and Insead. He has also received fifteen honorary degrees from universities around the world.

This is his fifteenth book, which revisits the subject of his first, *The Nature of Managerial Work* (1973). Others include *Structure in Fives* (1983), *Mintzberg on Management* (1989), *The Rise and Fall of Strategic Planning* (1994), *Managers Not MBAs* (2004), and *Strategy Safari* (with Joe Lampel and Bruce Alhstrand; second edition, 2009). He has also published about 150 articles, including two *Harvard Business Review* McKinsey prize-winners.

Henry Mintzberg has received awards from prominent academic and practitioner associations, including the Academy of Management, the Strategic Management Society, and the Association of Management Consulting Firms. He was the first person from a management faculty named to the Royal Society of Canada, and is an Officer of the Order of Canada and l'Ordre national du Québec.

He has been devoting much of his time in recent years to the development of a family of programs in which managers learn by reflecting in small groups on their own experience. These include the International Masters in Practicing Management (www.impm.org), the International Masters for Health Leadership (www.imhl.info), and the Advanced Leadership Program (www.impm-alp.com). This led to the establishment of www.CoachingOurselves.com, which enables groups of managers to learn in this way and drive change in their own workplace.

Henry Mintzberg is completing a monograph entitled "Managing the Myths of Health Care," and is about to devote his time to an electronic pamphlet entitled "Getting Past Smith and Marx . . . toward a Balanced Society," for which he has been collecting materials and doing workshops around the world the past ten years.

Preface

In 1973 I published *The Nature of Managerial Work*, based on my doctoral dissertation—a study of a week in the working lives of five chief executives. I claimed in the preface that, as a kid, I always wondered what my father, the president of a small manufacturing firm, did at the office. I found out some, but not enough.

So six years ago, thirty years later, I decided to revisit the subject, determined to find out what my wife, a manager in the world of telecommunications, did at the office. Not that I believed managing had changed; I changed, or at least I hope so. (Whoever reads both books can be the judge of what I learned over the years.)

This time I based the book on a day I had spent in the working lives of twenty-nine managers, of all kinds. So I must begin by thanking the twenty-nine people (named in a table a few pages forward) who opened up their jobs and their thoughts for this "fly on the wall." You will become aware of their contribution to this book from beginning to end.

Many other people have contributed profoundly in other ways. My personal assistant these past ten years, Santa Balanca-Rodrigues, outdid herself on this one. At one point she was going flat-out, almost literally around the clock, to get the manuscript to the publisher. I am deeply indebted to her, as much as a friend with her wise and concerned counsel as for her direct contribution to the manuscript.

Gui Azevedo, my superresourceful research assistant, contributed in a number of ways (not least in cracking the nut of how to show the model of managing in Chapter 3: "You call them planes," he said, "so why don't you show them that way?" I never thought of that!). Then, when Gui was called by the Amazon (river, not .com), Nathalie Tremblay stepped in to clean up the manuscript wonderfully well.

I ran the two trickiest chapters (4 and 6) past the members of our doctoral colloquium and received many helpful ideas. I want to single out Brian King, who provided a good deal of thoughtful comment. Jacinthe Tremblay also helped out on the conundrums of managing in Chapter 5.

I am blessed to have worked again on this book with people who continue to practice publishing in the old-fashioned way: with deep and respectful concern for the contents of their books and the thoughts of their authors. Steve Piersanti, who has created a very special operation at Berrett-Koehler in the United States, and Richard Stagg, who heads up a team of highly competent people in trade management at Pearson in the U.K., both offered much detailed input, especially in ways that have brought this book closer to its readers. Writers love words, or they wouldn't write. The trouble is that they love their own words best of all. At one point, I finally got the message of *their* words, and that turned this book around.

Both publishing houses also sent the book out to a number of reviewers who provided very useful feedback. I would like to mention especially Charlie Dorris, Jeff Kulick, Stefan Tengblad, and Linda Hill. Once again, Michael Bass and his team brought their considerable skills to production; my special thanks to Laura Larson for the copyediting.

Finally, a great big heartfelt thank you to the manager in my life. Saša, who knows all this far better than I do, was a constant source of subtle but for me "Gee whiz!" comments and contributed in so many other ways.

Henry Mintzberg
Montreal
May 2009

A Note to the Reader

This book is written for everyone interested in the practice of managing—managers themselves, people who work with managers (in selection, assessment, and development, etc.), and others who want to understand managing better (scholars, teachers, students, other nonmanagers). All have different needs, so let me offer some guidance.

Please note first that **I have highlighted key sentences throughout this book in boldface**, to serve as a running summary of its main points. (There are no summaries in the introduction or conclusion to each chapter; in my view, these boldface sentences do it more effectively and no less efficiently, by being embedded in the text that they summarize.) If you are one of those busy managers described in Chapter 2, or anyone else short of time, you can use these sentences to follow the thread of the argument, probing around the points you find of greatest interest.

The first two chapters of this book are its shortest and sharpest: they set the tone. The next two are longer and more involved, because they address the substance of managing, which is no simple matter. And the last two, of intermediate length, are more applied and in places more fun—at least for me to write and I hope for you to read. A few words on each follow.

Chapter 1: Managing Ahead   This introduces the book and my view of managing. I suggest you read all of this.

Chapter 2: The Dynamics of Managing   This should be easy reading—or scanning, for that matter. You might wish to give special attention to the last section, on "The Impact of the Internet" (starting on page 34).

Chapter 3: A Model of Managing   This is a more intricate chapter, presenting what I see as the essence of managing. You can get a good sense of it from the boldface sentences, but I cannot single out any special section; as I conclude, this is a model whose components cannot be isolated. Readers who know little about managing will find Chapters 2 and 3 the most helpful.

Chapter 4: The Untold Varieties of Managing   This was the toughest chapter to write and perhaps also to read—because, I like to believe, of the sheer varieties of managing. Again, the boldface sentences can help. The second-to-last section, on the "Postures of Managing" (starting on page 133), pull the ideas of this chapter together. A number of controversial points in this chapter, especially about the failure of ostensibly key factors (such as culture and personal style) to explain much of *what managers do* (from pages 102 and 121, respectively), may be of special interest to researchers and specialists in management development.

Chapter 5: The Inescapable Conundrums of Managing   I had a great time writing this chapter and suspect that you may especially enjoy reading it, particularly if you are a manager and so live with these things every day. This is the most applied chapter of the book; hence, managers, especially those who think there is some kind of magic bullet, should read this carefully.

Chapter 6: Managing Effectively   Much of this chapter should be easy and enjoyable reading, especially the opening on "The Inevitably Flawed Manager" (starting on page 196) and the closing on "Managing, Naturally" (page 232), as well as the discussion of "Where Has All the Judgment Gone?" (page 225). People who advise and support managers may wish to pay special attention to the section on "Selecting, Assessing, and Developing Effective Managers" (page 219).

Appendix   This describes a day in the life of eight of the managers discussed in the book. Full descriptions of all twenty-nine days observed, and my conceptual interpretations of them, are presented at www.mintzberg-managing .com.

1

Managing Ahead

We know more about the motives, habits, and most intimate arcana of the primitive people of New Guinea or elsewhere, than we do of the denizens of the executive suites in Unilever House.

Roy Lewis and Rosemary Stewart (1958:17)

A half century has passed since the words above were written, and they still hold true. Yet it is easy enough to find out what managers do. Observe an orchestra conductor, not in performance but during rehearsal, to break through the myth of the manager on a podium. Sit in as the managing director of a high-technology company joins the discussion of a new project. Take a walk with the manager of a refugee camp as he scans attentively for signs of impending violence.

Finding out what managers do is not the problem; interpreting it is. How do we make sense of the vast array of activities that constitute managing?

A half century ago Peter Drucker (1954) put management on the map. Leadership has since pushed it off the map. We are now inundated with stories about the grand successes and even grander failures of the great leaders. But we have yet to come to grips with the simple realities of being a regular manager.

This is a book about managing, pure if not simple. I have given it a broad title, *Managing*,[1] because it is meant to be basic and comprehensive, about this fundamental practice in its untold variety. We consider the characteristics, contents, and varieties of the job, as well as the conundrums faced by managers and how they become effective. My objective is straightforward. Managing is important for anyone affected by its practice, which in our world of organizations means all of us. We need to understand it better, in order for it to be practiced better.

Those befuddled by some or all of this practice—which hardly excludes managers themselves—should be able to reach for a book that provides insights from evidence, comprehensively, on the big questions. Few books even try; this one does. It addresses questions such as these:

- Are managers too busy managing to contemplate the meaning of management?

- Are leaders really more important than managers?

- Why is so much managing so frenetic? And is the Internet making this better or worse?

- Is the whole question of management style overrated?

- How are managers to connect when the very nature of their job disconnects them from what they are managing?

- Where has all the judgment gone?

- How is anyone in this job to remain confident without becoming arrogant? Or to keep success from becoming failure?

- Should managing be restricted to managers?

Whatever Happened to Managing?

I began my career on this subject: for my doctoral thesis, I observed one week in the working life of five chief executives. This led to a book called *The Nature of Managerial Work* (1973) and an article called "The

---

[1] The title was inspired by Studs Terkel's book *Working* (1974), in which he had all kinds of people describe the work that they do

Manager's Job: Folklore and Fact" (1975). Both were well received. My research also led to a stream of replication studies.[2]

But that stream died out, and today we find remarkably little systematic study of managing. Many books are labeled "management," but not much of their contents are about managing (Brunsson 2007:7; Hales 1999:339).[3] Look for the best evidence-based books on the subject, and you will likely settle on Len Sayles's *Leadership: What Effective Managers Really Do and How They Do It* (1979), John Kotter's *The General Managers* (1982), Robert Quinn et al.'s *Becoming a Master Manager* (1990), and Linda Hill's *Becoming a Manager* (first edition, 1992). Notice the dates.

As a consequence, our understanding of managing has not advanced. In 1916, the French industrialist Henri Fayol published *General and Industrial Administration* (English translation, 1949), in which he described managing as "planning, organizing, commanding, coordinating, and controlling." Eighty years later, a Montreal newspaper reported the job description of the city's new director-general: "responsible for planning, organizing, directing, and controlling all city activities" (Lalonde 1977:1). So remains our prevalent understanding as well.

For years I have been asking groups of people in this job, "What happened the day you became a manager?" The response is almost always the same: puzzled looks, then shrugs, and finally comments such as "Nothing." You are supposed to figure it out for yourself, like sex, I suppose, usually with equivalently dire initial consequences. Yesterday you were playing the flute or doing surgery; today you find yourself managing people who are doing these things. Everything has changed. Yet you are

---

[2] I was told that upon publication of this article in the *Harvard Business Review*, it elicited the highest request for reprints of any article the Review had published to that time. Some of the replication studies are cited in Chapter 2.

[3] A student of mine, Farzad Khan, did a search for the word *manager* in the citations and abstracts of articles published in the thirteen most prominent academic journals and the five most prominent practitioner ones from 1995 to 2004. Of those that came up, he considered how many were about the nature of managerial work: 27 out of the 669 articles in the academic journals and 53 out of the 793 articles in the practitioner journals (most of these in the *Harvard Business Review*, but still less than 10 percent of its total: 37 out of 400). There were 3/74 in the *Academy of Management Journal*, 1/25 in *Administrative Science Quarterly*, and 2/150 in the *Sloan Management Review*. In a 1986 article entitled "What Managers Do: A Critical Review," Hales included a table on "principal sources of evidence on managerial work." It listed twenty-six studies, three published in the 1980s, seven in the 1970s, and another seven in the 1960s; the most active decade was the 1950s, with nine. One notable exception today is Tengblad's work (2000, 2002, 2003, 2004, 2006).

on your own, confused. "The new managers learned through experience what it meant to be a manager" (Hill, second edition, 2003:9).

Accordingly, in this book I revisit the nature of managerial work, retaining some of my earlier conclusions (in Chapter 2), reconceiving others (in Chapters 3 and 4), and introducing new ones (in Chapters 5 and 6).

Some Sobering Reality

- Because he was Sales Manager for Global Computing and Electronics at BT in the U.K., you might have expected Alan Whelan to have been meeting customers, or at least working with his people to help them sell to customers. On this day, Alan was selling, all right, but to an executive of his own company, who was reluctant to sign off on his biggest contract. Was Alan planning, organizing, commanding, coordinating, or controlling?

- "Top" managers take the long view, see the "big picture"; "lower"-level managers deal with the narrower, immediate things. So why was Gord Irwin, Front County Manager of the Banff National Park, so concerned with the environmental consequences of a parking lot expansion at a ski hill, while back in Ottawa, Norman Inkster, Superintendent of the whole Royal Canadian Mounted Police, was watching clips of last night's television news to head off embarrassing questions to his minister in Parliament that day?

- And why was Jacques Benz, Director-General of GSI, a high-technology company in Paris, sitting in on a meeting about a customer's project? He was a senior manager, after all. Shouldn't he have been back in his office developing grand strategies? Paul Gilding, Executive Director of Greenpeace International, was trying to do just that, with considerable frustration. Who had it right?

- Fabienne Lavoie, Head Nurse on 4 Northwest, a pre- and postoperation surgical ward in a Montreal hospital, was working from 7:20 A.M. to 6:45 P.M. at a pace that exhausted her observer. At one point, in the space of a few minutes, she was discussing a dressing with a surgeon, putting through a patient's hospital card, rearranging her scheduling board, speaking with someone in reception, checking on a patient who had a fever, calling to fill in a vacancy, discussing some medication, and chatting with a patient's relative. Is managing supposed to be that hectic?

- Finally, what about the famous metaphor of the manager as orchestra conductor, magnificently in charge so that the whole team can make beautiful music together? Bramwell Tovey of the Winnipeg Symphony Orchestra stepped off his podium to talk about the job. "The hard part," he said, "is the rehearsal process," not the performance. That's less grand. And how about being in such control? "You have to subordinate yourself to the composer," he said. So, does the orchestra "director" actually direct the orchestra—exercise that famous leadership? "We never talk about 'the relationship,'" was the response. So much for that metaphor.

Twenty-nine Days of Managing

I could go on. This is the tip of the managerial iceberg. I spent a day with each of these and other managers—twenty-nine in all—observing, interviewing, reviewing their diaries over a week or a month, to interpret what was going on. The evidence from that research informs this book.

As shown in Table 1.1, these managers came from business, government, health care, and the social sector (nongovernmental organizations [NGOs], not-for-profits, etc.),[4] and from all sorts of organizations, including banking, policing, filmmaking, aircraft production, retailing, telecommunications. Some of these organizations were tiny, others huge (from 18 to 800,000 employees). These managers spanned all the conventional levels of the hierarchy, from the so-called top and middle to the base. Some worked in major urban centers (London, Paris, Amsterdam, Montreal); others, in more out-of-the-way places (N'gara, Tanzania; New Minas, Nova Scotia; the Banff National Park in western Canada). Some were observed singly; others, in clusters (e.g., three managers of the Canadian parks, who reported to each other, on three successive days).

For each day (or cluster of days), I described what I saw and then interpreted it in conceptual terms. I let each speak for itself. And speak

---

[4] Some of these managers could have been put elsewhere. Many of the health care managers worked for government (although the status of hospitals in the National Health Service of England was shifting to the social sector). Doctors Without Borders could have been put under health care, and the Paris Museum under government (since it was responsible to the city of Paris).

Table 1.1 THE TWENTY-NINE MANAGERS OBSERVED*

	BUSINESS	GOVERNMENT	HEALTH CARE	SOCIAL SECTOR
Management Overall ("Top")	*John Cleghorn* CEO Royal Bank of Canada *Jacques Benz* Director-General, GSI (Paris) *Carol Haslam* Managing Director, Hawkshead Ltd. (film company, London) *Max Mintzberg* Co president, The Telephone Booth (Montreal)	*John Tate* Deputy Minister, Canadian Department of Justice *Norm Inkster* Commissioner, Royal Canadian Mounted Police (RCMP)	*Sir Duncan Nichol* CEO, National Health Service of England (NHS) *"Marc"* Hospital Executive Director (Quebec)	*Paul Gilding* Executive Director, Greenpeace International (Amsterdam) *Dr. Rony Brauman*, Président Médecins sans frontiers (Paris) *Catherine Joint-Dieterle* Conservateur en chef, Musée de la mode et le la costume (Paris) *Bramwell Tovey* Conductor, Winnipeg Symphony Orchestra
Management in Between ("Middle")	*Brian Adams* Director, Global Express, Canadair (Bombardier, Montreal) *Alan Whelan* Sales Manager, Global Computing and Electronics Sector, BT (London)	*Glen Rivard* General Counsel, Family and Youth Law, Canadian Department of Justice *Doug Ward* Director of Programming CBC Radio, Ottawa *Allen Burchill* Commanding Officer, "H" Division, RCMP (Halifax) *Sandra Davis* Regional Director-General, Parks Canada (Calgary) *Charlie Zinkan* Superintendent Banff National Park (Alberta)	*Peter Coe* District General Manager (North Hertfordshire), NHS *Ann Sheen* Director of Nursing Services, Reading Hospitals, NHS	*Paul Hohnen* Director Toxic Trade, Forests, Economic and Political Units, Greenpeace International (Amsterdam) *Abbas Gullet* Head of Subdelegation, International Red Cross Federation (N'gara, Tanzania)
Management at the Base ("Bottom")		*Gordon Irwin* Front Country Manager, Banff National Park (Alberta) *Ralph Humble* Commander, New Minas Detachment, RCMP (Nova Scotia)	*Dr. Michael Thick* Liver Transplant Surgeon St. Mary's Hospital (London), NHS *Dr. Stewart Webb* Clinical Director (Geriatrics), St. Charles Hospital (London), NHS *Fabienne Lavoie* Head Nurse, 4 Northwest, Jewish General Hospital (Montreal)	*Stephen Omollo* Manager, Benac and Lukole Camps, International Red Cross Federation (N'gara, Tanzania)

*Note: In the text of this book, I sometimes refer to some of these managers by first name, and others by formal title, according to what seemed most natural to me.

they did—for example, about how old-fashioned managing by exception can be very up-to-date; about how the managers of Greenpeace have to give as much attention to the sustainability of their organization as to the sustainability of our environment; about how the real politics of government may happen on the ground, where the bears meet the tourists. These days also spoke to the wide variety of contexts in which management happens: I found myself holding on the back of a motorcycle for dear life at it raced through Paris, from one press interview to another; sitting alone in a concert hall of 2,222 velvet seats watching a conductor rehearsing an orchestra; lunching once in a restaurant established by an enterprising refugee in an African camp, and another time freezing in the Greenpeace cafeteria in Amsterdam; walking in a pristine park discussing "bear jams" (traffic jams caused by motorists who stop to see the bears that have ambled down to the highway). All of this, I assure you, provides a wonderful setting to contemplate management and life—since managing is about so much of life.

A single day, albeit reinforced by discussion of other days, is hardly a long time. But it is remarkable what can come from straight and simple observation, with no agenda other than letting reality hit you in the face. As Yogi Berra, the sage of American baseball, put it: "You can observe a lot just by watching." Combine all twenty-nine days, and you have a good deal of evidence about the practice of managing.

Throughout the book, I weave in illustrations from these twenty-nine days, both the descriptions of what happened and the conceptual interpretations of why it happened. Eight of these descriptions are reproduced in the appendix, to anchor the book. The descriptions and interpretations of all twenty-nine days have been made available on a Web site (www.mintzberg-managing.com). To give a sense of this, let me quote some of the titles of the write-ups that appear on the site and figure in the later chapters:

- "Managing on the Edges"—about the political pressures experienced by those managers in the Canadian parks

- "Managing Up, Down, In, and Out"—about the effects of hierarchical level on five managers of the huge National Health Service (NHS) of England, from the chief executive to two head clinicians in hospitals

- "Hard Dealing and Soft Leading"—about the contrast in the work of the head of a film company, between managing externally and internally

- "The Yin and Yang of Managing"—contrasting the work of two chief executives, one of a fashion museum, the other of Doctors Without Borders, both in Paris but worlds apart

- "Managing Exceptionally"—about two Red Cross managers in that refugee camp in Tanzania, managing by exception in exceptional ways

Before proceeding, it will be helpful in this opening chapter to revisit three other myths that get in the way of seeing managing for what it is: that it is somehow separate from leadership; that it is a science, or at least a profession; and that managers, like everyone else, live in times of great change.

Leadership Embedded in Management and Communityship

It has become fashionable to distinguish leaders from managers (Zaleznik 1977, 2004; Kotter 1990a, 1990b). One does the right things, copes with change; the other does things right, copes with complexity. So tell me, who are the leaders and who are the managers in the examples described earlier? Was Alan Whelan merely managing at BT, and Bramwell Tovey merely leading on, and off, the podium? How about Jacques Benz in that project meeting at GSI? Was he doing the right things or doing things right?

Frankly, I don't understand what this distinction means in the everyday life of organizations. Sure, we can separate leading and managing conceptually. But can we separate them in practice? Or, more to the point, should we even try?

How would you like to be managed by someone who doesn't lead? That can be awfully dispiriting. Well, then, why would you want to be led by someone who doesn't manage? That can be terribly disengaging: how are such "leaders" to know what is going on?[5] As Jim March put it: "Leadership involves plumbing as well as poetry" (2004:173).

I observed John Cleghorn, Chairman of the Royal Bank of Canada, who developed a reputation in his company for calling the office on his way to the airport to report a broken ATM machine and such things. This bank has thousands of such machines. Was John micromanaging? Maybe he was setting an example that others should keep their eyes open for such problems.

---

[5] "Leaders tend to be twice-born personalities, people who feel separate from their environment. They may work in organizations, but they never belong to them" (Zaleznik 2004:79). How is such a person supposed to lead an organization?

In fact, today we should be more worried about "macroleading"—people in senior positions who try to manage by remote control, disconnected from everything except "the big picture." It has become popular to talk about us being overmanaged and underled. I believe **we are now overled and undermanaged.**

Konosuke Matsushita, who founded the company that carries his name, claimed, "Big things and little things are my job. Middle level arrangements can be delegated." In other words, **leadership cannot simply delegate management; instead of distinguishing managers from leaders, we should be seeing managers *as* leaders, and leadership as management practiced well.**

Whether in the confines of academia or the columns of newspapers, it is a lot easier to muse about the glories of leadership than it is to come to grips with the realities of management. Obviously this comes at the expense of management, but it has also undermined leadership itself. **The more we obsess about leadership, the less of it we seem to get.** In fact, the more we claim to develop leadership in courses and programs (I counted the words *leader* and *leadership* over fifty times on the Harvard MBA Web site in 2007), the more we get hubris. That is because leadership is earned, not anointed.

Moreover, by putting leadership on a pedestal separated from management, we turn a social process into a personal one. No matter how much lip service is paid to the leader empowering the group, leadership still focuses on the individual: whenever we promote leadership, we demote others, as followers. Slighted, too, is the sense of community that is important for cooperative effort in all organizations. What we should be promoting instead of leadership alone are communities of actors who get on with things naturally, leadership together with management being an intrinsic part of that. Accordingly, **this book puts managing ahead, seeing it together with leadership as naturally embedded in what can be called *communityship.***

Managing as a Practice

After years of seeking these Holy Grails, it is time to recognize that managing is neither a science nor a profession; it is a practice, learned primarily through experience, and rooted in context.[6]

---

[6] What follows draws from my book *Managers Not MBAs* (2004b).

Certainly Not a Science   Science is about the development of systematic knowledge through research. That is hardly the purpose of management, which is about helping to get things done in organizations. Management is not even an applied science, because that is still a science. Management certainly *applies* science: managers have to use all the knowledge they can get. And they certainly use analysis, rooted in the scientific method (meaning here scientific proof more than scientific discovery).

But effective managing is more dependent on art, and is especially rooted in craft. Art produces the "insights," and "vision," based on intuition.[7] (Peter Drucker wrote in 1954 that "the days of the 'intuitive' manager are numbered" [p. 93]. Half a century later, we are still counting.) And craft is about learning from experience—working things out as the manager goes along.

Thus, as shown in Figure 1.1, managing can be seen to take place within a triangle when art, craft, and the use of science meet. Art brings in the ideas and the integration; craft makes the connections, building on tangible experiences; and science provides the order, through systematic analysis of knowledge.[8]

Most of the work that can be programmed in an organization need not concern its managers directly; specialists can do it. That leaves the managers with much of the messy stuff—the intractable problems, the complicated connections. This is what makes the practice of managing so fundamentally "soft," and why labels such as experience, intuition, judgment, and wisdom are so commonly needed to describe it. **Put together a good deal of craft with the right touch of art alongside some use of science, and you end up with a job that is above all a *practice*.** There is no "one best way" to manage; it depends on the situation.

Nor a Profession   It has been pointed out that engineering, too, is not a science or an applied science so much as a practice in its own right (Lewin 1979). But engineering does apply a good deal of science, codified and certified as to its effectiveness. And so it can be called a profession, which means that it can be taught in advance of practice, out of context. In a sense, a bridge is a bridge, or at least steel is steel, even if its

---

[7] "Art is the imposition of a pattern, a vision of a whole, in many disparate parts so as to create a representation of that vision; art is an imposition of order on chaos" (Boettinger 1975:54; see also Vail 1989).

[8] I refer here to being "scientific" in the popular usage, not practicing science, which itself involves a good deal of art and craft.

Figure 1.1 MANAGING AS ART, CRAFT, SCIENCE

use has to be adapted to the circumstances at hand. The same can be said about medicine. But not about management:

> Many medical skills of diagnosis, inference and treatment . . . assume that illness can be decomposed into separate problems that do not differ much between patients and can be treated by fairly standard remedies. . . . In contrast, much managerial work involves dealing with problems that are quite interdependent with other parts of the organization, are specific to this particular firm, market and industry and not readily reduced to a general, standard syndrome that can be treated by a specific technique. (Whitley 1995:92; see also 1989)

Little of management practice has been reliably codified, let alone certified as to its effectiveness. That is why Hill found that people "had to act as managers before they understood what the role was" (2003:45).

Ever since Frederick Taylor (1916) dubbed his work study method the "one best way," we have been searching for the Holy Grail of management in science and professionalism. Today that lives on in the easy formulas of so much of the popular literature, whether "strategic planning," "shareholder value," and so forth. Yet time and time again, the easy answers have failed, giving the illusion of progress while the real problems have continued to fester.

Because of their codified knowledge, engineering and medicine must be learned formally. And so the trained expert can almost always outperform the layperson. Not so in management. Few of us would trust the intuitive engineer or physician, with no formal training, yet we trust all kinds of managers who have never spent a day in a management classroom (and we have suspicions about many of those who spent two years).[9]

What does exist about managing is a good deal of *tacit* knowledge. But *tacit* means not easily accessible, which is why the practice has to be learned on the job, through apprenticeship, mentorship, and direct experience. Moreover, much of that kind of knowledge develops in context— the situation at hand—meaning that the learning cannot easily be carried from one managerial job to another, often not even from one function in a particular organization to another, let alone across organizations and industries. (Could Bramwell have run the bank or Fabienne conduct the orchestra?) Sure, there are managers who succeed at doing so, because they have the ability to learn what they need to know in a new context. But for every one of these, I'll show you many who failed trying.

The true professional knows better, as does the true scientist. The patient does not argue with the surgeon or, for that matter, the surgeon with the molecular biologist. In their own domain, each knows better. But managers who believe they know better get in the way of their practice, because it has to be largely one of facilitation. **The manager, by the definition used here, is someone responsible for a whole organization or some identifiable part of it** (which, for want of a better term, I shall call a unit). To use that old saying, attributed to Mary Parker Follett in the 1920s, managers get things done largely through other people— those in the unit who formally report to them as well as others around it who do not. Managers have to know a lot, especially about their specific contexts, and they have to make decisions based on that knowledge. But especially in large organizations and those concerned with "knowledge work," **the manager has to help bring out the best in other people, so that *they* can know better, decide better, and act better.**

Recently, while criticizing professional management, I was asked, Is there not something professional about the manager who treats his or her

---

[9] See my book *Managers Not MBAs* (Mintzberg 2004b) and Whitley (1989) for detailed arguments about why management is not, and is not likely to become, a profession; see also Brunsson (2007: Chapter 4).

practice nobly, responsibly? Something important, yes, but let's not mix up acting responsibly with practicing a profession. Instead, **let's recognize management as a *calling*, and so appreciate that efforts to professionalize it, and turn it into a science, undermine that calling.**

Managing in Times of Less Change Than You Think

This book draws on research from the 1940s through to the 2000s. My own twenty-nine days of observation took place in the 1990s. Books these days are not supposed to do such things—they are expected to be terribly up-to-date.

Let's try the reverse: terribly up-to-date can get in the way. We risk being mesmerized by the present, and biased by the stories we "know" all too well. A little time between us and the events can be a good thing. Moreover, does date really make a difference? Ask yourself if the examples used earlier struck you as out of date. Does that day in the working life of a sales manager, even in high technology, or a head nurse, not apply now because it happened in the 1990s?[10]

Attend some speech on management. It is likely to begin with the claim that "we live in times of great change." As you hear this, look down at the clothes you are wearing. Notice the buttons, and ask yourself if we really live in times of great change, how come we are still buttoning buttons? Indeed, how come we are still driving automobiles powered by internal combustion four-cycle engines? Weren't these used in the Model T?

Why didn't you notice those buttons when you dressed this morning, or that old technology when you drove to hear about living in times of

---

[10] In 2005, a colleague of mine took out a subscription to the *Harvard Business Review*. In return, he received a complimentary copy of a book of articles called *Leadership Insights*. First in the book was an article of mine from thirty years earlier (Mintzberg 1975b). While we are on this note, some concerns were expressed that none of the twenty-nine managers observed was American. Management writers are not supposed to do this, either. Yet, most management books discuss nothing but American managers. Does it really make a difference whether Bramwell Tovey conducted in Winnipeg instead of Wisconsin? (In Chapter 4, I shall present evidence that national culture has surprisingly little effect on the content of managing.) Maybe some researchers will find it refreshing, and American readers enlightening, to read about managers from other places for a change. One reviewer of this book, a former U.S. corporate chief executive, claimed that when people see the dates of the research and the absence of Americans in it, they will stop reading. I certainly hope so. Anyone who believes that managing has to be terribly up-to-date and necessarily American has picked up the wrong book.

great change? After all, when you arrived at work later, you *did* notice that Windows made another change in its operating system. **The fact is that we only notice what is changing. And most things are not.** Information technology has been changing; we all notice that, same with the economy of late. How about managing?

Managing Today and Yesterday "For all the fashionable hype about leadership, it is unfashionable management that is being practiced and its fundamental characteristics have not changed" (Hales 2001:54). Managers deal with different issues as time moves forward, but not with different managing. The job does not change. We buy new gasoline all the time and new shirts from time to time; that does not mean that car engines and buttons have been changing. Despite the great fuss we make about change, the fact is that basic aspects of human behavior—and what could be more basic than managing and leading?—remain rather stable. (If you doubt this, rent a good old movie about leadership.)

 I was struck during my own earlier study (published in 1973) that the behaviors I observed were probably indistinguishable from that of similar managers of earlier times. Much of the information they needed was different, but they sought it in much the same way—by word of mouth. Their decisions may have concerned the latest technology, but their procedures to make those decisions used little of that technology.

 Has any of that changed now? We might like to think so, but the evidence suggests otherwise.[11] Were management a science, even a profession, it would change. (Medical practice changes constantly.) But management is neither. So aside from the fads that come and go, many of them dysfunctional, managing carries merrily along. Even the new information technologies, especially e-mail—the one thing that does seem to be rendering significant change—may actually be reinforcing long-standing characteristics of managerial work (as we shall discuss in Chapter 2).

[11] Tengblad, for example, probably the most active researcher on managerial work today, concluded from one of his studies, "Managerial work appears to be a relatively stable and evolutionary phenomenon. . . . The many striking similarities between the work behaviors of Swedish CEOs during the forties and those of the nineties indicate the importance of traditions rather than modern technology or fashions in management for deciding the where, when, how, and why of their work" (2000:38).

A Variety of Vintages

Accordingly, I have not hesitated to draw material for this book—examples, evidence, concepts, quotations—from the sources that seem to be most helpful, regardless of their age. Indeed, I hope you agree that the old quotations used in this chapter are some of the best. They have survived for good reason; indeed, like fine wine, they have improved with age.

My book of 1973 described managerial work in two basic ways: the characteristics of the job—namely, its unrelenting pace, many interruptions, oral and action nature, and so forth; and the content of the job, in the form of various roles managers perform (such as figurehead, crises handler). I was more satisfied with the former than the latter, and so Chapter 2, on the "The Dynamics of Managing," draws extensively from that book. I have seen little subsequent evidence to change those conclusions—in fact, I cite a fair amount that supports them.

In contrast, Chapter 3—which is about the content of managing, what managers actually do in their jobs—breaks away from that book. Subsequent to it, I came to realize that it, like most other such books on the subject, offered a list of roles rather than an integrated description of managing. So in the 1990s, I undertook to develop "A Model of Managing" (the title of Chapter 3 here, first published in Mintzberg 1994b), which describes managing on three planes: information, people, and action. I used this model to help me interpret what I saw on those twenty-nine days, and this helps me to illustrate the material of Chapter 3.

The last three chapters, building on the first three, are new, fully up-to-date—but about my thinking, not about managing. (They could have been included in my 1973 book had I thought about them then. I'm the one who changed.)

Chapter 4 considers "The Untold Varieties of Managing." As I went through the conventional evidence, about how various factors, such as national culture, level in the hierarchy, and personal style, affect the practice of managing, I became increasingly dissatisfied. Something felt wrong: this was not capturing the fascinating variety I observed in the twenty-nine days. So I went back over those days and found that few factors—even personal style—explained much across all of the days. It was the combination of factors that proved revealing. Hence, I conclude this chapter by describing various "postures" that managers assume—such as maintaining the work flow, managing out of the middle, connecting to the external environment—as well as various postures of managing without managers.

Chapter 5 faces head-on "The Inescapable Conundrums of Managing"—basic concerns that managers have to face because they cannot be resolved, such as the Syndrome of Superficiality, the Quandary of Connecting, and the Dilemma of Delegating. I thoroughly enjoyed writing this chapter and hope you can say the same about reading it.

Finally, I am the one who had to face "Managing Effectively" in the last chapter. Many authors have ridden boldly into this subject, particularly on that white leadership horse, only to have ended up on the rear ends of misguided banalities. With trepidation I proceeded, and to my surprise I had a grand time. This chapter muses quite seriously about why every manager, like every other human being, is flawed, yet many succeed. It draws on some published material about happy and unhappy families to consider happily and unhappily managed units. And it concludes that to be an effective manager—even, dare I say, a great leader—maybe you don't have to be wonderful so much as normal, and clearheaded.

As I hope has become evident in this opening chapter, I have written this book not to reinforce conventional wisdom—add to all that stuffy managerial correctness—but to open up perspectives, to get us all probing, pondering, wondering about managing. I don't want you to leave this book knowing. I want you to leave it, as I do, imagining, reflecting, questioning. Managers are only as good as their ability to work things out thoughtfully in their own way. To repeat, this is a job of paradoxes, dilemmas, and mysteries that cannot be resolved. The only guaranteed result of any formula for managing is failure (including, of course, this one).

So ahead we go, to the delights, duties, and distresses of the ancient and contemporary practice of managing.

2

The Dynamics
of Managing

I don't want it good—I want it Tuesday.

Have a look at the popular images of managing—that conductor on the podium, those executives sitting at desks in *New Yorker* cartoons—and you get one impression of the job: well ordered, seemingly carefully controlled. Watch some managers at work and you will likely find something far different: a hectic pace, lots of interruptions, more responding than initiating. This chapter describes these and related *characteristics* of managing: how managers work, with whom, under what pressures, and so on—the intrinsically dynamic nature of the job.

I first described these characteristics in my 1973 book. None of them could have come as a shock to anyone who ever spent a day in a managerial office, doing the job or observing it. Yet they struck a chord with many people—especially with managers—perhaps because they challenged some of our most cherished myths about the practice of managing. Time and again, when I presented these conclusions to groups of managers, the common response was "You make me feel so good! While I thought that all those other managers were planning, organizing, coordinating, and controlling, I was constantly being interrupted, jumping from one issue to another, and trying to keep the lid on the chaos."[1]

---

[1] "I found Mintzberg's article both comforting and challenging. In spite of my various titles: vice-president, production manager, sales manager and mother, I never have been quite sure I was really acting as a manager. Certainly, it never seemed to me that I planned, organized, coordinated or controlled much of anything! If Mintzberg's definitions and observation, backed by his and others research, are true, then I am indeed a manager" (from a course paper written by a manager, not at my own university).

Knowing. And Knowing.   Why should there have been such reactions to what these managers doubtlessly knew already? My explanation is that, as human beings, we "know" in two different ways. Some things we know consciously, explicitly; we can verbalize them, often because we have so often read or heard about them. Other things we know viscerally, tacitly, based on our experience.

Surely we function best when these two kinds of knowing reinforce each other. In managing, they have all too often contradicted each other, requiring managers to live a myth—the folklore of planning, organizing, and so on, compared with the facts of daily managing. So **if we wish to make significant headway in improving the practice of managing, we need to bring the covert reality in line with the overt image.** That is the intention of this chapter.

Characteristics Then and Now

In this chapter I draw extensively on the conclusions of my earlier book because subsequent research has almost universally supported these conclusions. For example, in a parallel study of four senior executives a decade later, three from the same industries of my study, Kurke and Aldrich reported "an amazing degree of similarity" and called the original conclusions "surprisingly robust" (1983:977).[2] I will cite some of these studies as we go along and also use evidence from the twenty-nine days of my later research to illustrate these characteristics.[3] They are as follows:

- The unrelenting pace of managing

- The brevity and variety of its activities

- The fragmentation and discontinuity of the job

- The orientation to action

- The favoring of informal and oral forms of communication

- The lateral nature of the job (with colleagues and associates)

- Control in this job as covert more than overt

---

[2] See also Hales (1986, 2001), Hannaway (1989:51, 61), Boisot and Liang (1992), and Morris et al. (1982). Tengblad (2006) supported most of these characteristics but not all, as discussed later.

[3] I did not tabulate actual time allocations in this study so do not provide quantitative comparisons.

As noted in the last chapter, the basic processes of managing do not change much over time, these characteristics perhaps least of all. At the end of this chapter, I shall discuss the one development that should be having a significant impact—the new information technologies (IT), especially e-mail. My conclusion is that they are not so much changing the job as reinforcing these long-standing characteristics, all too often driving them over the edge.

As we go along, I identify a number of conundrums associated with these characteristics as a prelude to probing into each in Chapter 5.

Folklore: The manager is a reflective, systematic planner.

We have this common image of the manager, especially in a senior job, sitting at a desk, thinking grand thoughts, making great decisions, and, above all, systematically planning out the future. There is a good deal of evidence about this, but not a shred of it supports this image.

Facts: Study after study has shown that (a) managers work at an unrelenting pace; (b) their activities are typically characterized by brevity, variety, fragmentation, and discontinuity; and (c) they are strongly oriented to action.

The Managerial Pace   The reports on the hectic pace of managerial work have been consistent, from foremen averaging one activity every forty-eight seconds (Guest 1956:478) and middle managers able to work for at least a half hour without interruption only about once every two days (Stewart 1967), to chief executives, half of whose many activities lasted less than nine minutes (Mintzberg 1973:33). "Over forty studies of managerial work dating back to the 1950s have shown that 'executives just sort of dash around all the time'" (McCall, Lombardo, and Morrison 1988:55).

In my first study, I noted that the work pace of the chief executives I observed was unrelenting. They met a steady stream of callers and mail, from their arrival in the morning until their departure in the evening. Coffee breaks and lunches were inevitably work related, and ever-present people in their organization were ready to usurp any free moment. As one put it to me, **the work of managing is "one damn thing after another."**

In his study of general managers, John Kotter (1982a) referred to the overall demands of this job as adding up to "a particularly stressful situation and a very difficult time management problem," within "a rapid-pace, high-pressure environment." Here is how one manager put it:

> I feel guilty that I'm not doing the things that the management educators, trainers, and the things I read say that I should be doing. When I come out of one of these sessions, or after reading the latest management treatise, I'm eager and ready to do it. Then the first phone call from an irate customer, or a new project with a rush deadline, falls on me, and I'm back in the same old rut. I don't have time for time management. (Barry, Cramton, and Carroll 1997:26–27)

The work of managing an organization is just plain taxing. Morris et al., for example, found that most of the school principal's days were "spent on the run" (1982:689). The quantity of work to be done, or at least that managers choose to do during the day, is substantial, and after hours senior managers appear able to escape neither from a situation that recognizes the power of their position nor from their own predispositions to worry about outstanding concerns.

Why do managers exhibit such paces and workloads? One reason has to be the inherently open-ended nature of the job. Every manager is responsible for the success of the unit, yet there are no tangible mileposts where he or she can stop and say, "Now my job is finished." The engineer completes the design of a bridge on a particular day; the lawyer wins or loses a case at some moment in time. The manager, in contrast, must always keep going, never sure when success is truly assured or that things might come crashing down (see Hill 2003:50). As a result, **managing is a job with a perpetual preoccupation: the manager can never be free to forget the work, never has the pleasure of knowing, even temporarily, that there is nothing left to do.**

The Fragmentation and the Interruptions Most work in society involves specialization and concentration. Engineers and programmers can spend months designing a machine or developing some software; salespeople can devote their working lives to selling one line of products. Managers can expect no such concentration of efforts.

The search for patterns in managerial work—during the day, across the week, over the year—has not found much, aside from a few budgeting periods, and the like. One study of university presidents (Cohen and March 1974:148) noted that they tended to do administrative tasks early in the day and the week, and external and political tasks later, which is not terribly revealing. More so was a comment by Lee Iacocca about his highly visible CEO job: "Some days at Chrysler, I wouldn't have gotten up in the morning if I had known what was coming" (Iacocca, Taylor, and Bellis 1988). A surprising finding of my own initial study is that few of the chief executives' meetings and other contacts were held on a regularly scheduled basis. On average, thirteen out of fourteen were ad hoc.

What we find is a great deal of fragmentation in this work, and on top of that much interruption. Someone calls about a fire in a facility; a few e-mails are then scanned; an assistant comes in to inform about a challenge from a consumer group; then a retiring employee is ushered in to be presented with a plaque; after that it's more e-mails; and soon it's off to a meeting about a bid for a large contract. And so it goes. Most surprising is that **the significant activities seem to be interspersed with the mundane in no particular pattern; hence, the manager must be prepared to shift moods quickly and frequently.**

There are usually some longer meetings in most managers' days, but in my study even many of these tended to get cut short.[4] And they were typically surrounded by many shorter events—quick phone calls, short stints of desk work, spontaneous encounters in the office, trips down the hall, and so forth.

Carlson, in his 1940s study of Swedish managing directors, found that they could barely get twenty-three minutes without interruption once every third day "All they knew was that they scarcely had time to start on a new task or to sit down and light a cigarette before they were interrupted by a visitor or a telephone call" (1951:73–74). Aside from that cigarette, would Carlson find anything different today?

Two studies (Horne and Lupton 1965; Stewart et al. 1994) concluded that there is more fragmentation of managerial work at lower levels in the hierarchy, which is consistent with the Guest finding about foremen averaging forty-eight seconds per activity. And I saw something similar in the day I spent with the head nurse of the hospital ward. But two other first-line managers I observed in this later study—the Front

---

[4] Doktor (1990), who studied Korean and Japanese managers, and Tengblad (2003, 2006), who studied chief executives, reported more time in long meetings, although Tengblad saw fragmentation in another way—in terms of the traveling done by these managers.

County Manager of the Banff National Park and the Detachment Commander of the Royal Canadian Mounted Police—did not so stand out, while several of the chief executives I observed did, including the heads of Doctors Without Borders and the film company in London. Indeed, perhaps the most fragmented day I witnessed was that of another chief executive, the co-owner of the chain of telephone stores. I counted 120 distinct activities, among them the following sequence:

> • At 9:28, Max chats with Lorne, just outside the door, about a soldering problem on some telephones and then turns back to Traci, his assistant, to continue going through the pile of papers. Just then Pierre walks by, and Max requests that he not proceed with some plan, and fifteen seconds later, it is back to Traci with "OK, let's continue." Then Monique, who deals with Accounts Payable, sticks her head in to report back on an earlier request, and seconds later it is back to Traci. Anna, who deals with customer and store service, puts her head in to report with great joy that she has solved a problem. It's now 9:35—seven minutes have passed! (In a later meeting, the controller of the company said to Max, "Let me get a pad. You're throwing so many things at me I have to write it down.")

Carlson concluded in his early study (1951) that managers could free themselves from interruptions by making better use of their secretaries and being more willing to delegate work. But he begged an important question: is brevity, variety, and fragmentation forced on the managers, or do they choose this pattern in their work? My answer is yes—both times.

The five chief executives of my earlier study appeared to be properly protected by their secretaries, and there was no reason to believe that they were inferior delegators. In fact, there was evidence that they sometimes preferred interruption and denied themselves free time. For example, they—not the other parties—terminated many of their meetings and telephone calls, and they themselves often interrupted their quiet desk work to place telephone calls or to request that people come by. One chief executive I studied located his desk so that he looked down a long hallway. The door was usually open, and his reports were continually coming into his office.[5]

Why this preference for interruption? **To some extent, managers tolerate interruptions because they do not wish to discourage the**

---

[5] From Gonzáles and Mark: "Our data confirms previous studies that people interrupt themselves as often as they are interrupted" (2004:119).

flow of current information. Moreover, they may become accustomed to variety in their work, and so boredom develops easily.

More to the point, however, **managers seem to become conditioned by their workload: they develop a sensitive appreciation for the *opportunity cost* of their own time—the benefits forgone by doing one thing instead of attending to another.** They are also acutely aware of the ever-present assortment of obligations associated with their job—the mail that cannot be delayed, the callers that must be received, the meetings that require their participation. Managing, wrote Leonard Sayles in his study of American middle managers, is like "'keeping house' . . . where the faucets almost always drip and dust reappears as soon as it's wiped away" (1979:13).

In other words, **no matter what they are doing, managers are plagued by what they *might* do and what they *must* do.** As the head of a British football (soccer) association commented after the fans had been rioting on the continent: "In this job, one has to be permanently worried!" The realities of their job encourage some particular personality traits: to overload themselves with work, to do things abruptly, to avoid wasting time, to participate only when the value of participation is tangible, to be careful about too much involvement with any one issue. **To be superficial is an occupational hazard of managerial work,** certainly compared with the specialized work most managers did before they went into this job. **To succeed, managers have to become proficient at their superficiality.**

It has been said that an expert is someone who knows more and more about less and less until finally he or she knows everything about nothing. The manager's problem is the opposite: knowing less and less about more and more until finally he or she knows nothing about everything. We shall return to this "Syndrome of Superficiality," as well as other conundrums associated with these characteristics of managerial work, in Chapter 5.

The Action Orientation   Managers like action—activities that move, change, flow, are tangible, current, nonroutine. Don't expect many to spend a lot of time debating abstract issues at work; most prefer to focus on the concrete. And don't expect to find much general planning in this job, or open-ended touring; look instead for tangible delving into specific concerns. Even when it comes to scheduling, "One should never ask a busy executive to promise to do something e.g. 'next week' or even 'next Friday.' Such vague requests do not get entered into [the] appointment diary. No, one has to state a specific time, say, Friday

4:15 P.M., then it will be put down and in due course done" (Carlson 1951:71).

I found in my earlier study that mail processing was treated as a burden. Why? Because little of it was actionable. In those days, it was slow, too. E-mail has certainly changed that—now even the mail has become actionable. But as we shall discuss at the end of this chapter, this may be deceiving.

Managers like current information. It often receives top priority, interrupting meetings, rearranging agendas, and evoking flurries of activity. Of course, current information can be less reliable than that which has had a chance to settle down, get analyzed, and be compared with other information. But managers are often willing to pay this price in order to have information that is up-to-date.

If managers are so action oriented, how do they plan? Snyder and Glueck challenged my conclusion in the 1973 book that "managers do not plan" (1980:76), essentially by pointing out from their study that managers think ahead and consciously interrelate activities. Certainly they do. Managers all plan; we all plan. But that does not make managers the systematic planners depicted in so much of the traditional management literature: people who lock their doors and think great thoughts. Leonard Sayles is worth quoting at length in this regard:

> We . . . prefer not to consider planning and decision making as separate, distinct activities in which the manager engages. They are inextricably bound up in the warp and woof of the interaction pattern and it is a false abstraction to separate them. A good example of this is Dean Acheson's description of what he believed to be the naïveté of the then new Secretary of State [John Foster] Dulles' expectations concerning his job: "He told me that he was not going to work as I had done, but would free himself from involvement with what he referred to as personnel and administrative problems, in order to have more time to think. . . . I wondered how it would turn out. . . ." Later in this same essay, Acheson [commented]: "This absorption with the Executive as Emerson's 'Man Thinking,'" surrounded by a Cabinet of Rodin statues bound in an oblivion of thought . . . seemed to me unnatural. Surely thinking is not so difficult, so hard to come by, so solemn as all this. (1964:208–209)

So the real planning of organizations takes place significantly in the heads of its managers and implicitly in the context of their daily actions, not in some abstract process reserved for a mountain retreat or in a bunch of forms to fill out. This means the plans exist largely as intentions in their heads—a kind of agenda off-line, if you like (off *that* line). Of course, this raises the big question: how are managers to think strategically, to see the "big picture," take the long view? That, again, will be taken up in the conundrums of Chapter 5.

To conclude this point, managers appear to adopt particular activity patterns because of the nature of their work. This is an environment of stimulus-response, encouraging in the incumbent a clear preference for live action. **The pressures of the managerial environment do not encourage the development of reflective planners, the classical literature notwithstanding. This job breeds adaptive information manipulators who prefer the live, concrete situation.**

Folklore: The manager depends on aggregated information, best supplied by a formal system.

In keeping with the classical image of the manager perched on a hierarchical pedestal, managers are supposed to receive their important information from some sort of comprehensive, formalized management information system (MIS). But this has never proved true, not before computers, not after they appeared, not even in these days of the Internet.

Fact: Managers tend to favor informal media of communication, especially the oral ones of telephone calls and meetings, also the electronic one of e-mail.

Consider two surprising findings from earlier studies of managerial work, the first from Carlson on the Swedish managing directors:

> The only complaint heard from some of the chief executives [about the system of internal reports they received] was that the number or size of the reports had a tendency to grow more and more, and that it had become impossible to read them all. . . . These reports . . . form a part of that paper ballast on the executive's desk or in his briefcase, which is the cause of so much mental agony. (1951:89)

This study was done just when the first computer was being invented. Think of all the reports today!

Second is this comment from a study of MIS managers themselves:

> Mintzberg . . . found that chief executive officers placed little reliance on formal information sources. The results reported here, ten years later, suggest a quite similar phenomenon for information systems managers. These managers rarely referred to computer based information systems. . . . Like the shoemaker's children, information systems managers seem to be among the last to directly benefit from the technology they purvey. (Ives and Olson 1981:57)

Oral Communication   My earlier study and others found managing to be between 60 and 90 percent oral. One CEO I studied looked at the first piece of "hard" mail he received all week—a standard cost report—and put it aside with the comment, "I never look at this." It was much the same for the paper mail sent out, with another CEO commenting, "I don't like to write memos, as you can probably tell. I much prefer face-to-face contact." Another said, "I try to write as few letters as possible. I happen to be immeasurably better with the spoken word than with the written word."[6] (E-mail has certainly changed that. But here we are discussing *informal* information, and e-mail, if not its attachments, is often informal too—for example, done more quickly than conventional mail.)

It should be emphasized that, unlike other workers, **the manager does not leave the telephone, the meeting, or the e-mail to get back to work. These contacts *are* the work.** The ordinary work of the unit or organization—producing a product, selling it, even conducting a study or writing a report—is not usually undertaken by its manager. The manager's productive output has to be gauged largely in terms of the information he or she transmits orally or by e-mail. As Jeanne Liedtka of the Darden School has put it (in a talk I attended): "Talk is the technology of leadership."

Soft Information   The managers I studied seemed to cherish soft information. **Gossip, hearsay, and speculation form a good part of the manager's information diet.** Why? The reason appears to be its timeliness; today's gossip can be tomorrow's fact. The manager who is

---

[6] Once, while working with a group of managers, I was asked to offer some comments to their spouses, who were meeting in a nearby room. I talked about these characteristics of managerial work, again to nodding heads. One woman came up to me afterward and said, "My husband never reads the mail [at home]. He asks, 'What did we get today, dear?' I thought he was illiterate!"

not accessible for a quick message or an e-mail advising that the firm's biggest customer was seen golfing with its main competitor may read about it as a dramatic drop in sales in the next quarterly report. But then it's too late.[7] As one manager put it: "I would be in trouble if the accounting reports held information I did not already have" (in Brunsson 2007:17). Of course, plenty of managers have been in such trouble of late, and this point helps to explain why.

Consider these words of Richard Neustadt, who studied the information-collecting habits of Presidents Roosevelt, Truman, and Eisenhower.

> It is not information of a general sort that helps a President see personal stakes; not summaries, not surveys, not the *bland amalgams*. Rather . . . it is the odds and ends of *tangible detail* that pieced together in his mind illuminate the underside of issues put before him. To help himself he must reach out as widely as he can for every scrap of fact, opinion, gossip, bearing on his interests and relationships as President. He must become his own director of his own central intelligence. (1960:153–154; italics added)

Formal information is firm, definitive—at the limit, it comprises hard numbers and clear reports. But informal information can be much richer, even if less reliable. On the telephone, there is tone of voice and the chance to interact. In meetings, there is also facial expressions, gestures, and other body language. Never underestimate the power of these. E-mail does not offer these advantages, but it is a lot faster than conventional mail, and so is somewhat more interactive.[8]

Personal Access   In our master's program for practicing managers (www.impm.org), the participants pair up and spend a week on "managerial exchanges" at each other's workplaces. Time and again, managers who have gone to a foreign place where they did not speak the language reported on how rich was their learning, because they had to focus on these other aspects of communicating. I also heard a story about an

---

[7] Hannaway (1989) has noted some other advantages of oral forms of information: "managers can be sure that their messages are received"; it is less risky for managers, since "there is no unambiguous record" (p. 73); and "it requires less effort" (p. 74).

[8] In my opinion, however, this is less so than it seems. Personally, I have given up typing to use e-mail to do all but the simplest form of scheduling. Much of the time, one phone call works better than half a dozen e-mails because it allows for much greater adaptability to each other's needs.

employee at the Swiss office of an American company. She was disliked by the people at headquarters because she kept "demanding" this and that in her e-mails. Only when she visited the head office personally was the problem understood: she was misusing the word *demander*, which in French means "to ask."

This raises an important concern: those people working in close vicinity of their manager, because of face-to-face access, can communicate more effectively and so be better informed than others at a distance. **We can talk all we like about a global world, but most organizations—even the most international of corporations—tend to remain rather local at their headquarters.**

Of course, managers can always get into airplanes to meet others and find out personally what is going on. Tengblad noted that the Swedish CEOs he studied in the international companies were inclined to do just that, "despite the emergence of faster means of communication" (2002:549). But that takes time (as Tengblad noted), especially compared with banging out an e-mail. So the danger may be to stay home and communicate electronically.

The Real Data Banks   Two other concerns should be noted here as well. First, the types of information that managers favor tend to be stored in human brains. Only when written down can it be stored in electronic brains. But that takes time, and managers, as noted, are busy people. Even in their e-mails, the short reply seems generally to be favored over the more extensive debrief. As a consequence, **the strategic data banks of organizations remain at least as much in the heads of their managers as in the files of their computers.**

This raises the second concern. The managers' extensive use of such information helps to explain why they may be reluctant to delegate tasks. It is not as if they can hand a dossier over to someone; they must take the time to "dump memory"—to tell that person what they know about the subject. But this could take so long that it may be easier just to do the task themselves. And so a manager can be damned by his or her own information system to a "dilemma of delegation"—to do too much alone, or else to delegate to others without adequate briefing. We shall return to this conundrum, too, in Chapter 5.

Folklore: Managing is mostly about hierarchical relationships between a "superior" and "subordinates."

No one quite believes this statement, of course—we all know that plenty of managing happens outside and across hierarchies. But our very use of the awful labels of "superior" and "subordinate" does say something, just as does our obsession with leadership, the ubiquitousness of the label "top" management, and those stiff organizational charts. As Burns put it back in 1957, in a comment we have yet to fully appreciate: "The accepted view of management as a working hierarchy on organization chart lines may be dangerously misleading. Management simply does not operate as a flow of information up through a succession of filters, and a flow of decisions and instructions down through a succession of amplifiers" (p. 60).

Fact: Managing is as much about lateral relationships among colleagues and associates as it is about hierarchical relationships.

The management literature has long slighted the importance of lateral relationships in managerial work, and it continues to do so.[9] Yet study after study has shown that managers generally spend a great deal of their contact time—often close to half or more—with a wide variety of people external to their own units: customers, suppliers, partners, government and trade officials, and other stakeholders, as well as all kinds of colleagues in their own organization with whom they have no direct reporting relationship.

Figure 2.1 shows the breakdown of contacts via meetings, telephone calls, and mail for the chief executives of my earlier study. I found that these CEOs developed extensive networks of informers, who sent various reports and informed them of the latest events and opportunities. In addition, they maintained contacts with many experts (consultants, lawyers, underwriters, etc.) to provide specialized advice. Trade organization people kept them up-to-date on events in their industry: the unionization of a competitor, the state of impending legislation, the promotion of a peer. And as a consequence of their personal reputations and that of their organizations, these CEOs were fed with unsolicited information and ideas—a suggestion for a contract, a comment on a product, a reaction to an advertisement.

---

[9] One early and pathbreaking exception is Leonard Sayles's book *Managerial Behavior* (1964), which identified "the manager as participant in external work flows" as one of three key aspects of managerial work (the other two being "the manager as leader" and "the manager as monitor"). Sayles categorized these relationships as concerning trading, work flow, service, advising, auditing, stabilizing, and initiating.

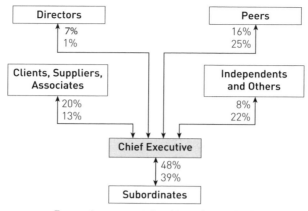

Top numbers: percent time in meetings and calls
Bottom numbers: percent of mail from each

Figure 2.1 CHIEF EXECUTIVE CONTACTS (from Mintzberg, 1973:46)

One might expect this of chief executives. But studies of other managers, in middle and even first-line positions, bear evidence of similar ranges and varieties of contacts. I noted this for a number of managers of my later study—for example, Brian Adams of Bombardier, whose job I described as lateral management with a vengeance. He had enormous responsibility yet not a great deal of formal authority over many of the people he had to work with in the "partner" organizations (subcontractors, responsible for parts of the aircraft). Likewise, Charlie Zinkan, who ran the Banff National Park, sat between all sorts of interests—developers, environmentalists, and so forth—and had to respond to many of them, as delicately as possible. (The full days of both are described in the appendix.)

We might thus characterize the manager's position as the neck of an hourglass, sitting between a network of outside contacts and the internal unit being managed. The manager receives all kinds of information and requests from insiders and outsiders, which are scanned, absorbed, and passed on to others, again both inside and outside the unit.

Folklore: Managers maintain tight control—of their time, their activities, their units.

The orchestra conductor standing on the platform waving the baton has, as noted, been a popular metaphor for managing. Here is how Peter Drucker put it in his 1954 classic book, *The Practice of Management*:

> One analogy [for the manager] is the conductor of a symphony orchestra, through whose effort, vision and leadership, individual instrumental parts that are so much noise by themselves, become the living whole of music. But the conductor has the composer's score: he is only interpreter. The manager is both composer and conductor. (pp. 341–342)

Drucker certainly spent a lot of time interviewing managers, but not (so far as I know) watching them conduct their work all day long. Sune Carlson did, and he came up with a rather different metaphor to describe what he saw:

> Before we made the study, I always thought of a chief executive as the conductor of an orchestra, standing aloof on his platform. Now I am in some respects inclined to see him as the puppet in the puppet-show with hundreds of people pulling the strings and forcing him to act in one way or another. (1951:52)

I often read these two quotes, and a third, to groups of managers and ask them to vote on which best describes their work. But they have to vote after I read each, before they have had a chance to hear the others. I add, however, that they can vote up to three times. How would you have voted on these two: For the first? The second? Both? Neither?

The orchestra conductor usually gets some hands, not too many (people are suspicious), and the puppet gets a few as well, hesitantly. Then I read the third quote, from Leonard Sayles—back to the orchestra conductor, but not as Drucker saw it:

> The manager is like a symphony orchestra conductor, endeavoring to maintain a melodious performance in which the contributions of the various instruments are coordinated and sequenced, patterned and paced, while the orchestra members are having various personal difficulties, stage hands are moving music stands, alternating excessive heat and cold are creating audience and instrumental problems, and the sponsor of the concert is insisting on irrational changes in the program. (1964:162)

All the hands go up!

Fact: **The manager is neither conductor nor puppet: control to the extent possible tends to be covert more than overt, by establishing some obligations to which the manager must later attend and by turning other obligations to the manager's advantage.**

If managerial work is like orchestra conducting, a point I investigated in my day with Bramwell Tovey of the Winnipeg Symphony (see the Appendix), then it is not the grand image of performance, where everything has been well rehearsed and everyone is on his or her best behavior, the audience included. It is rehearsal, where all sorts of things can go wrong and must be corrected quickly.

In my earlier study, I found that the chief executives initiated a little less than a third (32 percent) of their own oral contacts (meetings and calls) and sent only about one piece of correspondence for every four they received (26 percent), almost all of them responses. (I have found no subsequent, comparable data for e-mail.) The content of these meetings and calls appeared likewise to be more passive than active (42 percent vs. 31 percent, the rest in between)—for example, engaging in a ceremonial event versus negotiating a contract. In his study of U.S. presidents, Neustadt concluded:

> A President's own use of time, his allocation of his personal attention, is governed by the things he has to do from day to day: the speech he has agreed to make, the fixed appointment he cannot put off, the paper no one else can sign, the rest and exercise his doctors order. . . . A President's priorities are set not by the relative importance of a task, but by the relative necessity for him to do it. He deals first with the things that are required of him next. Deadlines rule his personal agenda. (1960:155)

But does all this tell the whole story? Do the findings that many of managers' meetings are set up by others, that they receive more mail than they generate, that they can be inundated with requests and are slaves to their appointment diaries, indicate that they are puppets who do not control their own affairs? Not at all. The frequency of requests, for example, may be a good measure of the status a manager has established for him- or herself, while the quantity of unsolicited information received may indicate the manager's success in building effective channels of communication.[10]

- I was struck by Marc, the head of the hospital, who faced enormous pressures, especially from a cost-conscious government on the outside and demanding physicians on the inside. The politics in and around any hospital can be intense. I referred to this day as "a state of siege." Yet Marc fought back, using every manner of maneuver to gain some control. Some of the other managers among the twenty-nine who seemed to be even more constrained, in fact, proved to be among the most proactive. (In Chapter 5, we shall discuss Peter Coe of the National Health Service of England, as he "managed out of the middle.")

Effective managers thus appear to be neither conductors nor puppets—they exercise control despite the constraints.[11] How do they do this? I concluded in my earlier study that they use two degrees of freedom in particular. They make a set of initial decisions that define many of their subsequent commitments (e.g., start a project that, once underway, demands their time). And they adapt to their own ends activities in which they *must* engage (e.g., by using a ceremonial occasion to lobby for their organization). In other words, managers create some of their obligations and take advantage of others.[12]

---

[10] Hannaway has suggested several advantages that managers can have in responding to the demands of others—for example, that the tasks in question "have already been processed to some degree, so they tend to be better defined and more suited to immediate action" than those initiated by the manager him or herself; and that "it is easier to react to demands than to sort out priorities and probabilities in a dynamic and ambiguous world" (1989:55). See also an early article by Tom Peters (1979) on the "sad facts and silver linings" of leadership.

[11] In their study of city mayors (1974:49–60), Kotter and Lawrence categorized their people's setting into four "patterns": "muddling through" with little control at one end, and "rational planning," with extensive control, at the other, the other two being a blend of these two. Eight managers were described as muddling through, none as rational planning, and twelve in between. See also Bowman and Bussard (1991), who questioned Stewart's conclusion "that agendas discriminate proactive and reactive managers" (1979:82), coming to a conclusion much like that here.

[12] Pitner and Ogawa (1981), in a study of the superintendents of school districts, came to a similar conclusion: that they use the sometimes unobtrusive strategies of (a) persuasion (convincing others of something, even when constrained by their context); (b) timing, or "opportunism"—for example, sensing when a "situation was ripe for movement"; and (c) diversion—for example, erecting strawmen—creating issues to draw attention away from one issue to another. As for control of the work, these researchers go back and forth. They found that the superintendents initiated 58 percent of their time in verbal contact (p. 53) but that "socio-cultural context

Perhaps this is what most clearly distinguishes successful and unsuccessful managers. **The effective managers seem to be not those with the greatest degrees of freedom but the ones who use to advantage whatever degrees of freedom they can find** (a point I shall develop in Chapter 4 and return to in Chapter 6). In other words, these people do not just *do* the job; they *make* the job. All managers appear to be puppets. Some decide who will pull the strings, and how, and then they take advantage of every move that they are forced to make. Others, unable to do so, get overwhelmed by this demanding job.[13]

The Impact of the Internet

There has been one evident change in recent times that should be having a great effect on all these characteristics of managing: the Internet, especially e-mail, a new medium of communication that has dramatically increased speed and volume in the transmission of information. Has its impact on managing been likewise dramatic?

Judging by all the e-mails flying about and the ambiguousness of BlackBerries, it would certainly seem so. But the question is whether this has changed managing fundamentally. And about this important issue there has so far been little evidence—a surprising finding in its own right.[14] I will draw here on what I can, including studies from outside management, but my comments will necessarily have to be seen as speculative.

My answer is yes and no. No, because the Internet may be mostly reinforcing the very characteristics that have long been prevalent in managerial work, as discussed in this chapter. And yes, because this may be driving some of the practice of managing over the edge.

---

defined, to a large extent, the specific issues to which [they] attended." Hence "while appearing on the surface to control much of their work, upon closer examination [they were] mere vehicles for translating community preferences into elements of their school districts' structures." Yet these managers "possessed their own ideas" and "did, indeed, steer their organizations in directions of their own choosing . . . [using the] array of strategies discussed above" (p. 58).

[13] See Stewart (1982) for a detailed discussion of the demands, constraints, and choices in managerial work—respectively, what managers have to do, limitations on what they can do, and what they elect to do.

[14] One exception is Tengblad (2000), who found that "approximately 90% of [the total working time of the Swedish chief executives he studied] was used for meetings, reading, writing, and talking on the telephone." E-mail accounted for less than half an hour a day, although the variation was wide. In particular, the younger CEOs devoted twice as much time to it (pp. 20–23), which suggests that these figures may change in the future.

The Internet for Better and for Worse   The advantages of the Internet are evident and quite astonishing. Managers can keep in current touch with people all over the world in ways that used to be unthinkable. They can also share large amounts of information with a great many people. These advantages enable them to greatly extend their informational networks and rather easily conduct their affairs across the globe.[15]

I needn't dwell on these advantages; they are profound and evident to all of us. But what effect does the Internet have on managing itself?

Better-informed managers, able to communicate more quickly, can develop faster-moving, more competitive enterprises—so long as they can handle these changes. Some may be able to take them in stride; others may be drawn into acting more quickly and less thoughtfully—conforming more and considering less. I fear that there is a growing number of the latter.

The Media and Its Messages   There are various aspects of the Internet; I will focus mainly on e-mail here, because that seems to be having the most direct impact on the practice of managing. (Of course, managers, like others, send large documents at the click of a key. But many of these documents are prepared by specialists, as are perhaps many of the Web searches required by a manager. But few managers these days escape the extensive use of e-mail.)

It is important to note, for starters, that this new medium remains thin. **Like conventional mail, e-mail is restricted by the poverty of words alone**: there is no tone of voice to hear, no gestures to see, no presence to feel—even images can be a nuisance to create. E-mail may simply limit the user's "ability to support emotional, nuanced, and complex interactions" (Boase and Wellman 2006). Managing is as much about all these things as it is about the factual content of the messages.

The danger of e-mail is that it may give a manager the impression of being in touch while the only thing actually being touched is the keyboard. This can aggravate a long-standing problem in managing: allowing a fancy new technology to give the illusion of control. Prime Minister Margaret Thatcher was criticized by some of her military officers for trying to direct the Falklands war via the use of telex in London. Imagine if she had e-mail. The head of a major department of the Canadian government did

---

[15] This may ultimately prove to have a democratizing effect on organizations. Sproull and Keisler (1986:1510) call it "status equalization," although it may have the opposite effect by diffusing information "neither universally nor uniformly" (Boase and Wellman 2006:3).

have e-mail: he told me that he used it to communicate with his staff every morning. I feared for his managing. Relying on the rapidity of e-mail is fine, so long as the manager is not fooled into believing that he or she understands a situation because some words have popped up on a screen.

On the telephone, people can interrupt, grunt, pounce; in meetings, they can nod in agreement or nod off in distraction. Effective managers pick up on such clues. With e-mail, you don't quite know how someone has reacted until the reply comes back, and even then you cannot be sure if the words were carefully chosen or sent in haste. Compare this with oral communication, where feelings are difficult to hide.[16]

So, does the Internet make managers better connected or less? Take your choice for now—we don't yet know the answer. But we had better be asking the question.

Is the Global Village a Community?   Marshall McLuhan (1962) wrote famously about the "global village" created by new information technologies. But what kind of a village is that?

In the conventional village, you chat with your neighbor at the local market: this is the heart of the community. In the global village, you click to send a message to someone on the other side of the globe, who you may never even have met. Like those fantasy-ridden love affairs on the Internet, such relationships may remain untouched and untouchable. In fact, Keisler et al. found that "people who communicated by computer evaluated each other less favorably than did people who communicated face-to-face" (1985:78). This is obviously not true for those electronic love affairs, so maybe the more accurate conclusion is that these detached forms of communication tend to exaggerate impressions of other people,

---

[16] In a laboratory experiment, Keisler et al. found that "computer-mediated communication technologies focus attention on the message" while they "transmit social information poorly." In fact, these technologies "do not have a well developed social etiquette. Therefore, [they] might be associated with less attention to others, less social feedback, and depersonalization of the communication setting" (1985:77). Hardly characteristics to be welcomed in management. Boase and Wellman took this etiquette point further with the claim "The rapidity of internet connections . . . may foster a high velocity of interpersonal exchanges, sometimes ill-considered" (p. 2). In conventional mail, the sender is more inclined to take time, redraft, even pull a letter from the out-tray before it goes. On the one hand, the rhythm of e-mail—so many at a time, such volume, the incentive to get it out, keep it moving—can discourage all that. On the other hand, Sproull and Keisler claim that "uninhibited behavior" can enhance the flow of new ideas, just as the "status equalization" of e-mail can allow wider access to information (1986:1510). See also Beaudry and Pinsonneault (2005) on the varying effects, emotional included, that IT can have on individuals.

one way *or* the other. The communicators, in other words, have little basis on which to judge each other.

Yet judging people is critically important to all managing. Organizations are communities, dependent on the robustness of their relationships. Trust and respect are absolutely key. So we have to be quite careful about this global village, not to confuse its networks with communities. **The Internet may be enhancing networks while weakening communities, within organizations as well as across them.**[17] Thus, Boase and Wellman have written about "networked individualism," where "people belong to more spatially dispersed and sparsely knit personal networks" (2006). Their point of reference is society in general, but this might help to explain the rise of the egocentric, heroic form of leadership that is wreaking so much havoc on today's organizations.

Let's now consider what may be the direct effects of the Internet on the characteristics of managing that have been discussed in this chapter.

The Pace and the Pressures   One thing alluded to throughout this discussion seems certain: **e-mail increases the pace and pressure of managing, and likely the interruptions as well.**

Of course, many people do e-mail in batches. But with their preference for instant information, managers may be inclined to do it frequently, in brief spurts, plus leave the computer open so they can respond to "You've got mail!" Add a BlackBerry in the pocket—the tether to the global village—and you've got interruptions, galore. (I heard one story about a meeting called by e-mail at 10:30 Sunday evening for 8:30 Monday morning.)[18]

---

[17] There is some contradicting evidence about this, at least in society at large. Hampton and Wellman (in Barney 2004:39) found that the residents of a town who were wired (because of availability, not just choice) "'neighbor[ed]' more extensively and more intensively than their non-wired counterparts." They concluded that the new communication technologies "may hold as much promise of reconnecting us to communities or places as they do in liberating us from them" (quoted in Barney 2004:39). In contrast, Boase and Wellman found that "the current body of internet research indicates that the internet has not caused a widespread flourishing of new relationships"; people mostly communicate with others they already know, and when they do meet people on line, the relationships that continue "tend to migrate offline" (2004:9).

[18] González and Mark found that managers (as well as analysts and software developers) in the field of IT averaged about three minutes on a task before switching to another or being interrupted, while on e-mail they averaged under two and a half minutes (2004:166).

When the American and British publishers of this book read an early draft of this chapter, without this section, both e-mailed that I had to discuss the Internet, which is driving managers crazy. Steve Piersanti of Berrett-Koehler wrote (on June 21, 2005), "Managers are interrupted more than ever, but now the interruptions are the frequent [e-mails] . . . that demand their attention." To quote another CEO, from a newspaper interview: "You can never escape. You can't go anywhere to contemplate, or think" (CAE's Robert Brown, in Moore 2006). Of course, you *can* go anywhere you wish in order to contemplate or think—if you *choose* to.

The Orientation to Action   For managers, who already exhibit an orientation to action, nothing about e-mail suggests a reduction in that characteristic. Quite the contrary. It is an interesting irony that **e-mail, technically removed from the action (picture the manager sitting in front of a screen), enhances the action orientation of managing.** There is, after all, lots of fire and brimstone (so to speak) in those brains, computer and human, with all their electrons flying about.

The Oral Nature of Managing   Of course, more time on the Internet can mean less time on everything else, which likely includes oral communication. There are only so many hours in every day. But then again, some of those hours have been devoted to sleep and to family, so we have to ask whether those have suffered as a result of the Internet. In other words, does the Internet just pile more pressures on top of an already pressured job? Do too many managers want it all?[19]

Again, we don't have evidence on this, but there is room for suspicion. Even if the communication may be less oral, it can be more frenetic, and perhaps more superficial as well. And with this can come greater conformity—just to get it done fast.

The Lateral Nature of the Job   People who report to a manager are few and fixed, in contrast to the network of people outside the unit that is far larger and potentially unlimited. So **this new medium that makes it so easy to establish new contacts, and to keep "in touch" with**

---

[19] Encouraging and discouraging in this regard is Tengblad's "striking" finding of "big increases in time spent traveling" for the Swedish CEOs he studied, "despite the emergence of faster means of communication" (2002:549), albeit perhaps because he was comparing them with the managers of the Carlson study whose operations were less international. So they were still inclined to go face-to-face—but was it at the expense of family time?

the ones already established, likely encourages the extension of managers' external networks at the expense of their internal communication.[20]

Might this weaken the strong ties a manager might otherwise have with the people in his or her own unit? With limited managerial time available, we might think so. (Consider the failures of so many financial institutions in 2008–2009.) Time in front of the screen is time not spent in front of someone down the hall. Indeed, as with that Canadian government manager, the person down the hall may now be the one on the screen.[21]

Control of the Job   Finally comes perhaps the most interesting question of all: does the Internet enhance or diminish the control managers have over their own work? Obviously it depends on the manager: As with most technologies, the Internet can be used for better or for worse. You can be mesmerized by it, and so let it manage you. Or you can understand its power as well as its dangers, and so manage it. I have written this section of the book to encourage the latter.

Still, there may be pervasive effects overall. Think of the power of e-mail to connect, the power of the Internet to access and transmit information. Think, too, of the pressures and pace of managerial work, the needs to respond, the nagging feeling of being out of control. **Might the Internet, by giving the illusion of control, in fact be robbing managers of control?** In other words, are the ostensible conductors becoming more like puppets after all?

Over the Edge?   Pinsonneault and Kraemer (1997) found something interesting in a study of 155 city governments: electronic communication reinforced already existing tendencies in the organization, specifically to centralize or else to decentralize. Might the same thing be true of the characteristics of managing? Combining this with just about every point thus far suggests one conclusion: **the Internet is not changing the practice of management fundamentally; rather, it is reinforcing characteristics that we have been seeing for decades.** In other words, the changes are in the same direction, of degree, not kind.

---

[20] Back to the Tengblad (2002) study of the Swedish CEOs: he noted, as a consequence of their flying, if not the Internet, that "the strong bond between their work and their own offices has vanished" (p. 559), leading to more reliance on "indirect forms of control" (p. 560).

[21] See Granovetter's (1973) classic article on "the strength of weak ties," about how weak ties within a community may be accompanied by strong ties outside of it, and vice versa.

But the devil can be in the detail. Changes of degree can have profound effects, amounting to changes of kind. **The Internet may be driving much management practice over the edge, making it so frenetic that it has become dysfunctional: too superficial, too disconnected, too conformist.** In India, I watched the managers of a high-technology company on an international program go nuts when their e-mail connections went down for a couple of days. Were they unable to manage because they were suddenly out of touch? Or did the way they have come to manage put them out of touch with managing itself? Perhaps the ultimately connected manager has become disconnected from what matters, while this overactivity is destroying the practice of managing itself.

Normally Calculated Chaos

To conclude, in this chapter we have seen the characteristics of managing, as they were then and remain now: the pace, brevity, variety, fragmentation; the interruptions; the orientation to action; the oral aspect of the information; the lateral nature of much of the communication; and the tricky problem of exercising control without quite being in control.

Does all this suggest bad managing? Not at all. It suggests normal managing—inevitable managing. "When asked to describe what a manager does, the new managers spoke feelingly about the stresses in their new positions. Management seemed a world of overwhelming confusion, of overload, ambiguity, and conflict. . . . Above all, they were struck by the unrelenting workload and pace of being a manager" (Hill 2003:50). Some of these managers expected this to slacken. "Once I get my arms around the job or should I say if . . . everything will fall into place. Then I'll be the coordinator, controller, not necessarily in that order, all the time" (p. 51). No such luck. Not even for those who make it to the so-called top, the "rapid-pace high-pressure environment" of the general managers that Kotter described.

But these characteristics are normal only within limits. Exceed them, and the practice of management can become dysfunctional. The Internet can cause this, but so can the characteristics themselves. We all know excessively frenetic managers. What one day seems normal can the next become hazardous.

Managing, even normal managing, is no easy job. A *New York Times* commentary on my original study (Andrews 1976) used two phrases that for me capture the nature of this well: "calculated chaos" and "controlled disorder." They tell of the nuance that is all effective managing—compared with the "confusing chaos" of "naïve managers" (Sayles 1979:19). With this in mind, we turn now to the content of managing—what managers actually do—and return to how managers can deal with these pressures in Chapter 5.

3

A Model of Managing

A good theory is one that holds together
long enough to get you to a better theory.

Donald O. Hebb (1969)

In search of a better theory, we turn now from the characteristics of managing to its content: what is it that managers actually do, and how?

We begin with the gurus, most of whom have seen the job in its component parts, not its integrated whole, and the academics, who have seen the whole as lists of disconnected parts. This chapter proposes a model of managing that positions the parts within the whole, by depicting managing as taking place on three planes: information, people, and action, inside the unit and beyond it. A final section describes the "well-rounded" job of managing as a dynamic balance.

Managing One Role at a Time   If you wish to become famous in management—one of those "gurus"—focus on one aspect of managing to the exclusion of all the others. Henri Fayol saw managing as controlling, while Tom Peters has seen it as doing: "'Don't think, do' is the phrase I favor'" (1990; on Wall Street, of course, managers "do deals"). Michael Porter has instead equated managing with thinking, specifically analyzing: "I favor a set of analytical techniques for developing strategy," he wrote in *The Economist* (1987:21). Others such as Warren Bennis have built their reputations among managers by describing their work as leading, while Herbert Simon built his among academics by describing it as decision making. (The *Harvard Business Review* concurred, for years pronouncing on its cover, "The magazine of decision makers.")[1]

Each of them is wrong because all of them are right: **Managing is not one of these things but all of them: it is controlling and doing and dealing and thinking and leading and deciding and more, not added up but blended together.** Take away any one of these roles, and you do not have the full job of managing. In that sense, by focusing on one aspect of the job to the exclusion of the others, each of these gurus has narrowed our perception of managing rather than broadening it.

An Abundance of Lists   Go beyond the gurus, to some of the less popular fare of the academics, and you find acknowledgment of this problem: they offer lists of managerial roles. The good news is that these are more comprehensive; the bad news is that they take the job apart without putting it back together. It feels like Humpty Dumpty, lying in broken pieces on the ground.

I was responsible for one of these lists. One chapter of my 1973 book, called "The Manager's Working Roles," presented what I thought was a model, which I later came to realize was just another list, albeit with arrows, as shown in Figure 3.1.[2] So while managers may have related well to my description of the characteristics of managing, they did not take particularly well to my list, or those of others (even if some academics did). As one manager commented: "the descriptions are lifeless and my job isn't" (in Wrapp 1967:92).

Thus, in 1990, I decided to revisit the content of managing. Since the publication of my 1973 book, I had been collecting new articles on the subject, which by then filled two boxes. I opened them and also looked at the books on the subject—about forty in all, from Barnard (1938) to Zaleznik (1989). I wanted to know what we formally knew about the content of managing.

---

[1] This was used from July 1967 to June 1981. Before that, it was for "thoughtful businessmen"; and just after that, for "the thoughtful manager."

[2] Thus I can hardly complain when Hales turned around my claim that the empirical studies of managerial work "paint an interesting picture, one as different from Fayol's classical view as a cubist abstract is from a Renaissance painting" (1975:50). He called the analogy "unfortunately apt, because the research picture does indeed appear as an assemblage of geometric shapes which do not always fit together" (1986:105).

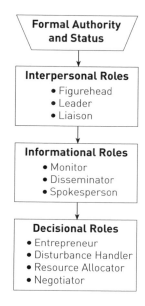

Figure 3.1 THE MANAGER'S WORKING ROLES (from Mintzberg, 1973:59)

The answer: on one hand, quite a bit; on the other, not much at all. All of this material together seemed to cover the things that managers do (Hales 2001:50), but it did not amount to much of a theory, or a model, to help managers understand their work.[3]

---

[3] In the first serious study of managerial work, Carlson commented near the end, in words that remain true, "Throughout the present study, I have, above all, lacked a theoretical system, in which to arrange the observations I have made. . . . As a first implication of the present study on further research I would therefore, place the desirability of developing a systematic theory of executive behavior" (1951:115; see also Martinko and Gardner 1985:688 and Lombardo and McCall 1982:50). True, here and there can be found a brilliant exposé, such as *The Functions of the Executive* written by Chester Barnard, himself an executive (1938). And then there have been a few researchers who devoted much of their careers to the subject, notably Leonard Sayles (1964, 1979), John Kotter (1982, and 1974 with Paul Lawrence), and Rosemary Stewart, who produced the largest stream of research (e.g., 1967, 1976, 1982). All have provided interesting insights; none, in my opinion, offers a comprehensive framework that captures fully the content of managerial work. In fact, Sayles, who I believe came closest in his 1964 book, commented on "our inability . . . to find proper pigeon holes . . . to both describe and explain what managers do" (1979:10). Later, and closer, came the work of Robert Quinn and his colleagues (e.g., Quinn 1988; Quinn et al. 1990), but this also really reduced to a list—of opposite pairs of eight managerial roles. Four quadrants are identified according to the evolution of management thought (Rational Goals, Internal Process, Human Relations, and Open Systems), along

What's the Problem?

How can this be so? We live in societies obsessed with management and especially leadership, now more than ever. We idolize "leaders"; we fill bookstores with biographies of them, under "Fiction" as well as "Business" (sometimes being unable to tell the difference); we pretend to train huge numbers of students to become them; we have even created a special class for them in airplanes (and beyond). Yet we cannot come to grip with the simple reality of what they do. Why?

Let me consider two possible explanations. The first is that, as in other primitive societies, we live in mortal fear of our own gods, or at least our own myths, and management/leadership is surely one of them. Perhaps we fear the consequences of revealing their nakedness, or our own. Of course, we write about "leadership," ad nauseum, but little of that touches on the everyday realities of managing.

Carlson offered another explanation in his early study: that "executive behavior" is "so varied and so hard to grasp" because "it is more a practical art than an applied science" (1951:109–110). How to theorize about that?

Whitley took this further, arguing that managerial tasks are specific to context, and thus dependent on knowledge of the particular organization and its problems, which are constantly changing (1989:213, 215). How, then, can we develop general theory about what managers do, instead of specific descriptions of what particular managers did?

I beg to differ. At some level of abstraction, we *can* generalize. Let me illustrate. To become a senior manager ("partner") in a consulting firm means to become responsible for selling, which is the work of specialists in most other businesses. Yet do we want to describe managerial work as selling? As Peter Drucker put it:

> Every manager does many things that are not managing. . . . A sales manager . . . placates an important customer. A foreman repairs a tool. . . . A company president . . . negotiates a big contract. . . . All these things pertain to a particular function. All are necessary, and

---

axes of flexibility and control, and internal and external. (e.g., the Open System Model being external and flexible). Laid across this, facing each other, are four sets "competing values" (e.g., Participation, Openness/Productivity, Accomplishment), with a role assigned to each (e.g., for the above, Facilitator/Producer). In their 1990 book, Quinn et al. included a final chapter called "Integration and the Road to Mastery," which comprised 17 pages out of the 345 total, but hardly addressing integration at all. Almost all the rest of the book was devoted to chapters on each of the eight roles.

have to be done well. But they are apart from that work which every manager does whatever his function or activity, whatever his rank and position, work which is common to all managers and peculiar to them. (1954:343)

Before we throw out the managerial baby with the selling bathwater, let's ask ourselves why senior managers of consulting firms do this selling. The obvious answer is that many consulting services have to be sold at senior levels in the buying company, and so they require the intervention of senior managers in the selling company. On one hand, therefore, the task is specialized and context-specific; on the other hand, it has to be done by managers and so is intrinsically managerial (see also Hales and Mustapha 2000:22).

Indeed, a good deal of what we generally accept as intrinsically managerial corresponds to specialized functions in the organization: managers brief subordinates, but their organizations have formal information systems; managers serve as figureheads at ceremonial events despite the presence of public relations specialists; managers have long been described as planners and controllers, while near them can be found planning departments and controllership offices. **A good part of the work of managing involves doing what specialists do, but in particular ways that make use of the manager's special contacts, status, and information.**

So let's get past our myths and our deities, and get on with understanding managing as it is practiced.

TOWARD A GENERAL MODEL

When I opened those boxes and looked at those books, my intention was not to find out what managers do—we knew that already—but to weave that into a comprehensive model. Hence, I did not set out to do more research, not yet (the twenty-nine days of observation mostly came later), but simply to draw together the results of existing descriptions and research. My focus was really quite simple: to get it all on one sheet of paper, in the form of a single diagram. This was not meant to trivialize the job or to suggest that all its nuanced complexity could be described on one page, only to offer the reader a place where the whole of managing could be seen all at once—comprehensively, coherently, interactively—even if that page required many more of explanation.

After perhaps a dozen efforts over many years, I developed that one page to my satisfaction, as reproduced in Figure 3.2.[4] The first time I showed it to a manager—a friend, over dinner—he immediately pointed to where were the strengths and the weaknesses of the managers in his company. That was exactly the response I wanted.[5]

The figure has come out looking a bit like an egg, perhaps in honor of Humpty Dumpty. In the spirit of the opening quotation of this chapter, my earlier effort had held together long enough to get me to this model, which I hope will hold together long enough to help others get to better models.

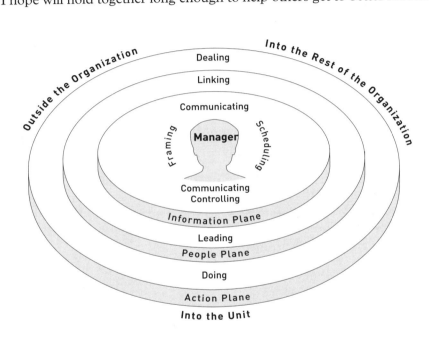

Figure 3.2 A MODEL OF MANAGING

---

[4] Anyone interested in tracing my thinking can see the sequence of diagrams on www.mintzberg .org/managingmodel.

[5] Likewise, a participant in our International Master's for Health Leadership program (www .imhl.ca), at the time a manager with the World Health Organization in Uganda, wrote that the model "resonated in several ways. First of all, because it explicitly recognizes the multi-layered and multi-faceted nature of our work . . . as if the mere acknowledgement of the fact somehow makes the work easier. Secondly, because I could instantly see the functions or roles from which I tend to shy away or not do so well. In that sense, it challenged me more. The question that continues to nag persistently is how to achieve balance in the face of so many different roles" (Rosamund Lewis, Reflection Paper, Module 1, July 28, 2006).

An Overview of the Model

Figure 3.2 puts the manager in the center, between the unit for which he or she has formal responsibility (by definition) and its surroundings, of two kinds: the rest of the organization (unless the manager is chief executive, responsible for the entire organization), and the outside world relevant to the unit (customers, partners, etc.).

The overriding purpose of managing is to ensure that the unit serves *its* basic purpose, whether that be to sell products in a retail chain or care for the elderly in a nursing home. This, of course, requires the taking of effective *actions.* Mostly other people in the unit do that, each a specialist in his or her own right. But sometimes a manager gets close to this *action*, as when Jacques Benz, Director-General of GSI, joined the meeting of a project team that was developing a new system for a customer.

More commonly, however, the manager takes one or two steps back from the action. One step back, he or she encourages other *people* to take action—the manager gets things done through other people by coaching, motivating, building teams, strengthening culture, and so forth. Two steps back, the manager gets things done by using information to drive other people to take action. He or she imposes a target on a sales team, or carries a comment from a government official to a staff specialist. So as shown in the figure, **managing takes place on three *planes*, from the conceptual to the concrete: *with information, through people*, and *to action* directly.**[6]

> • On the day of observation, Carol Haslam of Hawskhead could be
>   seen working on all three planes. On the action plane, she was
>   deeply involved with developing projects for new films—she was
>   doing deals galore. On the people plane, she was maintaining
>   her vast network of contacts used to promote these projects,
>   as well as building teams of filmmakers to execute them. And
>   on the information plane, all day long she was collecting and
>   disseminating ideas, data, advice, and other information.

Two roles are shown as being performed on each plane. On the information plane, managers *communicate* (all around) and *control* (inside). On the people plane, they *lead* (inside) and *link* (to the outside). And on

---

[6] More broadly, but similarly, Fine, in a 1973 report entitled "Fundamental Job Analysis Scales," distinguished for all work "scales" concerned with data, people, and things.

the action plane, they *do* (inside) and *deal* (outside). Also shown, within their own heads, managers *frame* (conceive strategies, establish priorities, etc.) and *schedule* (their own time). Each aspect of the model is discussed in turn before all of them are discussed together in conclusion.

THE PERSON IN THE JOB

Positioned at the center of the model is the manager, who personally carries out two roles in particular: framing and scheduling.

Framing the Job

Framing defines how a manager approaches his or her particular job. **Managers frame their work by making particular decisions, focusing on particular issues, developing particular strategies, and so forth, to establish the context for everyone else working in the unit.**[7] Alain Noël (1989) has called these the managers' *preoccupations,* as compared with their *occupations* (what they actually do)—which can sometimes amount to a single "magnificent obsession."

> • Brian Adams, Program Manager for the Global Express aircraft at Bombardier, had a magnificent obsession, imposed by the senior management: to "get it in the air" by June. "Then, we'll see," he commented. In contrast, John Cleghorn of the Royal Bank of Canada had a variety of preoccupations as its chairman, concerning the improvement and success of the company. (Both their days are described in the appendix.)

One of the new managers studied by Linda Hill quickly found out about the importance of framing: "I expected to come out of the starting gate with the knowledge . . . now I find I'm out here inventing the wheel" (2003:51). We return to framing in our discussion of managerial styles in Chapter 4 and strategy formation in Chapter 5.

---

[7] See Barnard on "The Formulation of Purpose and Objectives" (1938:231). He commented that "strictly speaking, purpose is defined more nearly by the aggregate of actions taken than by any formulation in words" (p. 231).

Scheduling the Work

Scheduling is of great concern to all managers: the agenda inevitably gets a lot of attention. A half century ago, Sune Carlson noted how managers "become slaves to their appointment diaries—they get a kind of 'diary complex'" (1951:71). **Scheduling is important because it brings the frame to life, determines much of what the manager seeks to do, and enables him or her to use whatever degrees of freedom are available** (Stewart 1979).

Needless to say, scheduling was evident in all twenty-nine days of observation. It has to be done in all managerial jobs, but as a means to other ends—namely, the performance of the other roles. Thus, the diaries were often out, and much juggling of schedules took place.[8]

The manager's schedule can have enormous influence over everyone else in the unit: whatever gets in the agenda is taken as a signal of what matters in the unit. In fact, when managers schedule, they are often allocating not only their own time but also that of the people who report to them.[9]

Scheduling amounts to what Peters and Waterman (1982) have called "chunking"—slicing up managerial concerns into distinct tasks, to be carried out in specific slots of time. The problem, of course (which we shall discuss under the Labyrinth of Decomposition in Chapter 5), is how to put back together that which has been taken apart. And this is where the frame comes in: if clear enough, it can function as a magnet to draw the distinct chunks into a coherent whole. As Whitley put it, managing is "not so much focused on 'solving' discreet, well bounded individual problems as in dealing with a continuing series of internally related and fluid tasks" (1989:216).

Despite the attention that has long been given to decision making, managerial agendas seem to be built around ongoing issues more than

---

[8] In the case of John Cleghorn of the Royal Bank, scheduling received particular attention. He was the only manager I knowingly came across among the twenty-nine who systematically tabulated and studied his own time allocation (perhaps is a throwback to his earlier work as a public accountant).

[9] Scheduling has received a good deal of attention in the research (e.g., Kotter 1982a; Kotter and Lawrence 1974:51–56; Barry et al. 1997; Noel 1989; Bowman 1986). Perhaps this is because the schedule is the most accessible manifestation of managerial work. However, Barry et al. (1997), in their excellent study of the agendas of forty-five managers, described these as "coming in many forms: subconscious mental notes, scribbled scraps of paper, elaborate lists and charts" (p. 27).

specific decisions—in the words of Farson (1996:43), "predicaments" more than "problems" (see also Pondy and Huff 1985). Just look at the agendas of a typical management meeting, or else ask a manager what is on his or her "plate."[10]

MANAGING THROUGH INFORMATION

We turn now to the three planes on which managing is manifested, beginning with that of information. **To manage through information means to sit two steps removed from the ultimate purpose of managing: information is processed by the manager to encourage other people to take the necessary actions.** In other words, on this plane the manager focuses neither on people nor on actions directly, but on information as an indirect way to make things happen.

Ironically, while this was the classic view of managing, which dominated perceptions of its practice for most of the last century, it has again become prevalent, thanks to current obsessions with the **"bottom line" and "shareholder value": both encourage a detached, essentially information-driven practice of managing.**

Two main roles describe managing on the information plane, one labeled *communicating,* to promote the flow of information all around the manager, and the other labeled *controlling,* to use information to drive behavior mainly within the managed unit.

Communicating All Around

Watch any manager and one thing readily becomes apparent: the amount of time that is spent simply *communicating*—namely, collecting and disseminating information for its own sake, without necessarily processing it. Barnard, himself a chief executive (of New Jersey Telephone), identified the "first executive function" as "to develop and maintain a system of communication" (1938:226).

---

[10] Bowman (1986), in a study of twenty-six managers, found that they averaged a small number of issues (what he called "concerns"), about five or six at a time, even if these encompassed a great many items on the agenda (see also Bowman and Bussard 1991; Wrapp 1967:92). In the previous chapter, I noted that the number of issues managers juggle appears to be many more. Perhaps the difference lies in the agenda: many issues may be active, but only a few get represented in the agenda at a given time.

In my 1973 study, I estimated that the five chief executives spent about 40 percent of their time simply communicating in one way or another. In his study of Swedish corporate chief executives, Tengblad (2000) put 23 percent of their time at "getting information"—"the single most frequently recorded activity"—plus another 16 percent "informing and advising" (p. 15).

I did not tabulate the time spent on various activities by the twenty-nine managers of my later study, but communicating was no less evident: Norm Inkster, head of the RCMP, going over press clippings of the past twenty-four hours; someone dropping in on RCMP Division Commander Burchill "to tell you what's going on"; John Cleghorn briefing institutional investors on happenings at the bank; Stephen Omollo in the refugee camp inspecting the reconstruction of a fence that had been blown over in a recent storm; and much more.

The communicating role exists in the model as a kind of membrane all around the manager, through which all managerial activity passes. "Communicating is not simply what managers spend a great deal of time doing but the medium through which managerial work is constituted" (Hales 1986:101). Managers take in information through what Sayles (1964) has called *monitoring* activities, which enable them to be the *nerve centers* of their units, and they send their information out through what can be called *disseminating* activities inside the unit and *spokesperson* activities outside it.

Monitoring   As monitors, managers reach out for every scrap of useful information they can get—about internal operations and external events, trends and analyses, everything imaginable. They are also bombarded with such information, significantly as a consequence of the networks they build up for themselves. Thus, Morris et al. wrote about high school principals spending "a good deal of time 'on the go'": touring the halls, visiting the cafeteria, quick checks in the classrooms and libraries, etc.—a "constant bobbing" in and out, in order to "gauge the school climate" and "anticipate and quell potential trouble" (1981:74).[11]

Nerve Center   Everyone reporting to a manager is a specialist, relatively speaking, charged with some particular aspect of the unit's work. The manager, in contrast, is the relative generalist among them, overseeing

---

[11] See Alvessan and Sveningssan (2003) on "the importance of listening and informal chatting" in managerial work.

it all. He or she may not know as much about any particular specialty as the person charged with it, but usually more than any of them about the whole set of specialties together. And so the manager develops the broadest base of information within the unit. As a consequence of the monitoring activities, **the manager becomes the *nerve center* of the unit—its best-informed member, at least if he or she is doing the job well** (Barnard 1938:218).

This can apply to the president of the United States compared with the cabinet secretaries and the CEO of a company compared with the vice presidents no less than to a first-line manager compared with the workers. As Morris et al. put it about those school principals: "Inside the building, the principal is the key exchange point, the information switchboard through which all important messages pass" (1982:690).

- At a lunchtime briefing of investors of the Royal Bank, John Cleghorn drew on anecdotes from his morning in the branches. The rest of the day likewise saw a great deal of communicating in and out. Mostly John was learning, picking up all sorts of scraps of detail, and in some cases more aggregated figures. But he also spent time telling people about broader issues of the bank—a pending acquisition, for example—and imbibing a sense of its values. (The full day is described in the Appendix.)

The same holds true for external information. By virtue of his or her status, the manager has access to outside managers who are themselves nerve centers of their own units. The president of the United States can call the prime minister of Great Britain, much as one factory foreman can call another factory foreman. Consider the following descriptions, the first about leaders of street gangs in America, the second about a president of the United States of America:

Since interaction flowed toward [the leaders], they were better informed about the problems and desires of group members than were any of the followers and therefore better able to decide on an appropriate course of action. Since they were in close touch with other gang leaders, they were also better informed than their followers about conditions in [the town] at large. (Homans 1950:187).

The essence of Roosevelt's technique for information-gathering was competition. "He would call you in," one of his aides once told me, "and he'd ask you to get the story on some complicated business, and you'd come back after a couple of days of hard labor and present the juicy morsel you'd uncovered under a stone somewhere, and *then* you'd find out he knew all about it, along with something else you *didn't* know. Where he got his information from he wouldn't mention, usually, but after he had done this to you once or twice you got damn careful about *your* information." (Neustadt 1960:157)

Disseminating   What do managers do with their extensive and privileged information? A great deal, as we shall see in the other roles. But still on this one, they simply disseminate much of it to other people in their unit: they share it. **Like bees, managers cross-pollinate.** As Commanding Officer Allen Burchill of the RCMP reported on his way to a management meeting with his reports: "I'm informed. But this is a go-around to make sure they're informed."

Spokesperson   The manager also passes information externally, from people in the unit to outsiders, or from one outsider to another—for example, between customers, suppliers, and government officials. More formally, **as spokesperson for the unit, the manager represents it to the outside world, speaking to various publics on its behalf, lobbying for its causes, representing its expertise in public forums, and keeping outside stakeholders up-to-date on its progress.**

> • Charlie Zinkan, as Superintendent of the Banff National Park, met with the owner of a campground concerned about Indian land claims. Patiently Charlie described the government's position. The man was grateful: finally someone had explained the situation to him. At N'gara, Stephen Omollo of the Red Cross met the representative of a major donor organization who was there to audit the use of its money in the refugee camps. Stephen's knowledge of the operations, illustrated in his detailed replies to many of the questions, was impressive—informed, articulate, and straightforward.

The Verbal, the Visual, and the Visceral   It should be evident from our discussion of Chapter 2 that the manager's advantage lies not in documented information, which can be made available to anyone, but in the current, not (yet) documented information transmitted largely by word of mouth—for example, the gossip, hearsay, and opinion discussed in that chapter. Indeed, much of an informed manager's information is not even verbal so much as visual and visceral—in other words, seen and felt more than heard, representing the art and craft of managing more than its science. Effective managers pick up tone of voice, facial expression, body language, mood, atmosphere.

- I observed this especially in the day I spent with Stephen Omollo as he walked through the refugee camps, using every means possible to sense what was going on. Stephen greeted everyone he passed, smiling and laughing—in front of their homes, on the streets, in the markets and the fields. No few came up to shake his hand and chat. "My job is to assist and train the local staff," Stephen said, "but there is a need to tour on foot. You need to laugh with the people."

To conclude this discussion of the role of communicating, **the job of managing is significantly one of information processing, especially through a great deal of listening, seeing, and feeling, as well as a good deal of talking.** But that can damn a manager to a job of overwork or one of frustration. On one side of the managerial coin, there is the temptation to get in there and find out personally what is going on—to "avoid the sterility so often found in those who isolate themselves from operations" (Wrapp 1967:92). The danger, of course, is that this can encourage micromanaging: meddling in the work of others. But on the other side of that coin is "macroleading": simply not knowing what is going on. We shall return to this under our conundrums of Chapter 5.

Controlling Inside the Unit

One direct use of the managers' information is to "control"—that is, to direct the behavior of their "subordinates." As noted earlier, for the better part of the last century, managing was considered almost synonymous with controlling. This view began with Henri Fayol's book of 1916, based on his experience of managing French mines in the previous century, but it really flourished in the conventional manufacturing of products, such as automobiles, and then in government, as expressed in Gulick and Urwick's (1937) popular acronym POSDCORB: planning, organizing, staffing, directing, coordinating, reporting, and budgeting. Four of these words are clearly about controlling, while the other three—*staffing, coordinating,* and *reporting*—reflect important aspects of controlling. Hence, this long-dominant description of managerial work has not so much been wrong as narrow, focusing on one restricted aspect of the job: control of the unit through the exercise of formal authority.

Controlling may have lost its preeminent status after 1960, as the people plane of managing rose to prominence. But thanks to the recent surge in "bottom line" and "shareholder value" thinking, controlling is back—with a vengeance.

I chose to leave controlling out of the ten roles of managing I described in my earlier book (although I did include one labeled "resource allocator"—an aspect of controlling). Perhaps this was my overreaction to the excessive attention it had received earlier. In any event, I include it here, but in a tangible way: in terms of how managers exercise control.

- In the refugee camps of N'gara, controlling was front and center, simply because so much that happened had to be kept under tight wraps for fear of a small incident blowing into a major crisis. "You just need to put your ear to the ground, Stephen, and find out more about what the feelings are among the refugees," Abbas Gullet told Stephen Omollo at a meeting in the Red Cross compound. On top of this were the many Red Cross systems, procedures, rules, and regulations. In contrast, the day with orchestra conductor Bramwell Tovey exhibited much less overt controlling. He hardly "directed" this day, in the sense of giving orders, delegating tasks, or authorizing decisions. Controlling, like the other roles of managing, does vary in importance.

Administration, in some ways seen as synonymous with controlling, has for some time been put down in managerial work, as routine, boring, "bureaucratic." Indeed, in the 1950s, Peter Drucker (1954) distinguished "managers" from "administrators" much as leaders are now distinguished from managers. Instead of rushing to glorify leadership, however—"cast[ing] off the dowdy feathers of administration for the rich plumage of leadership" (Hales 2001:53)—and thus reducing management to administration, we should be recognizing controlling as an inevitable component of all effective management and leadership.

Linda Hill found that the new managers she studied had negative connotations of "administration," which they nevertheless reluctantly accepted as part of their job (2003:22).[12] Presumably this is because, first, if the manager of the unit does not take responsibility for getting it organized and instituting the necessary controls, who will; and second, because the manager is the person in the unit held accountable for its performance. **The trick is not to avoid the controlling role but to avoid being captured by it—which is true for all the roles of managing.**

The *Oxford English Dictionary* traces the word *manage* to the French—specifically, the word *main*, meaning "hand," in reference to "the training, handling, and directing of a horse in its paces."[13] This is essentially the role of controlling, which is about handling and directing "subordinates" to ensure that they get their work done. But *how* do managers do this? To help answer this, we can turn to decision making.

Controlling through Decision Making   Decision making is generally considered to be a thinking process in the head of the decider—in organizations, usually taken to be the manager. This may be true of many actual choices, but there is more to decision making than that. In fact, **decision making can be seen as encompassing the various aspects of controlling.**[14]

Consider the model of decision making shown in Figure 3.3 in three stages: (1) defining (and diagnosing) the issue, (2) developing possible courses of action to deal with it, and (3) deciding on the final outcome. Around these stages are shown five aspects of controlling, described next: designing, delegating, designating, distributing, and deeming.

---

[12] Hales and Mustapha (2000:13ff.) found that expectations for administration to be common for all the managers they studied (in the form of planning the work, allocating duties and resources, monitoring work performance, giving instructions, etc.). Indeed, they found this to be far stranger than were the expectations for staff development, in the form of training, mentoring, and so forth.

[13] This usage has hardly disappeared, as in the "bear management plans" I heard about in the Banff National Park.

[14] See Tengblad (2000), who has made a similar distinction, contrasting the chief executive as decision maker with that as leader, and discussing the "potential drawbacks of obtaining effective control by the use of decision-making" (p. 1). He found in his study of eight Swedish corporate chief executives that only 7 percent of their activities could be categorized as decision making. He concluded, "If decision-making is not seen as the task for the top manager but rather as *a* means of control a different picture emerges. In this article *influencing* is suggested to be the main task for the top manager" (p. 26).

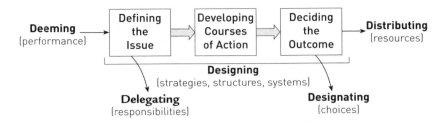

Figure 3.3 CONTROLLING THROUGH DECISION MAKING

Designing   **The field of management's most eminent thinker, Herbert Simon, considered designing to be the essential function of management**: intervention to create or change something (1969).[15] Managers sometimes engage in the design of tangible things, as when they head up a task force to develop a new product (which we shall discus on the action plane). Of concern here is designing the infrastructure of the unit, through strategies, structures, and systems to control the behaviors of its people.[16]

Designing Strategies   A favored metaphor for the manager is "architect" of organizational purpose (Andrews 1987): the person who designs on paper so that everyone else can build—in the language of strategic management, formulates strategies for others to implement. This assumes that strategy making is a process of deliberate design, in order to control behavior. (In Chapter 5, we shall contrast this with strategy making as a process of emergent learning.)

Designing Structures   Managers also design organizational structures: they divide up the work in their unit; allocate responsibilities for it to individual members; and then organize this around a hierarchy of authority, as depicted in those "organizational charts." Such structures help to set people's agendas, and so control their actions (see Watson 1994:32–33).

---

[15] See also Keough et al. (1992) on an interview with Jay Forrester about "The CEO as Organization Designer."

[16] Peter Senge (1990a) has referred to such designing as creating the social infrastructure of the unit, first by conceiving basic purpose, vision, and core values; next by setting up (policies), strategies, and structures that translate these into decisions; and finally by establishing the learning processes by which all of these are continuously improved.

Designing Systems   More directly, managers can take charge of designing, and sometimes even running, various systems of control in their units—concerning plans, objectives, schedules, budgets, performance, and so on. In fact, Robert Simons (1995) found in his research that corporate chief executives tend to select one such system (e.g., profit planning) and make it key to their exercise of control. In a similar vein, Morris et al. noted that the principals they studied "created and established a system for administering discipline in the school"—for example, using index cards so that "students learned there was a written record of their misbehavior" (1981:104). Note the "hands-off" nature of this form of controlling: the manager sets it up, and then the system does the controlling (much as deliberately designed strategies do the guiding).

Delegating   In delegating, the manager assigns a task to someone else on an ad hoc basis: a specific individual is directed to carry out a specific activity. This is thus shown in Figure 3.3 as emanating from the first stage of decision making. **In delegating, the manager identifies the need to get something done but leaves the deciding and the doing to someone else** (perhaps reserving the right to authorize that person's final choice).

The tricky thing about delegating is the dilemma noted in the last chapter (and discussed at length in Chapter 5): how to delegate when the manager, as nerve center, is better informed but lacks the time to do the task or even to pass on the information needed by someone else to do it.

Designating   If delegating focuses on the first stage of decision making, then **designating, including authorizing, focuses on the last stage—the making of specific choices.** Sometimes these concern issues that just arise and can quickly be resolved, as when a manager authorizes or refuses a decision proposed by someone else in the unit. Of course, it is not necessarily that simple.

- Catherine Joint-Dieterle of the fashion museum was asked by her assistant about hiring someone for an open position. "Oh, no, I know this guy. I don't want him," she replied. But at her assistant's insistence, she agreed to meet him, which she did later in the day. Then she hired him on the spot, commenting, "He's been through a hard time—had to give him a break." Many of the requests for authorization during the twenty-nine days came in administrative meetings, often about pending expenditures, as when Dr. Webb,

> head of the geriatric service in the hospital, met with his business
> manager: she was asking the questions, and he was giving quick
> short answers, mostly yes or no.

This designating can happen formally or informally, with the latter probably a lot more common and highly varied. Consider the comment by Andy Grove of Intel:

> To be sure, once in a while we managers in fact *make* a decision.
> But for every time that happens, we *participate* in the making of
> many, many others, and we do that in a variety of ways. We provide
> factual inputs or just offer opinions, we debate the pros and cons of
> alternatives and thereby force a better decision to emerge, we review
> decisions made or about to be made by others, encourage or dis-
> courage them, ratify or veto them. (1983:50–51)

Distributing   Distributing—namely, allocating resources as a result of other decisions—is a form of designating, too. But it merits separate attention because of its importance in managerial work.

Managers spend a good deal of time using their budgeting systems to allocate resources—money, materials, and equipment, as well as the efforts of other people. But they allocate resources in many other ways too—for example in how they schedule their own time and design the organization structures that determine how other people allocate their time.

Note that to treat something as a "resource" is to consider it as information—often numerical—for the purpose of control. So to "allocate resources" is to function on the information plane of managing, in the role of controlling. Indeed, **treating employees as "human resources" means to deal with them as if they are information, not people: they get reduced to a narrow dimension of their whole selves.** Later we shall discuss how much that today is considered interpersonal management on the people plane in fact reduces to the impersonal control of people on the information plane.

Deeming   Finally we come to deeming, which has become an increasingly popular form of controlling these days, but hardly under that label. ("Management by objectives" is a better-known one.) By deeming, I mean imposing targets on people and expecting them to perform accordingly: "Increase sales by 10 percent," or "Reduce costs by 20 percent"—and

"Do it in my first hundred days." The manager pronounces and then steps back. Indeed, such targets are often distant even from strategies themselves, since deeming is often favored when a manager lacks a clear frame. **All too often, when managers don't know what to do, they drive their subordinates to "perform."**

For much the same reason, a good deal of so-called strategic planning these days amounts to deeming. Treated as a formulaic process rooted in analysis rather than synthesis, strategic planning often discourages the creation of strategies, as managing gets reduced to "number crunching"—the setting of performance targets to drive behaviors (see my 1994 book *The Rise and Fall of Strategic Planning*). "Increase sales by 10 percent" is not a strategy.

During the twenty-nine days, I observed several planning meetings that had little to do with strategy, more with organizing or budgeting, even scheduling, as discussed in the accompanying box.

I do not wish here to dismiss the setting of targets, which is often necessary, but rather to make the point that deeming cannot stand alone. Managers have to get beyond the targets—inside them, and past them, into the workings of their units. So-called stretch goals are fine so long as the manager puts some personal walk behind the general talk. Put differently, **some deeming is fine; management by deeming is not.**

Deeming is easy—too easy for managers who are out of touch. Targets are fine when combined with ideas. When not, they can demean organizations, which have to be managed as integrated wholes, not collections of disconnected parts.

To conclude, controlling, on the information plane, is important, but not when it is removed from the people and action planes or, worse, used as a replacement for other roles on these planes.

MANAGING WITH PEOPLE

To manage *with* people, instead of *through* information, is to move one step closer to action but still to remain removed from it. On this plane, the manager helps other people make things happen: *they* are the doers.

Managing on the people plane requires a wholly different attitude from managing on the information plane. There the manager's activities

"Strategic" Planning as Framing? Deeming? Scheduling?

At one point, Paul Gilding, the Executive Director of Greenpeace, was joined by two of his reports, Annelieke, who arrived with a big pile of flip charts, and Steve. (The full report of this day appears in the appendix.) Annelieke put up the charts, the first titled "Basic Planning Exercise," and began explaining them. (The charts had labels such as "Finance and Implications of Strategic Planning," "Political Structure," and "Communication Structure.") But Paul interrupted: "Before we start, what's the aim of the whole exercise?" Annelieke answered: to have a work plan for the whole organization—who does what. As they discussed the charts, Paul commented, "We need to think through the Strategic Plan before implementation," and "We should have performance targets for the Strategic Plan."

Then Annelieke listed on the board, "(1) Objectives/mission; (2) Break down targets; (3) Communication," and they discussed how to proceed. "Are we brainstorming or just going through it systematically?" she asked at one point, and remarked at another that "I think we should move on; we can discuss [campaigns, the first chart] for two days, I'm sure. Resource allocation [the second chart]," she announced.

Were these three directors of Greenpeace directing, let alone strategizing? They were certainly trying to get some order in their own heads, to come to grips with the complexities of directing Greenpeace. Yet strategy, whether as broad perspective or specific positions, was barely mentioned. The exercise seemed to reduce to decomposition: of the organization into a collection of parts and the charts into a collection of wishes. These managers were not getting strategy from structure any more than they were getting ideas from planning.

Maybe, therefore, planning is really about "prioritizing"—getting things into order for the purposes of deciding what has to be done when, which in the model of this chapter is called *scheduling*. As Aaron Wildavsky put it: "Alone and afraid, man is at the mercy of strange and unpredictable forces, so he takes whatever comfort he can by challenging the fates. He shouts his plans into the storm of life. Even if all he hears is the echo of his own voice, he is no longer alone. To abandon his faith in planning would unleash the terror locked in him" (1973:151–152).

are instrumental, using information to drive people to specific ends. Here people are not driven so much as encouraged, often to ends they favor naturally. Thus, Linda Hill contrasted "I must get compliance for my subordinates" with "compliance does not equal commitment" (2007:3), and she continued later, "Management has just as much, if not more, to do with negotiating interdependence as it does with exercising formal authority. . . . 'being a manager' means not merely assuming a position of authority but also becoming more dependent on others," insiders and outsiders—and more so in senior positions (2003:262).

After several decades of POSDCORB thinking and Tayloristic techniques, the Hawthorne experiments of the 1930s (Rothlesburger 1939) demonstrated with dramatic impact that management has to do with more than just the control of "subordinates." People entered the scene, or at least they entered the literature, as human beings with concerns, and so to be "motivated" and later "empowered" by their managers. Influencing thus began to replace informing, and commitment began to vie with calculation. Indeed, by the 1960s and into the 1970s, the management of people, quite independent of the substance of their work, became a virtual obsession in the literature, through a succession of fashionable labels, such as "human relations," "Theory Y," "participative management," "quality of work life," and "total quality management." And then came "human resources"—back we went.

For all this time, however, these **people remained "subordinates": "participation" kept them subordinate, because this was seen as being granted at the behest of the manager, still fully in control. And the later term** *empowerment* **did not change that, because the term itself indicated that the power remained with the manager.** Truly empowered workers, such as doctors in a hospital, even bees in a hive, do not await gifts from their managerial gods; they know what they are there to do and just do it. You "have to be careful when talking 'empowerment'" to the people working in the Banff National Park, Charlie Zinkan, its Superintendent, told me: "We have mechanics reading the *Harvard Business Review!*" As Len Sayles put it: "Intrinsic job satisfaction can only be obtained by the employees themselves. It can't be handed out on a platter" (1964:53). In fact, a good deal of what is today called "empowerment" is really just getting rid of years of disempowerment (see Hales 2000 and Peters 1994:6).

People remained subordinates in another way, too. The focus of all this attention was on those inside the unit, who reported formally to its manager. Only after the beginning of serious research on managerial work did the obvious become evident: that managers generally spend at least as much time with people outside their units as they do with their own so-called subordinates. This section thus describes two managerial roles on the people plane: *leading* people within the unit and *linking* to people outside it.

Leading People Inside the Unit

When a specialist becomes a manager, the biggest change often is (or should be) the shift from "I" to "we." Having become responsible for the performance of others, the first instinct, as Hill found out, is to think, "Good, now I can make the decisions and issue the orders." Soon, however, comes the realization that "formal authority is a very limited source of power," that to become a manager is to become "more dependent . . . on others to get things done" (2003:262). Enter the role of *leading*.

More has been written about leadership than probably all other aspects of managing combined. The United States, in particular, is obsessed with it, now more than ever. (When I went on the Harvard MBA website in 2007, I counted the words *leader* and *leadership* more than fifty times.) As Hill noted:

> From their first days on the job, [the new managers] sprinkled the word "leadership" throughout their conversations, announcing, for example, that they intended to lead the organization. Leadership seemed to be a catch-all phrase. They were not [however] able to articulate with much confidence what they meant by it. (2003:105)

Find an organization with a problem and you will find all kinds of people proposing leadership as the solution. And if a new leader comes in and things improve, no matter what the cause (a stronger economy, a bankrupt competitor), they will have been proven right. This is part of our "Romance of Leadership" (Meindl et al. 1985).

Leadership can certainly make a difference. But it is no more the be-all and end-all than is controlling or strategizing. Leadership has to work alongside such other factors, plus especially "communityship," to make an organization effective. In fact, many organizations these days could use less leadership (see Raelin 2000; Mintzberg 2004a).

The word *leadership* tends to be used in two different senses. The first is with regard to position and the led: the leader is in charge, motivates and inspires, elicits shock and awe, turns around ailing companies. This is where that distinction between leaders and managers comes in. It is also where those courses on "leadership" come in: spend a few days in a classroom or a couple of years in an MBA program, and (if you believe the hype) out you pop, all ready to exercise leadership. Try to do so, however, and you discover, as did the new managers Hill (2003:92) studied, that **leadership is earned as well as learned, not granted.**

In the second sense, leadership is seen more broadly, often beyond formal authority: a leader is anyone who breaks new ground, sets direction that shows others the way. A great inventor is a leader (even if he or she is a recluse); so is anyone who takes the lead in an organization, regardless of position, as in those stories about "skunkworks" that have changed companies.

I appreciate both views—we need all the creative direction setting we can get. But in this book and especially this chapter, I wish to describe leadership as a necessary component of management—specifically about helping to engage people in the unit to function more effectively. In this spirit, Lombardo and McCall have written about managers "who do not speak of themselves as leaders" so much as "taking leadership" in specific situations (1981:23); in the next chapter, in a section called "Managing beyond the Manager," we shall discuss the second view of leadership.

Managers exercise such leadership with *individuals*, one-on-one, as the saying goes; with *teams*; and with the *whole unit or organization*, in terms of its culture. We shall begin with the individual, in two aspects: energizing people and developing them (see Raelin 2000:155).[17]

Energizing Individuals   Call it what you like, managers spend a good deal of time helping to bring about more effective behavior on the part of their reports: they motivate them, persuade them, support them, convince them, empower them, encourage them, engage them. But perhaps all of this is better put another way: **in the leading role, managers help to bring out the energy that exists naturally within people.** To quote the words of a prominent CEO: "It's not [the manager's] job to supervise or to motivate, but to liberate and enable" (Max DePree of Herman Miller, 1990).

---

[17] A third set of related managerial activities—including hiring, judging, remunerating, promoting, and dismissing individuals—falls under the role of controlling, not leading, because these are about making decisions. Of course, *how* a manager carries out these activities can put him or her on the people plane. But that is true of every managerial role, doing and dealing no less than controlling and communicating.

Developing Individuals   Also on the individual level, managers coach, train, mentor, teach, counsel, nurture: in general, they help develop the individuals in their units. Again, the vast array of labels indicates just how much attention this aspect of leading has received. But again, **the job of development is perhaps best seen as managers helping people to develop themselves.** (For our own efforts in this regard, see www .CoachingOurselves.com.) And not only managers: consider these lovely words of two schoolteachers in Calgary: "We lose patience with the idea that the teacher is there mainly to 'facilitate' children's development. . . . We are there for something more subtle and profound than that: we help mediate the knowledge, problems and questions the children already possess" (Clifford and Friesen 1993:19).

- This aspect of leadership came out most clearly in the days I spent in the refugee camps. Every "delegate" with the International Red Cross Federation, most of them experienced in disaster relief, had a "counterpart" in the Tanzanian Red Cross whom he or she trained. Abbas Gullet appeared to be spending a good deal of his time on such training, alongside the more regular tasks of reviewing performance, posting jobs, and interviewing applicants.[18] (See the appendix for a full description of Abbas's day.)

Sometimes as part of this developmental work, managers "do" in order to develop—in other words, they take action, not to get something done so much as to set an example for the taking of action by others. Andy Grove of Intel claimed that "nothing leads as well as example," adding that "values and behavioral norms are simply not transmitted easily by talk or memo, but are conveyed very effectively by doing and doing *visibly*" (1983:52).

Building and Maintaining Teams   On the group level, managers build and maintain teams inside their own units. **This involves not only bonding people into cooperative groups but also resolving**

---

[18] The time managers spend on such training seems to vary considerably. Hales and Mustapha, in their study of Malaysian middle managers, found that "expectations to *maintain* staffing levels and performance were stronger than expectations to *improve* staff performance" (2000:13), while Hill found that the new managers in the United States "were more comfortable" with the formal people management skills (e.g., training) than with their more informal ones (such as counseling and leadership) (2003).

conflicts within and between these groups so that they can get on with their work. "The leader . . . is one who can organize the experience of the group—whether it be the small group of the foreman, the larger group of the department, or the whole plant . . . and thus get the full power of the group. The leader makes the team" (Follett 1949:12).

A great deal has been written about this, which, again, need not be repeated here. But one observation by Hill is worth mentioning. The new managers she studied initially conceived of their "people-management role as building the most effective relationships they [could] with each *individual* subordinate," and so they "fail[ed] to recognize, much less address, their team-building responsibilities." But over time, after mistakes, they realized the importance of this (2003:284).

Perhaps this occurs because "new managers get fooled" by organizational structure: "they assume that if all workers do their jobs according to some master plan or direction, there will be no need for contact or human intervention" (Sayles 1979:22). In other words, the controlling role will take care of the necessary coordination. Not so, wrote Sayles, and this was evident to me as Fabienne Lavoie worked to knit her nurses into a smoothly functioning team and Abbas Gullet brought the delegates and counterparts to work together in the refugee camps.

Hill (2003:289) cited Peter Drucker (1992) on the difference between managing people who play *on* a team (as in baseball) versus those who play *as* a team (as in football or an orchestra). Kraut et al. likewise commented on successful athletics teams that have an "almost uncanny ability to perform as a single unit, with the efforts of individual members blending seamlessly together." Management as "a team sport . . . makes similar demands on its players" (2005:122).

Establishing and Strengthening Culture   Finally, in the full unit, and more commonly for the chief executive of an entire organization, managers play a key role in establishing and strengthening the culture.

Culture is intended to do collectively what other aspects of the leading role do for individuals and small groups: encourage the best efforts of people, by aligning their interests with the needs of the organization. **In contrast to decision *making* as a form of controlling, culture is decision *shaping* as a form of leading.** "One principal roams the school reminding teachers and students of their duties and exhorting all participants in the learning process to strive for good work and exemplary performance" (Morris et al. 1982:691). John Cleghorn did much the same in the time he spent in the Royal Bank branches in Montreal, promoting the bank's values to everyone who came his way.

Earlier the manager was described as the nerve center of information in the unit. Here **the manager can be described as the energy center of the unit's culture.** As William F. Whyte put it in his classic study of street gangs:

> The leader is the focal point for the organization of his group. In his absence, the members of the gang are divided into a number of small groups. There is no common activity or general conversation. When the leader appears, the situation changes strikingly. The small units form into one large group. The conversation becomes general, and unified action frequently follows. (1955:258)

In the 1980s, with the great success of the Japanese enterprises came a great deal of attention to what was seen as key to that success: corporate culture (e.g., Pascale and Athos 1981). But as Japan subsequently encountered economic difficulties, that message got lost; indeed, it was swamped by the rise of the bottom-line mentality (i.e., controlling). This was a mistake: the great enterprises remain those with the great cultures, in Japan and elsewhere. Just consider the enormous success of Toyota, a company that has remained largely faithful to the Japanese view of corporate culture.

Perhaps no one has written more eloquently about the manager's role in building culture than sociologist Phillip Selznick, in a little book published in 1957 called *Leadership in Administration*. He used other labels, but his focus was clear: the leader shapes the "character of the organization"; he or she builds "policy" (now called strategy) "into the organization's social structure" through the "institutional embodiment of purpose" and the infusion of the system "with value." That is how an "expendable" organization becomes a responsive "institution."[19]

---

[19] Selznick distinguished this cultural aspect of leadership from the individual and group aspects discussed earlier, which he called "interpersonal," where the leader's "task is to smooth the path of human interaction, ease communication, evoke personal devotion, and allay anxiety," for the "efficiency of the enterprise. The *institutional* leader, in contrast, is concerned with "the promotion and protection of values" (1957:27–28).

Others have referred to this as the "management of meaning," which obviously goes beyond the processing of information and even the development of strategy, to a sense of vision as the driving force of the organization as a community. Bolman and Deal have written that "the task of leaders is to *interpret experience*": the lessons of history, what is happening in the world, and so forth, to "give meaning and purpose . . . with beauty and passion" (1991:43).[20]

In Mary Parker Follett's words, leadership can transform "experience into power. . . . The ablest administrators do not merely draw logical conclusions from the array of facts of the past. . . . They have a vision of the future" (1949:52, 53), which helps "interpret our experience to us," leading "us to wise decisions" instead of the leaders imposing "wise decisions upon us. We need leaders, not masters or drivers. . . . This is the power which creates community" (1920:229, 230).

Consider in this regard the queen bee in the hive: "She issues no orders; she obeys, as meekly as the humblest of her subjects, the naked power . . . we will term the 'spirit of the hive'" (Maeterlinck 1901). But by her very presence, manifested in the emitting of a chemical substance, she unites the members of the hive and galvanizes them into action. In human organizations, we call this substance culture; it is the spirit of the human hive.

The culture of an organization may be rather difficult to establish, and to change—that can take years, if ever—but it can be rather easy to destroy, given a neglectful management. That is why the sustaining of culture was front and center on several of the days I spent with managers of long-established organizations:

- In the refugee camps, Abbas Gullet, as head of delegation and its most experienced member, was the carrier of the Red Cross culture, as concerned about getting others to appreciate it as he was in training for disaster relief. In a police force, we might expect to see a good deal of conventional controlling, in the form of rules, performance standards, and forms to fill out. There was no shortage of that on the days I spent with the three RCMP managers. But greater emphasis seemed to be put on culture: controlling behavior through the sharing of norms, based on

---

[20] Cohen and March have similarly written that the university president "is expected to capture the historic truths of the university as an institution" (1986:39).

careful socialization. Thus, Commissioner Inkster visited the officer training school and spoke extemporaneously for a half hour, followed by a blunt period of questions and answers.

To conclude this discussion of the role of leading, we can return to the metaphor of the leader as conductor, on the platform, fully in control. Does that actually constitute the exercise of leadership? Read the accompanying box.

Some Myths of the Conductor as Leader

In the conductor of the symphony orchestra, we have leadership captured perfectly in caricature. The great chief stands on the podium, with the followers arranged nearly around, ready to respond to every commend. The maestro raises the baton, and they all play in perfect unison. Another motion and they all stop. Absolutely in charge—a manager's dream. Yet all of it is a perfect myth.

For one thing, as Bramwell Tovey, conductor of the Winnipeg Symphony, was quick to point out, this is an organization of subordination, and that includes the conductor. (See the appendix for the full description of Bramwell's day, including his comments.) Mozart pulls the strings. Even that great maestro, Toscanini, was quoted as saying, "I am no genius. I have created nothing. I play the music of other men" (Lebrecht 1991: Chapter 4, p. 1). How else to explain the phenomenon of the "guest conductor"? Try to imagine a "guest manager" in almost any other kind of organization.[21]

Watching rehearsals reinforced this message. I saw a lot more action than affect. Bramwell Tovey was *doing*. Rehearsing is the work of the organization, and he was managing it directly, like the project that it really is. He was managing it for results: about pace, pattern, tempo, sound—smoothing it, harmonizing it, perfecting it. (Bramwell wrote to me later, in response to these comments: "In the traditional sense, I do most of my *leading* during performance, when, by means of physical gesture, I completely control the orchestra's timing—and timing is everything." For him perhaps, but hardly for most managers.) Here, if you like, he was orchestra *operating*, not orchestra leading, not even orchestra *directing*.

---

[21] Actually, Inkson et al. (2001) have written an article on the "interim manager."

Yet if we have to get past leading in the foreground, then perhaps we need to place it in the background. Bramwell himself used the label "covert leadership."[22] As noted earlier, when asked about his leadership, Bramwell replied, "We never talk about 'the relationship.'" Yet leadership was certainly on his mind: all that "doing" was influenced by various affective concerns—a feud between players, their sensitivities, aspects of the union contract, fear of censure in his role as first among equals.

Leading on the individual, team, and unit or organization-wide level can easily be distinguished in most managerial jobs. Not here.

As Bramwell made clear, direct leadership intervention concerning individuals was largely precluded during rehearsals. On the *group* level, there was something most curious here: a team of seventy people. Of course, there are "sections" within an orchestra, each with its own head, but these are players, not managers. When the orchestra plays, or even rehearses, there is only one manager, and only one team. So conventional team building is hardly possible. Bramwell said in jest at a presentation we later did together, "I don't see my job as a manager. I look on it more as a lion tamer!" It was a good line that got a good laugh, but it hardly captures the image of seventy rather tame pussycats sitting in neatly ordered rows ready to play together at the flick of a wand.

That leaves culture building. What does this mean here? Seventy people come together for rehearsals and then disperse. When is the culture built? Again, perhaps covertly: through the energy, attitude, and general behavior of the conductor. But beyond this, culture is built into the very system. In other words, I was observing the culture, not just of the Winnipeg Symphony Orchestra, but of symphony orchestras in general, developed over more than a century. So the culture of this particular orchestra did not have to be created so much as enhanced. "The conductor is no more than a magnifying mirror of the world in which he lives, *Homo sapiens* writ large" (Lebrecht 1991:5).

So beware, all you "leaders" (and leadership mavens). One day you may wake up to find that Bramwell Tovey is what a good deal of contemporary managing and its covert leadership is all about. Then you will have to step off your hierarchical podiums, lay down your budgetary batons, and get down on the ground, where the real work of your organization takes place. Only there can you and the others make beautiful music together.

---

[22] Which so appealed to the editors of the *Harvard Business Review* that they used it for the title of an article on this research (Mintzberg 1998).

Linking to People Outside the Unit

"Nothing legitimates and substantiates the position of leaders more than their ability to handle external relations. Above all else, leaders control a boundary, or interface" (Sayles 1979:38). Still on the people plane, **linking looks out the way leading looks in: it focuses on the web of relationships that managers maintain with numerous individuals and groups outside their units, whether in other units of the same organization or outside of it entirely.**

"When compared to non-managers, managers show wider organizational membership networks—they belong to more clubs, societies, and the like" (Carroll and Teo 1996:437). Homans (1958) referred to these as "exchange" relationships and Kaplan as "reciprocating" ones (1984)—see also his excellent description of what he called the managers' "trade routes"—because the manager gives something in order to get something else in return, immediately, or as an investment in a sort of interpersonal bank.

- The intricacies of linking were most evident during the days I spent with the three managers of the Canadian parks. As illustrated in Figure 3.4, they all managed on the edges—between their units and the external context—but in each case a different one. Sandy Davis, head of the western region, managed especially on a *political edge*, shown horizontally above her, particularly between her parks in western Canada and the administrators and politicians in Ottawa. She connected politics to process. Charlie Zinkan, head of the Banff National Park, who reported to Sandy, managed especially on a *stakeholder edge*, shown vertically to either side of him, as various outsiders brought pressures to bear on him. He connected influence to programs. And Gord Irwin, Front Country Manager in the Banff National Park, who reported to Charlie, functioned especially on an *operating edge*, between the operations and the administration, shown horizontally across the bottom of the figure. He connected action to administration.

It is surprising how little attention linking has received in the writings on management, despite the evidence from study after study, over several decades, that managers are external linkers as much as they are internal leaders (e.g., Sayles 1964; Mintzberg 1973; Kotter 1982a, 1982b). "The most important products of [the effective executives'] approach were

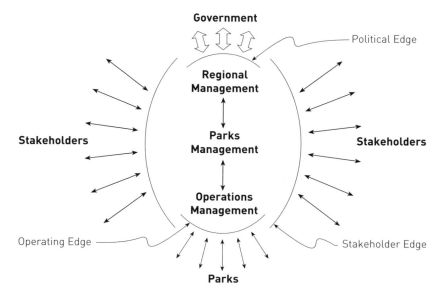

Figure 3.4 MANAGING ON THE EDGES (in the Canadian parks)

agendas and networks, not formal plans and organizational charts" (Kotter 1982a:127). This lack of attention is even more surprising now given the extent to which contemporary organizations engage in alliances, joint ventures, and other collaborative relationships.[23]

Many of these linking relationships develop on a peer level; in other words, "social equals tend to interact with one another at high frequency" (Homans 1950:186). But they extend well beyond that, to include links with more senior people (including the managers' own managers) and other staff and line people in the same organization, and a great many outsiders in the workflow (customers, suppliers, partners, union officials, etc.), as well as trade association and government officials, experts, community representatives, and a host of others.[24] Morris et al., for example,

---

[23] Interestingly, Hill found that the people reporting to the manager tended to be most aware of this role, in their expectations that their manager would protect them. "[T]he subordinates thought of the manager as their liaison with the outside world," especially as "buffer and advocate" (2003:33).

[24] In his 1979 book, Sayles categorized these as workflow relationships, service relationships, advisory relationships, stabilizing relationships, and liaison relationships.

found a school principal who "cultivate[d] . . . grandmothers"—neighborhood residents who knew the community well and so could act as "spotters" for the school, "warn[ing] him of unusual developments" (1982:689).

- A great variety of people linked to the managers during the twenty-nine days of observation. Fabienne Lavoie on the ward connected to doctors, patients, and families of patients. John Cleghorn lunched with financial investors of the Royal Bank, informing them for the purpose of influencing them, while Brian Adams had to work with partner companies of Bombardier from all over the world (Mitsubishi in Japan, BMW/Rolls-Royce in Europe, Honeywell in the United States, etc.). Marc, as head of the hospital, sat in a web of intense forces—his office almost felt like a state of siege. This included a government intent on cutting hospital expenditures and doctors who did not hesitate to go around him to members of the board. In the Red Cross camps, Abbas Gullet and Stephen Omollo interacted with their Tanzanian counterparts, NGO people, UN officials, representatives of refugees and the donor agencies, and by mail and phone with Red Cross officials in Africa and Switzerland.

A model of the manager's linking role is shown in Figure 3.5. It comprises the activities of networking, representing, conveying and convincing, transmitting, and buffering, each discussed in turn.

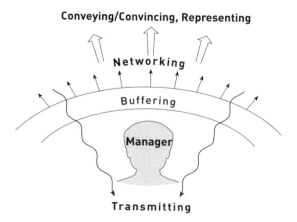

Figure 3.5 A MODEL OF LINKING

Networking   One thing is clear. **Networking is pervasive: almost all managers spend a good deal of time building up networks of outside contacts and establishing coalitions of external supporters.** Kotter noted that the general managers he studied "all allocated significant time and effort early in their jobs [as well as later] to developing a network of cooperative relationships," and that "the excellent performers . . . approached network building more aggressively and built stronger networks" (1982a:67, 117).

> - Carol Haslam, Managing Director at the film company Hawkshead, brokered between customers and producers, drawing on what seemed to be an immense web of contacts and a finely tuned understanding of the British television industry. Her diary was thick, mostly because of a handwritten telephone directory of contacts. In the Red Cross, Abbas Gullet exhibited a particular ability to bridge, not only between English and Swahili as well as Africans and Europeans, but also between a head office in a wealthy European city and the delegation compound office in an impoverished African township. In Gouldner's terms (1957), Abbas was a cosmopolitan and a local, able to combine his formal knowledge of the institution with his tacit knowledge of the situation.

Once again, it is enlightening to read two descriptions of this networking activity that are so remarkably similar even though one is about a president of the United States of America and the other about the leader of an American street gang.

> [President Franklin D. Roosevelt's] personal sources were the product of a sociability and curiosity that reached back to the other Roosevelt's time. He had an enormous acquaintance in various phases of national life and at various levels of government; he also had his wife and her variety of contacts. . . . Roosevelt quite deliberately exploited these relationships and mixed them up to widen his own range of information. He changed his sources as his interests changed, but no one who had ever interested him was quite forgotten or immune to sudden use. (Neustadt 1960:156–157)

> The leader [of the street gang] is better known and more respected outside his group than are any of his followers. His capacity for

social movement is greater. One of the most important functions he performs is that of relating his group to other groups in the district. Whether the relationship is one of conflict, competition, or cooperation, he is expected to represent the interests of his fellows. The politician and the racketeer must deal with the leader in order to win the support of his followers. The leader's reputation outside the group tends to support his standing within the group, and his position in the group supports his reputation among outsiders. (Whyte 1955:259–260)

Representing   On the external front, **managers play a *figurehead* role, representing their unit officially to the outside world,** whether it be a company CEO presiding at some formal dinner, a university dean signing diplomas for graduating students, or a factory foreman greeting visiting customers. (Someone once said, only half in jest, that the manager is the person who meets the visitors so that everyone else can get their work done.) "[T]he President of the United States, besides being a leader of the political party in power, is 'head of the Nation in the ceremonial sense of the term, the symbol of the American national solidarity'" (U.S. Committee Report, cited in Carlson 1951:24).[25]

> • Bramwell Tovey spent the evening at the home of the most generous supporter of the orchestra, who was hosting "The Maestro's Circle." There he socialized with about fifty of the orchestra's supporters, gave a short speech, and then entertained them at the piano. Detachment Commander Ralph Humble of the RCMP met with some local people to update them on the handling of a complaint, which he saw as a kind of public relations gesture.

Conveying and Convincing   Managers use their networks to gain support for their unit. This may simply entail, on the information plane, *conveying* nerve center information to appropriate outsiders—for example, telling those grandmothers in the vicinity of the school to watch out for drug dealers. Or, on the people plane, managers seek to *convince*

---

[25] Selznick (1957) referred to these representing activities as defending the "institutional integrity" of the organization, although defending its "legitimacy" has since become the more fashionable term. See also Goodsell (1989) on "Administration as Ritual."

outsiders about what is important for their unit—for example, encouraging accounting to increase its budget, or using pageants to "orchestrat[e] community involvement" at school (Morris et al. 1981:78). In the popular vocabulary, **managers *champion* the needs of their unit, *lobby* for its causes, *promote* its products, *advocate* on behalf of its values—and just plain *peddle influence for it.*[26]**

- A good part of Rony Brauman's day was spent in press and media interviews, representing the views of Doctors Without Borders on the situation in Somalia, to influence public opinion. He was "speaking out" more than just speaking. In N'gara, Stephen Omollo spent an hour and a half with Ben, a representative of the European Community Humanitarian Assistance office, who grilled him on the use of the funds it supplied for the Red Cross camps. At one point, Stephen said that 98 percent of the householders got the food they were supposed to get. "What actually ends up in their stomachs?" Ben wanted to know, as opposed to being bartered for sale or perhaps "taxed" away. Ben's knowledge of the details and the conscientiousness with which he pursued his auditing responsibilities were impressive, but so were Stephen's informed and articulate responses.

Transmitting   Linking is a two-way street: **managers who peddle influence out are the targets of influence coming in, a good deal of which has to be *transmitted* to others in the unit.**

- For Brian Adams of Bombardier to get that new airplane in the air as promised, everything had to come together on a tight schedule. So he had to pass to his engineers the pressures that came to him from suppliers and his own senior management, to ensure that they were dealt with promptly. Likewise, Carol Haslam of Hawskhead had to ensure that the internal making of the films was responsive to the external concerns of the clients.

These activities of conveying, convincing, and transmitting can require a rather intricate blending of information and influence, values

---

[26] See Dutton and Ashford (1993) on "issue selling," Bower and Weinberg (1988) on "statescraft."

and visions. Years ago, the Greek economist (and later prime minister) Andreas Papandreou described the corporate chief executive as a "peak coordinator," who consciously and unconsciously brings "the influences which are exerted on the firm" into some sort of "preference function" (1952:211). What form this might take is difficult to specify, but years earlier, Mary Parker Follett expressed the same idea more practically, and rather eloquently, in the case of a community leader:

> He must be able to interpret a neighborhood not only to itself but to others. . . . He must know the great movements of the present and their meaning, and he must know how the smallest needs and the humblest powers of his neighborhood can be fitted into the progressive movements of our time. . . . He must be always alert and ever ready to gather up the many threads into one strand of united endeavor. He is the patient watcher, the active spokesman, the sincere and ardent exponent of a community consciousness. (1920:230–231)

Buffering   It is in this combination of all these linking activities that we can especially appreciate the delicate balancing act that has to be built into the art and craft of managing. Managers are not just *channels* through which pass information and influence; they are also *valves* in these channels, which control what gets passed on, and how. To use two other popular words, **managers are *gatekeepers and buffers* in the flow of influence.** To appreciate the importance of this, consider five ways by which managers can get it wrong:

- Some managers are *sieves* who let influence flow too easily into their unit. This can drive their reports crazy, forcing them to respond to every pressure. We see this commonly these days when the demands of stock market analysts cause the chief executives of publicly traded companies to force everyone to manage for short-term performance.

- Other managers are *dams* who block out too much of the external influence—for example, from customers asking for product changes. This may protect the people inside the unit, but in so doing detaches them from the outside world—and external support.

- Then there are the *sponges*—managers who absorb most of the pressures themselves. This may be appreciated by others, but it is only a matter of time before these managers burn themselves out. I have seen this in some chiefs of hospital departments who are overprotective of the physicians.

- Managers acting as *hoses* instead put great pressure on the people outside, who may as a consequence become angry and less inclined to cooperate. This is common when a company squeezes its suppliers excessively.

- Finally, there are the *drips*, who exert too little pressure on the people outside, so that the needs of the unit are not well represented. Examples are those managers who ask too little of their suppliers and so get taken advantage of.

The effective manager may act in each of these ways some of the time but does not allow any of them to dominate all of the time. In other words, **managing on the edges—the boundaries between the unit and its context—is a tricky business: every unit has to be protected, responsive, and aggressive, depending on the circumstances.**

- A number of the managers I observed seemed to manage on the edges with a good deal of subtlety. Doug Ward, head of the CBC radio station in Ottawa, was "nudged" extensively by other parts of the organization, but he was quite clear on what to pass into his unit and what to hold back, also how to "nudge" back (e.g., about a proposed information system that he found questionable). "It's nice having a job at the interface," Doug said in response to a comment I made about such linking. The buffer par excellence was Marc, who protected his hospital and advocated for it aggressively. Had he acted as the government's agent, or even that of the board, the hospital's difficulties in coming to grips with its disparate inside forces would only have multiplied.

MANAGING ACTION DIRECTLY

If managers manage through information—conceptually, from a distance—and with people—closer, personally, with affect—then on a third plane they manage action directly: more actively, and concretely. Here we have a popularly recognized view of managing, at least in practice—"Mary-Anne is a doer"—if not in a literature that has long overemphasized controlling and leading.

Again, Len Sayles is one of the few to have insisted on the importance of this role (1964, 1979), alongside Tom Peters. The manager must be the focal point for action, Sayles argued, with direct involvement having to take precedence over the pulling force of leading and the pushing force of controlling. "The essence of management," he wrote, is not "making key decisions, planning, and 'motivating' subordinates," so much as "endless negotiations, trade and bargaining" as well as the "redirection of one's own and one's subordinates' activities" (1964:259–260).

Linda Hill's new managers recognized this only after they were well into their jobs. "When asked at the end of the first months, what is a manager, the new managers no longer responded 'being the boss' or 'being the person in control.' Instead, the most common observations included being a 'trouble-shooter,' a 'juggler,' and a 'quick-change artist'" (2003:57). If, from a distance, managing looks like controlling on the information plane, then close up, getting involved on the action plane looms a lot larger.

- Catherine Joint-Dieterle of the fashion museum played a major role in the bringing in of new garments and reviewing each as it arrived; she was personally involved in the public tours of the museum; she wrote the proposals for new exhibitions. This was unlike Carol Haslam, head of Hawskhead, who did the deals but let others make the films.

We have seen repeatedly in this chapter that the most common managerial roles have generated many vernacular expressions. And so it is here, too. Managers "champion change," "manage projects"; "fight fires"; "do deals." Some of this pertains to actions taken within the unit, discussed here as *doing on the inside*; some others happen beyond the unit, discussed as *dealing on the outside*.

Doing on the Inside

What does it mean for a manager to be a doer? Many managers, after all, hardly "do" anything. Some don't even place their own phone calls. Watch a manager at work and what you see is a lot of talking and listening, not doing.

Doing in the context of managing usually means *almost* doing—that is, getting close to the taking of action: managing it directly, rather than indirectly by encouraging people or processing information. So **the manager as "doer" is really the person who "gets it done,"** as in the French expression *faire faire* (literally, "to make something get made").

What is it that managers actually do? This has to relate to what the unit gets done, the actions that it takes—whether to produce a product in a company, deliver a baby in a hospital, or head up a study in a consulting firm—but in the sense of changing directly the way these things get done. Key here is that the manager's involvement is not passive. This is not about sitting in an office and giving orders, ("Joe, ship twenty of those to Acme") or making judgment on those actions. Deeming is not doing. Nor is it about designing strategies, structures, and systems to drive other people. All of that is controlling. In the doing role, the manager gets personally involved in those actions, "hands-on": he or she becomes part of the designing of actions that change the unit's output.

> • Delays in the delivery of food to the refugees brought Abbas Gullet into one camp to investigate, and a complaint by a refugee about a camp manager brought Stephen Omollo into another camp to meet with a representative of the refugees.

When the time came some years ago to redesign Pampers, Proctor & Gamble's most important product, the chief executive of the whole company headed up the task force. When Johnson & Johnson faced a crisis after someone tampered with a few of its Tylenol packages, it was the CEO who headed up the response effort (Bennis 1989). These examples suggest that **there are two aspects of the doing role: managing projects proactively and handling disturbances reactively.**

Managing Projects   Managers choose to head up projects themselves, or to join others on them, for a variety of reasons. Sometimes it is *to learn*: to inform themselves about something they need to know. Other times it is to *demonstrate*—that is, manage actions to encourage others to take action, or show them how to do so. And most commonly, perhaps, managers involve themselves in projects because they are concerned about the *outcomes*. Thus, in the Pampers example, the CEO may have acted personally to find out more about the product and its customers, to demonstrate project management skills, or else—likely in this case—because the project was so important that the CEO simply felt he had to lead it.

> • Jacques Benz, Director-General of GSI, was an active participant in a meeting about a software platform being developed for the French Post Office. After listening for some time, he commented, "There's a choice to make"; later he gave some advice; and at the

end of the meeting, he pushed for what was needed at the next meeting. Asked why he attended, Jacques replied that the project was setting a precedent for the company, "the beginning of a strategy." At Greenpeace, doing meant not only taking actions but also "staging events" (in the words of its executive director), in which the senior managers were sometimes involved. "Hugging trees" was a common expression here. In the case of Brian Adams at Bombardier, doing, dealing, and linking all came to-gether. He searched for problems—anything that could have impeded getting that plane off the ground on schedule—and then set out to resolve them.

Of course, few managers can take personal charge of all their unit's projects, even all the key ones. But the suggestion in some of the literature that managers should "do" nothing—doing being dismissed as micro-managing—stems from a sterile view of the job: the manager on a pedes-tal, out of literal "touch," simply pronouncing strategies for everyone else to implement. As reported by an executive in the motorcycle business: "The Chief Executive of a world famous group of management consul-tants tried hard to convince me that it is ideal that top level management executives should have as little knowledge as possible relative to the prod-uct. This great man really believed that this qualification enabled them to deal efficiently with all business matters in a detached and uninhibited way" (Hopwood 1981:173).

This might work fine in a simple world. Ours, unfortunately (actu-ally, fortunately), is a messy one. So managers have to get out and find out what's going on, and one sensible way to do this is to get involved in specific projects. The projects benefit from the managers' nerve cen-ter information, while the managers learn their way to new strategies. **Strategies are not immaculately conceived in detached offices so much as learned through tangible experiences** (more on this in Chapter 5). Put differently, projects don't just execute strategies; they help to establish them in the first place, as in the example of Jacques Benz just cited. Managers *off* the ground often don't learn—and thus turn out to be dreadful strategists.

The last chapter described managers as "jugglers" who get involved in many projects. For one chief executive of my earlier study, during the week of observation I noted several, concerning public relations, possible acquisitions, setup of a new overseas manufacturing facility, resolution of a problem with an advertising agency, and so on.

With all sorts of responsibilities, most managers cannot allow themselves to focus on one project—that "magnificent obsession" noted earlier from Noel's study (1989). But there can be important exceptions—for example when the unit is in crisis or is facing a magnificent opportunity. And then there are the project managers, such as Brian Adams at Bombardier, whose job focuses on one project.

For most managers, however, a variety of projects demand attention. Since these tend to proceed in fits and starts anyway, with many delays, the manager can work on each intermittently, occasionally giving it a boost and then turning to other concerns until another boost later becomes necessary. Marples described this with an apt metaphor:

> The manager's job can usefully be pictured as a stranded rope made of fibers of different lengths—where length represents time—each fiber coming to the surface one or more times in observable "episodes" and representing a single issue. . . . A prime managerial skill may be the capacity to keep a number of "issues" in play over a large number of episodes, and long periods of time. (1967:287)

Handling Disturbances   If managing projects is largely about initiating and designing proactive change in the unit—essentially exploiting opportunities—then handling disturbances is about reacting to changes forced on the unit. An unforeseen event, a problem long ignored, the appearance of a new competitor may precipitate a disturbance, and a correction becomes necessary. "Management is a contingency activity; managers act when routines break down, when unexpected snags appear" (Sayles 1979:17).

- Alan Whelan's day at BT, as described earlier, was largely one of dealing with what for him was a major disturbance—the failure to get a sign-off on a large contract. Brian Adams of Bombardier had to intervene with a "problem supplier" of the airplane, and Abbas Gullet faced a crisis in the camp hospital, due to the inadvertent firing of its head nurse. (All three days are described at length in the Appendix.)

As noted earlier, in the words of Farson, as managers advance to senior positions, they "deal increasingly with predicaments, not problems." These "require interpretative thinking . . . [because of] paradoxical courses and consequences. Alas, predicaments cannot be handled smoothly" (1996:43), as we discuss in Chapter 5 under the labels of conundrums.

Why must the manager be the one to respond? Aren't others in the unit there to do that? Sure, and they often do. But some disturbances require the manager's formal authority, or his or her nerve center information. And others link to concerns that no one else in the unit can appreciate—the reaction of a key stakeholder, for example. Moreover, problems often degenerate into disturbances precisely because they have fallen between the cracks: no one in the unit has taken responsibility. So the manager has to do so. Hence, research has indicated that "leaders have more influence during periods of crisis than during non-crises periods" (Hamblin 1958:322). Returning to the Johnson & Johnson story, in the words of the company's chief executive, who "took charge immediately" after poison was found in some of those Tylenol capsules:

> I knew I had to and I knew I could. . . . I knew the media. I was a news freak, and I'd dealt with the networks several times. I knew the heads of news, who to call, how to talk with them. . . . I was in this room twelve hours a day. I solicited advice from everyone, because no one had ever dealt with this kind of issue before. It was brand-new. . . . We put together the new packaging overnight practically, when it would have normally taken two years. (in Bennis 1989:152–154)

There is no shortage of reported stories about disturbances that arose because of incompetent or at least neglectful management. Fair enough, much of this time. Less discussed, but equally worth noting, is the other side of this coin: that disturbances occur naturally in every organization (as in this example). In fact, **the effective organizations may be not only those that avoid many disturbances but also the ones whose managers deal effectively with the unexpected disturbances that do arise.** Indeed, the more innovative the organization, the more likely are disturbances to occur unexpectedly. The organization that doesn't take risks may avoid all disturbances, until the one that sinks it in the end. So judge the manager by the response and not just by the event.

- When a boat overturned on Lake Victoria, causing almost a thousand deaths, as soon as he heard the news Abbas Gullet (as he described to me) called the Tanzania Red Cross office in

> Dar-es-Salaam. Realizing that they were unprepared for this and that in N'gara he was relatively close to it, Abbas collected nine other Red Cross people, grabbed what supplies they could—body bags, stretchers, disinfectants—and headed there by road, arriving one day after the accident, the first NGO on site. They stayed two weeks, working long hours, arranging for body recovery, setting up a morgue in a nearby stadium, and helping the bereaved families.

One other aspect of disturbance handling merits mention here. Sometimes a manager substitutes for someone in the unit who is ill, has quit unexpectedly, or otherwise cannot do the job. Here the manager engages in the regular work of the unit. But since he or she is disturbance handling—filling in by exception—this should be considered part of the job of managing.

There are times, of course, when managers simply choose to do some of the regular operating work of their organization: the pope leads prayers; a hospital chief does clinical work on Fridays; Catherine Joint-Dieterle organized museum exhibitions herself. Perhaps they simply enjoy this work and would otherwise miss it, in which case it is no more managing than is a weekly game of tennis (at least without a client). But there may be managerial reasons behind these activities, too: the pope may be acting as figurehead, and the hospital head may be keeping in touch.

To conclude this discussion of the doing role, Chester Barnard has written: "Executive work is not that of the organization, but the specialized work of *maintaining* the organization in operation" (1938:215). It sounds right; the tricky part is distinguishing one from the other.[27]

Dealing on the Outside

Dealing is the other side of doing, its external manifestation. Sometimes it is called "doing the deal" or "wheeling and dealing" (although these

---

[27] Braybrooke has written, "[As] one investigates, one seems to discover that an executive can be said to do something clearly identifiable only when he is doing something that in a larger or more perfect organization would be done by a subordinate, or, in other words, it would seem that the more specialized the role of leadership becomes, the more difficult it is to say what a leader does. For in a perfect organization, would not every specialized power be delegated to some specialized functionary? The man at the top would be left with nothing, or what seems to approach nothing, to do. He would simply approve the decisions of subordinates; in a smoothly running organization, he would never have any occasion to disapprove" (1964:534). Remember this when we get to the perfect organization that runs smoothly.

suggest the too-common disconnection of the dealing from the doing, as in the CEO who does the deal—negotiates the acquisition—and then dumps its ill considered consequences into the laps of others). Managers do deals with outsiders, such as suppliers, but also with other managers inside their own organization.

> - As Doug Ward noted about the CBC: "This place has become very entrepreneurial, much more deal oriented," with a philosophy of "If you can help me, I'll help you." His proudest "done deals" seemed to have been his replacements of weak staff, involving considerable negotiations, not only with the individuals in question, but also with the managers of other CBC units willing to take them.

There are two main components of the dealing role: *building coalitions* **around specific issues—sometimes called** *mobilizing support***—and then using these coalitions together with established networks to** *conduct negotiations.* I shall discuss them together.

Much doing requires dealing: to get projects going usually requires considerable negotiating—with suppliers, customers, partners, government officials, and many others. But there are also deals that are primarily external, as when a corporate CEO works out a stock issue with investment bankers, or is called in to close the negotiations on a union contract. Sayles has written that "sophisticated [middle] managers place great stress on negotiations as a way of life" (1964:131). But so, of course, do senior managers:

> - As head of Hawkshead Films, Carol Haslam had to put together projects across TV networks, even around the world, pitching ideas to her potential clients and convincing them of her firm's ability to execute them. This was a particularly intricate process, involving a great deal of connecting and juggling. As director of the Global Express program at Bombardier, Brian Adams had to negotiate all kinds of arrangements with the partner/suppliers, to ensure smooth flow in designing and building the airplane.

Managing partners of consulting firms as well as chief executives of some high-technology firms, such as a Boeing and Airbus, often act as salespeople to secure contracts with customers. Here they are carrying out what is considered to be operating work in most other industries, but, as noted at the outset of this chapter, sometimes only they have the status and authority to close the deal. Put differently (now that we have introduced some new labels), **as figureheads, managers add credibility to the negotiations; as nerve centers, they can bring comprehensive information to bear on them; as distributors, they are able to commit the necessary resources in real time.** A key to understanding managerial work, therefore, is to appreciate not only *what* managers do, but also *why* they do it.

> • John Tate, as Deputy Minister of the Canadian Justice Department, not only managed the making of policy but also was an expert on it and so had to act in that capacity with other government departments and beyond. Because dealing was fundamental to the mission of Greenpeace (negotiating with companies and governments to reduce pollution, etc.), it was especially important in the jobs of the two managers I observed there.

Too Much Micromanaging?   We can conclude this discussion of the action plane by returning to that micromanaging versus macroleading discussed earlier. **Managers who don't do and deal, and so don't know what is going on, can become incapable of coming up with sensible decisions and robust strategies.** We no more need managers who never do and deal than we need managers who only do and deal. All around every manager, the world of action has to connect to the world of people, which has to connect to the world of information.

WELL-ROUNDED MANAGING

I noted at the outset of this chapter that many of the best-known writers in management have emphasized one aspect of managing to the exclusion of the others. Now it can be appreciated why each of them is wrong: heeding the advice of any one can lead to the lopsided practice of managing. Like an unbalanced wheel at resonant frequency, the job risks oscillating out of control.

Accepting Tom Peters's emphasis on doing can cause a centrifugal explosion of the job, as it flies off in all directions, free of the anchoring effect of a strong frame at the center. Opting instead for Michael Porter's view of the manager as analyzer, who focuses on formulating strategy at the center, can encourage centripetal implosion, as the job closes in on itself, far from the tangible actions that are its ultimate purpose.[28] **Thinking is heavy—too much of it can wear a manager down—while acting is light—too much of that and the manager cannot stay put.**

By the same token, **too much leading can result in a job free of content—aimless, frameless, and actionless—while too much linking can produce a job detached from its internal roots—public relations instead of tangible connections. The manager who only communicates never gets anything done, while the manager who only "does" ends up doing it all alone. And the manager who only controls risks controlling an empty shell of "yes" men and women.** We don't need people-oriented, information-oriented, or action-oriented managers; we need managers who operate on all three planes. **Only together do all these roles on all three planes provide the balance that is essential to the practice of managing.**

A corny metaphor, in the light of Figure 3.2 of our model, might thus make for some good advice: **the manager has to practice a well-rounded job.** Sure, the roles can sometimes substitute for each other—for example, by pulling employees via leading instead of pushing them through controlling. There are different ways to get this job done. But these roles do not constitute a portfolio from which managers can freely pick and choose: all of them must be somewhat present in every managerial job. Doing inside cannot be separated from dealing outside, any more than leading inside can be separated from linking outside, or getting information from working with people and taking action. Likewise, it makes no sense to conceive a neat frame, say an impressive strategy, and then expect to "implement" it through controlling, without leading. We have seen enough of this so-called strategic planning.

We have all experienced lopsided managing, whether due to the detachment of strategizing, the heavy-handedness of controlling, or the self-absorption of leadership. On one hand, "researchers have found that ineffective organizational leaders tended to have profiles [of managing] that were badly out of balance" (Quinn et al. 1990:310). On the other hand, Hart and Quinn found that CEOs with "the ability to play multiple, competing roles . . . produce the best firm performance" (1993:543; see

---

[28] Tom Peters made an interesting point on a panel with Michael Porter at the Strategic Management Society Conference in Montreal in 1991, that while Porter might look externally (to the competitive environment) and Peters internally (to the organization's operations), Porter really focuses internally, on thinking, while Peters really focuses externally, on behavior.

also Kraut et al. 2005:127).That is why the model of this chapter has been shown on a single page: as a reminder that this is one job, which has to be *seen* holistically.

To use another corny metaphor, also related to the image of the model, every manager has to swallow the whole pill. In a sense, the model can be likened to one of those time-release capsules: the outer layer offers quick action, while the successively inner ones, about people and then information, release their effects more slowly.

This may be a lot to swallow, but the problem is in the practice, not the theory. As I warned at the outset, this book is about managing, pure if not simple. Table 3.1 lists all the roles and subroles introduced in this chapter, while Table 3.2 lists various competencies (drawn from many sources in the literature) that accompany these roles. Can any manager

Table 3.1 ROLES OF MANAGING

	Framing the Job and Scheduling the Work	
	Internal	**External**
Information plane	Communicating	
	• Monitoring • Nerve center	• Spokesperson • Nerve center • Disseminating
	Controlling • Designing • Delegating • Designating • Distributing • Deeming	
People plane	**Leading** • Energizing individuals • Developing individuals • Building teams • Strengthening culture	**Linking** • Networking • Representing • Convincing/Conveying • Transmitting • Buffering
Action plane	**Doing** • Managing projects • Handling disturbances	**Dealing** • Building coalitions • Mobilizing support

Table 3.2 COMPETENCIES OF MANAGING

A. Personal Competencies
1. Managing self, internally (reflecting, strategic thinking)
2. Managing self, externally (time, information, stress, career)
3. Scheduling (chunking, prioritizing, agenda setting, juggling, timing)

B. Interpersonal Competencies
1. Leading individuals (selecting, teaching/mentoring/coaching, inspiring, dealing with experts)
2. Leading groups (team building, resolving conflicts/mediating, facilitating processes, running meetings)
3. Leading the organization/unit (building culture)
4. Administering (organizing, resource allocating, delegating, authorizing, systematizing, goal setting, performance appraising)
5. Linking the organization/unit (networking, representing, collaborating, promoting/lobbying, protecting/buffering)

C. Informational Competencies
1. Communicating verbally (listening, interviewing, speaking/presenting/briefing, writing, information gathering, information disseminating)
2. Communicating nonverbally (seeing [visual literacy], sensing [visceral literacy])
3. Analyzing (data processing, modeling, measuring, evaluating)

D. Actional Competencies
1. Designing (planning, crafting, visioning)
2. Mobilizing (firefighting, project managing, negotiating/dealing, politicking, managing change)

Source: Compiled from various sources; adapted from Mintzberg (2004:280)

master all of this? The short answer is no. But as we shall discuss in Chapter 6, the world has been functioning pretty well with managers who, like other human beings, are flawed. It has no other choice.

Managing across the Roles

When a pill decomposes, its different layers blend into each other. So, too, is it for this model: **when managers manage, the distinctions between their roles blur at the margins.** In other words, it may be easy to separate these roles conceptually, but that does not mean they can always be distinguished behaviorally.

- At GSI, when Jacques Benz's work was not strictly *doing*, it was often on the line between *doing* and some other role: *communicating, controlling, leading,* and especially *framing.* Jacques was being a doer—involving himself in project work—but in this he seemed to be facilitating these other roles.

Does this negate the model? No, not any more than the blending of the layers of a pill negate the need for its different ingredients. To understand the practice of managing, we need to understand each of its component parts, even if they cannot always be executed distinctly. This blurring can happen in three ways.

Activities in Multiple Roles   Earlier were examples of managing that happen at the interfaces of the different roles—for example, a manager who gives a boost to a project may be leading as well as doing. Andy Grove of Intel has described "nudging" at the interfaces of leading, controlling, communicating, and doing:

> You often do things at the office designed to influence events slightly, maybe making a phone call to an associate suggesting that a decision be made in a certain way. . . . In such instances you may be advocating a preferred course of action, but you are not issuing an instruction or a command. Yet you're doing something stronger than merely conveying information. Let's call it "nudging" because through it you nudge an individual or a meeting in the direction you would like. This is an immensely important managerial activity in which we engage all the time, and it should be carefully distinguished from decision-making that results in firm, clear directives. In reality, for every unambiguous decision we make, we probably nudge things a dozen times. (1983:51–52)

Roles Crossing Over into Others   Second, the roles can cross over the neat lines in the model. For example, I described managers as being able to control insiders but having to convince outsiders. Employees, after all, are paid to accept managerial authority. But insiders who are highly skilled, such as physicians in a hospital or researchers in a laboratory, often need to be convinced more than controlled by their managers, while captive suppliers of a company can sometimes be controlled like subordinates. As a consequence, managers sometimes have to *deal* on the inside, while they can sometimes *do* on the outside.

> • This was most evident with Brian Adams of Bombardier, for whom meeting the target had to matter more than the formalities of hierarchy. This led to what might be called extended controlling. It is interesting, for example, that the few directives Brian gave in a morning meeting went to people over whom he had no formal authority, while he flew past a subcontractor to the Los Angeles location of a subcontractor that was having problems.

As a consequence, in recent years the vertical lines from "superiors" to "subordinates" have been weakening in many organizations, while the horizontal lines to partners and colleagues have been strengthening (see Figure 3.6). This means that the roles of controlling and leading, long so dominant in the literature of managing, have been giving way to those of linking and dealing.

All this, to my mind, does not undermine our basic model—there are still plenty of outsiders to convince and insiders to control—but rather illustrates how it can be used to comprehend changes that are taking place in the practice of managing.

This crossing over of roles can also happen inadvertently, when managerial messages get misinterpreted. Burns noted in his study that

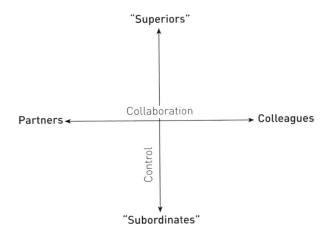

Figure 3.6 VERTICAL AND HORIZONTAL RELATIONSHIPS IN MANAGING

"half the time, what the manager thought he was giving as instructions or decisions [controlling] was being treated as information or advice [communicating]" (1954:95). Carlson in his study noted exactly the opposite: "I observed that a conversation between a chief executive and a subordinate, which from the former's point of view merely means the getting of information, may very well be regarded by the latter as decision taking or even as the receiving of orders" (1951:117–118).

Roles Infusing Each Other   Third, we have one role flowing into others and infusing them. Leading is most obvious in this regard: everything a manager does is likely to be screened by reports for clues about his or her leadership (Hill 2003:31). But this can be true for other roles, too; for example, how a manager leads can be screened as an indicator of how he or she wishes to control. "Feel free to criticize," claimed the CEO of one company I know, while he fired someone who did. No ambiguity there.

In his review of my 1973 book, Karl Weick called the leading role the "least convincing," even questioning its inclusion: "concern with motivation can be legitimately attached to other roles" (1974:117). Sure it can. But there are also activities distinct to the leading role (such as mentoring and training), just as there are activities distinct to the controlling one (such as delegating and deeming).[29]

Weick's point would seem to be strongest with regard to thinking— what is called *framing* in this model. After all, when does any of us stop thinking? Yet Weick, in another publication (1983), distinguished disengaged thinking—which can be called "reflection"—from "thinking that [is] inseparably woven into and occurs simultaneously with action" (p. 222). Accordingly, "managerial acts of any kind can be done more or less thinkingly" (p. 223). We shall return to this intriguing idea in the final chapter.

---

[29] For example, McCall et al. wrote that planning takes "place in between or during a huge variety of activities. The same is true of 'decision making'" (1978:37). On the latter, in the words of a Sony executive: "To be truthful, probably 60 percent of the decisions I make are my decisions. But I keep my intentions secret. In discussions with subordinates, I ask questions, pursue facts, and try to nudge them in my direction without disclosing my position. Sometimes I end up changing my position as a result of the dialogue. But whatever the outcome, they feel a part of the decision. Their involvement in the decision also increases their experience" (Maital 1988:57).

Tilting toward a Posture

To insist that all managers have to perform all the roles in the model—swallow the whole pill—is not to suggest that managers do not favor some roles over others. Every manager has specific needs to which he or she has to respond, and that gives rise to that person's particular "posture" of managing, as we shall discuss in the next chapter. Moreover, all managers have their own predispositions: each exhibits his or her own style, as we shall also discuss in the next chapter. Many opportunities arise in managing to substitute, combine, and nuance the various roles. Accordingly, **effective managers do not exhibit perfect balance among the roles; they tilt toward certain ones, even if they cannot neglect the others** (Quinn et al. 1990:316).

Consider some obvious examples (to which we shall return in the next chapter). Managers of professionals, as in hospitals and universities, may favor linking over leading, let alone controlling, since these professionals tend to act more like colleagues, or even suppliers, than subordinates. They need little encouragement or supervision from their managers, but they can require considerable support. In contrast, entrepreneurs who run their own businesses often emphasize doing and dealing, while senior executives of large corporations often give greater attention to controlling, particularly through their systems of performance control. The latter can be true of other managers as well:

- The Red Cross delegation in N'gara had to help sustain life for the refugees and avoid blowups in the camps. To ensure this, its managers emphasized communicating and controlling in order to minimize their own doing (namely, having to handle disturbances). In other words, the less doing they had to do, the more they were succeeding. That is why they kept themselves so carefully informed and the operations under such tight control.

The Dynamic Balance

I have observed in this closing section, first, that managing has to be well rounded, to avoid imbalance, and then that it inevitably tilts one way or another. But I do not see these as contradictory. **Over time managing has to function in a *dynamic* balance.** Managing that is well rounded can tilt back and forth according to the pressures of the moment. "Managerial work . . . [is] not a discrete, static, one-decision-at-a-time process, rather there is a timed 'ebb and flow' of meetings, requests, pressures, and negotiations" (Weick 1983:26).

- I was struck during a number of the twenty-nine days of observation by this dynamic balance. The remarkable thing about Fabienne Lavoie's day on the nursing ward, for example, was how everything just flowed together in a natural rhythm. I could find clear examples of each of the roles, yet she mixed them in such short snatches that they all just blended together. A short conversation with a nurse seemed to combine subtle controlling with sympathetic leading; then she was on the telephone with a patient's relative (linking); all the while, she was constantly doing, yet that was difficult to distinguish from her leading and her communicating. (See the appendix for a description of the full day.)

It is this dynamic balance that renders futile the teaching of management in a classroom, especially one role or competency at a time. Even mastering all the competencies do not a competent manager make, because the key to this work is the blending of all of its aspects into this dynamic balance. And that can only happen on the job, because no simulation I have ever seen in a classroom—case, game, in-basket exercise—comes remotely close to replicating the job itself. (Just read the descriptions of the management days in the appendix.)

Practicing managers can certainly benefit from coming into a classroom that encourages them to reflect, alone and together, on the experience they have already acquired in the job (as we shall discuss in Chapter 6; see also Mintzberg 2004b). But that experience can be so varied, as we shall discuss next, that the focus of such a classroom has to be more on the managers' learning than on the professors' teaching.

4

The Untold Varieties of Managing

Not chaos-like together crush'd and bruis'd
But as the world, harmoniously confus'd:
Where order in variety we see,
And where, though all things differ, all agree.

Alexander Pope, "Windsor Forest"

Spend a few hours with a variety of managers, and you will likely be struck by how varied this job can be: a bank chairman visiting branches; a Red Cross delegate on the lookout for tensions in a refugee camp; an orchestra conductor in rehearsal and then performance; an NGO head engaging in formal planning while fighting off a political challenge. Managing is almost as varied as life itself, because it is about so much that happens in life itself.

The last two chapters looked at the common characteristics and roles of managing. This one considers its sheer variety. How to find order in the variety we see? That is the intention of this chapter.

Managing—One Factor at a Time

Our inclination has been to proceed one factor at a time. Academics call this "contingency theory," and they call the factors "variables." In research, these variables are isolated (size of organization, or level in hierarchy), and their impact on the practice of managing is studied. For example: "The larger the overall organization, the more time the top manager spends in formal communication" (from my 1973 book, p. 130).

But academics are not alone on this. The same inclination exists in practice. Just think of how often you have heard, or asked, questions about how Japanese managers differ from American ones, how managing in government is different from managing in business, how "top" managing differs from "middle" managing.

So that is how I set out to write this chapter. I isolated twelve factors commonly found in the literature, both research and practitioner (see also Fondas and Stewart 1992), and sought to summarize the evidence about each. As listed here, they fell into five groups:

- *External context:* national culture, sector (business, government, etc.), and industry

- *Organizational context:* form of the organization (entrepreneurial, professional, etc.), and its age, size, and stage of development

- *Job context:* the level in the hierarchy and the work (or function) supervised

- *Temporal context:* temporary pressures and managerial fashion

- *Personal context:* background of the incumbent, tenure (in the job, the organization, the industry), and personal style

But as I began to consider this evidence, something felt wrong. I was not getting the insights I wanted, certainly not commensurate with the richness of the twenty-nine days of managing that I had observed.

Managing—One Day at a Time

So I reversed the process. I took the twenty-nine days and asked myself, for each, which of the factors seemed to be particularly influential for what these managers did.

The answers surprised me: for many of the days, few of the factors. And a number of the most prominent factors in the literature (such as national culture) seemed hardly influential at all.

Table 4.1 tabulates these results. They are impressionistic—personal assessment of what I saw—but as we proceed, I think you will appreciate my point (if not necessarily agreeing with each particular assessment). The factors that seemed highly influential for each day are shown with a fully shaded box; the modestly influential ones, with a dot; and the incidental ones, which seemed to explain little (if rarely nothing at all), with a blank. Notice all the blanks in the table.

Of the twelve possible factors, an average of three appeared particularly influential per day, the most being five, the least one. By far the most prominent factor was form of organization, which figured in twenty of the twenty-nine days, followed by industry, in twelve of the days. At the other extreme, fashion was especially influential in only one of the days and culture in two; managerial style appeared to be prominent in just five of the twenty-nine days. Thus, **the factors that have had the greatest attention in the literature, both academic and practitioner (such as national culture and personal style), may be less significant in what managers do than is generally believed, while some that have received little attention (form of organization, also industry and tenure) may be of greater significance.** Moreover, some of the factors that sound so clear alone proved to be rather intertwined when discussed with others in context.[1] An example illustrates:

- Did it much matter that Bramwell Tovey, as conductor of the Winnipeg Symphony, was British, or conducting in Canada? He was a "top" manager, even a chief executive, yet he was also the first-line supervisor, since this was a small organization, with no managerial hierarchy. But it was a big unit: seventy people reporting to one manager. And how about his personal style? That was a factor—it's always a factor—but more about *how* Bramwell did his job than *what* he essentially did: he conducted an orchestra, much like other conductors. The two factors that did seem particularly explanatory—which actually complement each other, almost as one factor—were the industry (namely, the fact that this was a symphony orchestra) and the form of organization (that it comprised highly trained professionals).

Managing—One Manager at a Time

Two conclusions about these factors emerge from this discussion. First, we cannot dismiss any of them (except perhaps fashion), since each appears to have had a strong influence on some of these days of managing if not necessarily on many of them. But second, and more to the point, **what we can dismiss is the effort to understand managing one**

---

[1] See Noordegraaf (2005) on the interplay of sector, size of organization, form of organization, and temporal pressures in a study of Dutch health care executives.

Table 4.1 MANAGERIAL DAYS BY FACTOR

	John Cleghorn—Royal Bank	Jacques Benz—GSI	Carol Haslam—Hawkshead	Max Mintzberg—C. Tel.	John Tate—Justice	Norm Inkster—RCMP	Sir Duncan Nichol—NHS	"Marc"—Hospital	Paul Gilding—Greenpeace	Dr. Rony Brauman—MSF	Catherine Joint-Dieterle—Museum	Bramwell Tovey—Orchestra	Brian Adams—Bombardier	Alan Whelan—BT	Glen Rivard—Justice
I External Context															
Culture						•				•					
Sector	•	•	•	▓	•		•	•						▓	•
Industry		•	▓	•		•			▓			•	•		
II Organizational Context															
Form of Organization		▓	▓	▓	▓	▓	▓		▓		▓	▓			
Age, Stage, Size	▓			▓		▓	▓				▓	▓	•		•
III Job Context															
Level	▓				•		▓		•	•					
Function (Work Sup.)		•			•	•			•	•		▓	▓		▓
IV Situational Context															
Temporary Pressures									▓	▓			▓		
Fashion															
V Personal Context															
Background					▓				▓				•		
Tenure	▓							•					•		▓
Style	•		•	•	•	•		•	▓		•	•	•	•	
Major Influence	3	1	3	3	4	2	2	3	5	1	3	4	4	5	4
Posture	6	6	2	3	9	5	2	2	4	2	3	1	3	8	3

▓ major influence   • modest influence   ☐ little influence

(continued)

Table 4.1 (continued)

	Doug Ward—CBC	Allen Burchill—RCMP	Sandra Davis—Parks	Charlie Zinkan—Parks	Peter Coe—NHS	Ann Sheen—NHS	Paul Hohnen—Greenpeace	Abbas Gullet—Red Cross	Gord Irwin—Parks	Ralph Humble—RCMP	Dr. Michael Thick—NHS	Dr. Stewart Webb—NHS	Fabienne Lavoie—Hospital	Stephen Omollo—Red Cross	Major Influences
I External Context															
Culture		●						■			●			■	2
Sector			■		●						●	●	●		5
Industry		●		●		■	■		●	●	■	■	■	■	12
II Organizational Context															
Form of Organization	■					●	■	■		■	■	■	■	■	20
Age, Stage, Size						■									8
III Job Context															
Level			■		●	■				●	●		●		6
Function (Work Sup.)	●	●				●			■	■			■		7
IV Situational Context															
Temporary Pressures					■				■					■	7
Fashion						■									1
V Personal Context															
Background							■				■	■			6
Tenure		●	■	●			●	■			●		●		9
Style			●		■				●				■	●	5
Major Influences	2	1	3	2	4	3	2	5	2	2	3	4	4	4	
Posture	3	7	7	7	8	1	3	1	1	1	4	4	1	1	

■ major influence   ● modest influence   ☐ little influence

factor at a time. Even if each can help explain some of the variance in management practice, none alone captures the essence
of managing in context. These factors thus have to be considered
together, one practice at a time.[2]

This chapter divides into four sections. The first looks briefly at
some evidence about eleven of the factors listed—how each seemed to
impact, or not, the twenty-nine days of managing. The second focuses on
one factor in particular, personal style, and especially its impact on *how*
managers perform their roles more than on *what* roles they perform. The
third combines the factors to delineate various *postures* that managers
seem commonly to adopt (e.g., "maintaining the workflow," or "managing out of the middle"), while the fourth carries this discussion into
various postures of "managing beyond the manager."

THE EXTERNAL CONTEXT

Every managerial job is situated in some external context, which can be
taken to mean its cultural milieu, its sector in general, and its "industry"
in particular.

Cultural Milieu

Most of us like to think that we live in places that have unique cultures.
And if we are interested in management, we are particularly interested
to know how this affects its practice. So there has been a good deal of
research on the effect of culture on managing, which draws conclusions
such as "Communication of German middle managers with their subordinates is primarily task oriented, while that of their British counterparts

---

[2] McCall (1977), who came to a similar conclusion (especially about leadership style), explained
it this way: "it is a mistake for leaders or researchers to assume that the 'situation' is comprised
of a small number of fixed parts. The organization, and its environment, are dynamic. An act of
Congress, a new invention, or new corporate president may change all existing cause and effect
relationships overnight." Kaplan suggested a similar reason: "The dilemma is that the more
abstract we make a theory of the job in order for it to encompass the wide range of instances of
it, the further the theory retreats from accurately representing any concrete instance" (1986:28).
Kaplan was in fact making a plea for contingency theory, but his words can also be taken as a
criticism of that theory.

concentrates on motivation" (Stewart et al. 1994:131).[3] Yet a surprising number of such studies also ended up finding striking similarities across management practices in different cultures.[4] And likewise in my own research, while each of the twenty-nine managers was situated in his or her own cultural milieu, in only two cases did this seem to be a compelling factor in what they did—and these were not even managers from the local culture:

- Abbas Gullet and Stephen Omollo were in the Red Cross Camps in N'gara, Tanzania, because of the tragic events that had taken place just across the border, in Rwanda. This had a major effect on their managing, causing them to be supersensitive about security and so emphasizing the role of *controlling*. Contrast this with the two Australians observed at the Greenpeace headquarters in Amsterdam: they could have been anywhere, since Greenpeace's cultural milieu is the whole world. John Cleghorn, as head of the Royal Bank of Canada, and Max Mintzberg, of The Telephone Booth in Montreal, had vastly different days despite both being Canadian. Glen Rivard's job of developing family law in the Canadian Justice Department was certainly all wrapped up in his country's culture. That affected the content of his work, but did it affect his managing—would someone in his position in, say, Chile, have necessarily managed differently?[5]

Linda Hill, in reviewing an earlier draft of this manuscript, asked, "Cultures do matter, don't they?" I like to think so—I have speculated

---

[3] See also, for example, Boisot and Liang (1992) on Chinese managers, Luthans et al. (1993) on Russian ones, Hales and Mustapha (2000) on Malaysian ones, Pearson and Chatterjee (2003) on ones in four Asian countries, and Tengblad (2002) on Swedish ones. Especially widely cited has been Hofstede's (1980, 1993) study of cultural difference among IBM employees in forty different countries, although these are about aspects of culture (such as individualism in America) more than managerial practices per se.

[4] For example, the "Chinese enterprise managers in this sample share many behavioral characteristics with their U.S. counterparts" (Boisot and Liang 1992:161). Yu et al. (1999) strongly reinforce this conclusion. See also Lubatkin et al. (1997) and Doktor (1990). As Hales and Mustapha put it: "While managerial work is not universally homogenous, neither is it infinitely variable" (2000:20).

[5] Culture milieu was noted to have a moderate effect in the case of the three officers of the RCMP, whose normative approach to policing might be expected in a liberal country such as Canada. Similarly noted was Rony Brauman's highly political day in a country rather inclined to power politics.

about a Canadian style of managing. But perhaps, we are mostly inclined to exaggerate our differences. Or perhaps culture has more influence on *how* the roles are performed than on which ones are performed (as we shall discuss for personal style).

Sector

The first table of this book, in Chapter 1, showed the twenty-nine managers by sector: business, government, health care, and the social sector. This is a common way to think about organizations, and it was a convenient way to present the twenty-nine days. But is it key to understanding managerial work—is managerial behavior profoundly influenced by working in, say, government as opposed to business? We have been trained to think so. After all, economic forces predominate in the private sector and political ones in the public sector, etc. But here again, generalizations can break down in specific situations.

> • There were certainly competitive (economic) pressures in all the private sector organizations of my study, but they were in particular evidence only on the days of Max Mintzberg in The Telephone Booth, Brian Adams at Bombardier, and Alan Whelan at BT. In the public sector, intensive political pressures were evident only on Charlie Zinkan's day in the Banff National Park. (Being in government also figured prominently in the work of Sandy Davis of the parks, but not so much on the political dimension.) In fact, the most intensive politics were encountered on the days of Rony Brauman of Doctors Without Borders and Paul Gilding of Greenpeace, both in the social sector. But I could not otherwise categorize the social sector managers in any common way. In health care, the professional nature of the work was clearly influential for the managers close to the operations, but less so for those in higher reaches of the hierarchy (as will be discussed later).

There are no doubt differences in managing across sectors, as there are across cultures—*on average.*[6] But given the variance within sectors, as within cultures, how useful are these difference in understanding

---

[6] See Noordegraaf and Stewart (2000) on managing in the public versus private sectors, and Duncan et al. (1994) on managing in health care versus business.

management and advising managers? The message here is that **if we wish to understand the varieties of managing, we need to climb off our generalizations and dig into the worlds of podiums, products, and programs.** And this raises another point of consequence: **treating one sector as superior—"business knows best"—hardly makes sense when management practice in business itself varies so widely.**

Industry

Using the term *industry* in a broad sense (e.g., the "orchestra industry"), there is obviously a wide range of industries in which managers work, and so here general conclusions are difficult to draw even if specific ones can be found in particular industries. For example, "the school principal is obliged to manage in a more open, more cordial, literally more visible fashion" because of the need to deal with teachers and students "coexisting in a state of uneasy harmony" (Morris et al. 1981:79).

Industry figured prominently in twelve of the days—for example, filmmaking in Carol Haslam's day, orchestra conducting in Bramwell Tovey's day, the Justice Department in days of the two managers observed there. But this intertwines with hierarchy: the effect of industry was strong for most of the first-line managers (four of six, and moderate for the other two), but fewer of the middle (four of eleven) and senior managers (four of twelve). This suggests that **industry influences managing most where it gets close to the production of products and the delivery of services.**[7] At any level, however, at least how I see management, tacit knowledge of the industry remains critical.

THE ORGANIZATIONAL CONTEXT

Next we look at the organization in which the managing is embedded—specifically, the form that it takes as well as its age, size, and stage of development.

---

[7] In fact, two of the four senior managers strongly influenced by industry—Carol Haslam and Bramwell Tovey—headed up small organizations and so were also close to the operations, while for a third, Paul Gilding of Greenpeace, the "industry"—environmental protection—permeated everything.

Form of Organization

It is interesting that **form of organization proved to be the most prominent factor by far in understanding what the managers of this study did.** I recorded it as prominent for twenty of the twenty-nine days. Yet it is commonly ignored, for a simple reason.

Species of Organizations   Imagine biology with no vocabulary to discuss species: how to distinguish, for example, beavers from bears without any word beyond *mammal?* This is the state we are in when it comes to organizations, in practice as well as research: we have little vocabulary beyond the word *organization*. How is a chief executive to explain to a consultant or a board member, "You are treating us like an A kind of organization, but we are really a B kind of organization," when there are no commonly understood words for A and B? As a result, "one best way thinking" continues to prevail in management: if it's good for the Royal Bank of Canada, it must be fine for Greenpeace (strategic planning anyone?).

Years ago, I proposed a vocabulary to help, which I used here to understand the impact of organization on the twenty-nine days of managing:[8]

- *The Entrepreneurial Organization*: centralized around a single leader, who engages in considerable *doing* and *dealing* as well as strategic visioning

- *The Machine Organization*: formally structured, with simple repetitive operating tasks (classic bureaucracy), its managers functioning in clearly delineated hierarchies of authority and engaging in a considerable amount of *controlling*

- *The Professional Organization*: comprising professionals who do the operating work largely on their own, while their managers focus more externally, on *linking* and *dealing,* to support and protect the professionals

- *The Project Organization (Adhocracy)*: built around project teams of experts that innovate, while the senior managers engage in *linking* and

---

[8] See Mintzberg (1979, 1983a, 1983b, 1989: Part II). I use the latter here. More recently, this has been elaborated on with regard to strategy (2007: Chapter 12).

dealing to secure the projects, and the project managers concentrate on *leading* for teamwork, *doing* for execution, and *linking* to connect the different teams together

- *The Missionary Organization*: dominated by a strong culture, with the managers emphasizing *leading* to enhance and sustain that culture

- *The Political Organization*: dominated by conflict, with the managers sometimes having to emphasize *doing* and *dealing* in the form of firefighting[9]

Although aspects of all these forms can be found in most organizations, many tilt toward one form or another. For example, hospitals favor the professional form, with the physicians more as colleagues of the managers than as subordinates, while much retailing is entrepreneurial, especially in its early stages, just as much filmmaking is adhocracy in nature.[10]

- The nature of *adhocracy* was most evident in the project work of Brian Adams on the new aircraft, Glen Rivard on government family law policies, Jacques Benz on GSI's systems for customers, and Carol Haslam on filmmaking. In Glen's case, for example, lawyers and other professionals worked in project terms to draft legislation. As he noted, this drew him personally into the project work: overseeing it, reviewing it, pushing it along, and sometimes doing it himself. Max Mintzberg of The Telephone Booth was the classic *entrepreneur*, while the controlling nature of the *machine* organization was most evident in the work of Abbas Gullet in the Red Cross refugee camps. *Missionary* characteristics of the RCMP showed up strongly in the work of its commissioner, and political

---

[9] These last two forms can also be seen as infusing the other four—for example, as a political adhocracy or a machine origination with a strong culture. Another type, the Diversified or Divisionalized Form, exists when a headquarters sits over divisions in different (i.e., diversified) businesses, each with its own form, which I believe most commonly to be the Machine Form (as discussed in Mintzberg 1989:155–172).

[10] Some research on managerial work related to this includes Chandler and Sayles (1971: Chapter 10), who described the work of the project manager in what amounts to adhocracy, and Hales and Tamangani (1996), who reviewed the sparse empirical evidence on the relationship between organization and managerial work in general. Hales himself (2002), using case study evidence, questioned the belief that organizations in general are moving toward what amounts to adhocracy, with managerial practices shifting from "command and control" to "facilitate and coordinate." Instead, he makes the case that the real movement is only a partial shift, to "bureaucracy-lite." (More on this later.)

characteristics of Greenpeace in the work of its executive director. But **the strongest impact of organization on managing showed up in *the professional* organizations, especially for the managers close to the operating professionals**—the two managers of nursing, the two of medicine, and the conductor of the orchestra.

Size, Age, and Stage of Organization

We would normally expect managing in small and young organizations to be more intense and less formalized (Stieglitz 1970; Stewart 1967; Mintzberg 1973:130). But some of the evidence of the twenty-nine days mixed this up:

- An orchestra is a small organization, even if composed of one large unit, and the newest of them conform to centuries of formalized protocol. The huge size of the National Health Service of England certainly influenced the work of its chief executive,[11] but would the work of its medical and nursing managers have been much different had they been in autonomous, even small hospitals?

In most cases, it was difficult to isolate these three factors. For example, how to separate large size from significant age in the Royal Bank of Canada, both of which go with the stage of maturity?[12] But even together, these three factors seemed significant in only eight of the twenty-nine cases, six of them for chief executives (out of the twelve in total). For example, John Cleghorn was dealing in a highly organized way with a large, old, mature bank, and Max Mintzberg in a much more intense way with a small, young retail chain. (The other two managers most affected by the size of their organizations, both at middle levels, were Peter Coe of the NHS and Alan Whelan of BT.)

---

[11] See Noordegraaf et al. (2005) on how "size counts" in the work of executives dealing with reform in health care.

[12] I should add that there were no really new organizations in the study. But there were many new projects and some new units in the older organizations. It is worth noting that the camps in Tanzania were the youngest units in this study, yet they had been established very quickly. To do so, Abbas Gullet had to be one of the most entrepreneurial managers of all, even if this was social intrepreneurship, practiced within the large and mature Red Cross Federation.

THE JOB CONTEXT

When we think of managing, beyond the style of the person in the job, our inclination has been to focus on the job itself—specifically, its level and function.[13]

Level of the Job

Level refers to the location of the job in the formal hierarchy of author-ity—typically "top," "middle," and first-line supervision at the base (never called "bottom"). All of this, of course, refers to the location on a chart printed on a piece of paper. Don't go necessarily looking for middle management in the middle of anything, or top management "on top of things," let alone sometimes even of the building they inhabit. (Hospital heads often sit near the main entrance, perhaps to make a quick getaway.)

Basically, to be a top manager—let's use the word *senior*—means to have everyone else in the organization reporting to you, which means to have formal responsibility for the activities of the entire place. To be a bottom manager, in contrast, means to have only operating work-ers—no other managers—reporting to you. So to be in middle manage-ment should mean that you have managers above and below you on that chart—some reporting to you and you reporting to other(s)—although, as we shall see, greater liberties are often taken with this term.

"Top" versus "Bottom"   In my 1973 book (p. 130), I hypothesized, conventionally, that the higher a manager's level in the hierarchy, the more unstructured and long-range the job, and the less brief and frag-mented its activities, also that senior managers work longer hours, while lower-level managers are more concerned with the maintenance of the workflow, in "real time." The chief executives I studied there averaged twenty-two minutes per activity; the foremen Guest (1955–1956) stud-ied averaged forty-eight seconds. Senior managers negotiate acquisitions, while the middle managers of Sayles's study (1964) "negotiated delivery dates on orders" (1964:42).[14]

---

[13] Early on, Shartle cited a study in which "less than half of the performance could be associated to [the person in the job] and a little over half to the demands of the particular job" (1956:94). In his own study, Shartle found that "differences among naval and among business organiza-tions were more pronounced than differences between the naval and business groups" (p. 90).

[14] Hales found the job of first-line manager to be more stable and consistent than those at more senior levels, and more concerned with performance-oriented supervision—with its decision

The picture seems consistent. So how did the twelve senior managers of my later study compare with the six managers at the base? (We'll get to the eleven middle managers later.) They conformed and they didn't. Concerns with maintaining the workflow and responding in real time were certainly evident in the jobs at the base. As for working hours, however, managers such as Fabienne Lavoie in the hospital probably worked at least as long as most chief executives. And Paul Gilding, Executive Director of Greenpeace, may have tried to focus on long-term planning, but he was also forced to respond to real-time concerns.

John Kotter has written that "lower-level management jobs do not have long-run responsibilities" (1982a:221; see also Allan 1981:615). Why, then, as noted in Chapter 1, was Gord Irwin of the front country office of the Banff National Park so concerned with the environmental impact of a parking lot, while Norm Inkster as head of the RCMP was watching clips of the previous day's newscasts to avoid embarrassing questions to his minister in Parliament that day? Indeed, why do so many corporate CEOs now spend so much time on their company's quarterly reports?

Add in size of organization, and more of the generalities about level become questionable. For example, the work of some of the chief executives of the smaller organizations (Max Mintzberg in the retail chain, Bramwell Tovey in the orchestra, etc.) looked much like first-line supervisors: the hierarchy was so compressed that the "top" and "bottom" came together. Moreover, Max's hectic work pace matched that of Fabienne Lavoie on the hospital ward. So **size of organization can sometimes trump level in organization for its effects on managing.**

"Middle" Management   In its popular usage, *middle management* can be an awfully broad term (Carlson 1951:58–59; Stewart 1976), and so the subject of much confusion. For example, it often includes a hodgepodge of pretty much everyone beside the most senior and junior managers and workers in the organization—such as specialists in staff jobs who manage no one.

In this book, I restrict the term *manager* to people responsible for units staffed with other people, and the term *middle manager* to people who both report to manager(s) and have other managers reporting to

---

making "confined largely to operating routines" (2005:471). Consistent with this, Morris et al. found that school system superintendents, compared with school principals, spent more time on scheduled and ceremonial activities and on written communication, and less time on decision making (1981:8, 9).

them. This includes eleven of the twenty-nine managers. But even they comprised quite a mixture, with responsibilities for (1) a geographic area (e.g., Nova Scotia in the RCMP), (2) a product or service line, or particular customers (e.g., big IT contracts at BT), (3) a basic function (e.g., nursing in a hospital), (4) specific programs, projects, or policies (e.g., family law in the Canadian Justice Department), and (5) staff units (e.g., the Economics Unit at Greenpeace). Such variety has not, however, discouraged a great deal of generalization in the literature about "the job" of middle manager.[15]

Middle management has been under attack for some years now, accused of having been bloated and therefore subjected in many corporations to repeated **"downsizings." This looks to be a contemporary form of bloodletting—the cure for every corporate disease**. While some of this has perhaps been appropriate, its faddish nature should have been raising suspicions about throwing out the managerial babies with the financial bathwater. How come so many companies discovered the problem all at once? Were their senior managers that inattentive before— or after?

Accordingly, a number of publications have sought to redeem the job of middle manager, especially with regard to its role in the strategy process. Floyd and Wooldridge, for example, questioned the view of middle managers as "subversives" and "drones" (1996:47–49) and the dismissal of them as people who merely "translate strategies defined at the higher levels into action at operating levels" (1994:48). Instead, as Quy Huy put it, **middle managers are often "far better than most senior executives . . . at leveraging the informal network at a company that makes substantial, lasting change possible."** They know "where the problems are," yet can also "see the big picture" (2001:73; see also Nonaka 1988).

- Doug Ward, manager of the radio station in Ottawa, sat between the tangible operations of radio programming and the intricacies of the CBC's formal hierarchy. "It's nice having a job at the interface," he said. Thanks to his earlier experience (he had been head of the entire radio network), Doug could both challenge the rest of the organization and act in ways beneficial to it—for example, by helping to create a new radio program later adopted by the network.

---

[15] See, for example, Paolillo, who had "top, middle, and low-level managers . . . rate the various roles required by their positions" (1981:91)

Nature of the Work Supervised (Including Function)

If chief executives manage whole organizations, then what do other managers manage? A whole list has been suggested here, which indicates the wide variations possible.[16] Of the items on this list, functions, projects (including programs and policies), and staff groups[17] touch especially on the work supervised.

Of course, every managerial job is influenced by the nature of the work supervised. The question here is, for how many of the twenty-nine days was this particularly prominent? For the chief executives, this appeared to be a prominent factor in only two of the days: Catherine Joint-Dieterle in the museum and Bramwell Tovey in the orchestra, both heading small organizations. (Bear in mind that chief executives of large organizations can be distant from the operations, and they can also focus on other things—like Rony Brauman of Doctors Without Borders, who spent much of the day on outside work.) For the middle managers, this factor appeared prominent in only two of the eleven days, both in project management: Brian Adams at Bombardier and Glen Rivard at the Justice Department. (Alan Whelan, for example, in charge of a clear function— selling—was seen this day to be more concerned with selling one of his unit's contracts to his own senior management at BT than to its customers.) At the base level, this factor was a bit more common, three of the six: Gord Irwin in the parks, Ralph Humble in the RCMP, and Fabienne Lavoie in the hospital.

The word *function* has mostly been used to describe the classic components of business: production, marketing, sales, and so forth.[18] But function has to be seen in a more generic way, as one component in a chain of

---

[16] Hales and Mustapha found in their study in Malaysia that "variations in middle managers' work were linked most strongly to their functional specialisms." But they also concluded that "commonalities in managerial work should not be underestimated" (2000:20; see p. 3 for a review of studies that have addressed this factor). Carlos Losada of the Esade Business School in Spain has carried out a particularly interesting and detailed study that compared the work of political managers (ministers) with civil service managers in the Catalan government—essentially functional differences. He found, for example, that the former spent more time on interpersonal relationships and in the liaison role, and in the conceiving role, but less time in the spokesperson role.

[17] Strictly speaking, there were no full-time staff managers among the twenty-nine, although (as shall be discussed later) John Tate of the Justice Department had some of these responsibilities, as did Paul Hohnen, to whom reported the Greenpeace Economics and the Political Units. For findings about these managers, see Alexander (1979) and McCall and Segrist (1980).

[18] There have been some studies of this. McCall and Segrist (1980), for example, found that sales managers emphasized the linking role; manufacturing managers, aspects of the doing and

operating activities leading to a final output. Sales in a manufacturing firm is a function because it cannot stand alone, without production, but so is nursing in a hospital, which cannot exist without medicine (and vice versa). Indeed, by the same token, what are labeled "divisions" in some companies are really functions, such as the mining activity of an aluminum company that transfers all of its bauxite downstream for refining.

Here again, in the job context, the simple categories did not hold up well in the light of a nuanced reality. *Level* focuses on the hierarchy of authority, the limitations of which have been mentioned several times, while *function* is an overly restrictive term.[19] So perhaps a reframing of these, in terms of "scale and scope," might help.

Scale and Scope

Scale refers to the size of the unit managed, which, as noted earlier, can be quite different from the size of the overall organization: a tiny unit can exist in a large organization (Dr. Thick's kidney transplant team in the NHS), while a large unit can exist in a tiny organization (Bramwell Tovey's single team of seventy musicians).

Scope refers to the breadth of a managerial job—in particular, the manager's degrees of freedom in it.[20] Scale may seem to provide scope: the bigger the unit, the greater the manager's ability to maneuver. But did Sir Duncan Nichol atop the massive NHS hierarchy have greater maneuverability than Dr. Thick at its base, with his tiny research unit? The former, trying to move an organization of almost a million people, was constrained on all sides; the latter, with his responsive little team, engaged in the practices that interested him. Bramwell Tovey chose the pieces to be played, but within limitations (including what the audience would accept). To understand scope, we can compare vertical scope—up and down the hierarchy—with horizontal scope—out to other units and beyond.

---

controlling roles; and finance managers, aspects of the communicating role. (See also Paolitto 1987, and DiPietro and Milutinovich 1973:109.) But they also found consistencies in managerial work across both functions and levels.

[19] To quote Rosemary Stewart, who has done the most research on managing, especially at middle levels: "The traditional ways of distinguishing between managerial jobs by level in the hierarchy and by function are not adequate for effective selection, appraisal, training, development, and career planning" (1987:390–391).

[20] Fondas and Stewart (1992) saw this a little differently, defining a job's scope as "its area of formal responsibility," after which they refer to its "scale of responsibility," as indicated by number of subordinates, turnover, and size of budget.

Vertical Scope   John Cleghorn was CEO of the largest bank in Canada, yet he could be seen *suggesting* that a sign be fixed in a bank branch. Could Sir Duncan Nichol have done likewise in an NHS hospital? Indeed, how much influence did he have over Dr. Thick? Or, for that matter, looking up the hierarchy, how much influence did Dr. Thick have over the rest of his hospital, let alone the upper reaches of the NHS hierarchy? Alan Whelan spent a good part of his day trying to do precisely that at BT—and he eventually succeeded in getting sign off on that contrast. So he did have vertical scope, up the hierarchy, although not as much as John Cleghorn, down it.

Horizontal Scope   How about influence to the sides—for example, in the flow of work to and from the unit? Some managers are able to reach out and, if not technically control others in the workflow, at least influence them significantly. Recall Brian Adams's influence over Bombardier's "partners"—really, suppliers to the airplane. Abbas Gullet at the Red Cross camps and Doug Ward at the CBC seemed quite able to influence people around them, perhaps because both were so experienced in their organizations. Compare this with Allen Burchill in the Nova Scotia division of the RCMP and Sandy Davis in charge of the western Canadian parks, whose geographic jobs may have been more restrictive of their horizontal scopes.

Scope in Terms of Frame   Chapter 3 introduced the frame of the manager's job; here we can use scope to understand a manager's control over it.

Along the top of the matrix shown in Figure 4.1, the managerial frame can range from (1) rather sharp and clear ("expand the unit by ten salespeople this year") to (2) rather vague ("strengthen the team"). A vague frame can offer considerable scope ("Oh, boy, I can do anything") or hardly any at all ("What am I supposed to do now?"), while a sharp frame can focus attention (to the point of that "magnificent obsession" discussed earlier), but in so doing narrow the manager's perspective.

- Brian Adams and Abbas Gullet had perhaps the sharpest frames of this study —one to get the plane in the air by a certain date, the other to keep the lid on conflict in the refugee camps. Peter Coe in the NHS world of purchasers and providers had a rather vague frame, which he used to his unit's advantage.

And down the side of the matrix is the source of the frame, which can range from being (1) *imposed* by the nature of the job itself (Brian

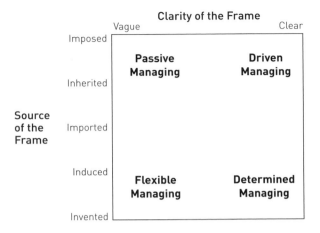

Figure 4.1 SCOPE IN MANAGING

and Abbas); (2) *inherited* from the previous manager (Norm Inkster, with respect to the RCMP culture); (3) *imported,* in the sense that the frame comes from other organizations (Bramwell Tovey of the orchestra); (4) *induced* by the manager him or herself (Peter Coe, in how he dealt with the purchaser/provider structure); and (5) *invented* by the manager (Alan Whelan in how he pursued his unit's mission at BT).

While every managerial job has aspects of its frame that range from sharp to vague and imposed to invented, most also have some overall tendency, four of which are labeled in Figure 4.1. **Managing with respect to frame can be *passive* (a vague frame forced on the manager), *driven* (a clear frame forced on the manager), *flexible* (the manager has chosen a vague frame), and *determined* (the manager has chosen a clear frame).** We shall return to examples of these in our discussion of styles of managing later in this chapter.

THE TEMPORAL CONTEXT

Next we come to the conditions of the moment, the situation at hand. These are difficult to categorize, because they can relate to so many happenings: a strike, a merger, a lawsuit, a sudden competitive attack, and so forth. So I will discuss them in general, except for one factor, fashion— the flavor of the managerial month.

Temporary Pressures

We know from long-standing research that crises—imminent bankruptcy, sudden hostilities, collapse of a currency—can cause an organization to centralize power to enable one person to act quickly and decisively (Hamblin 1958), especially using the roles of *doing* and *controlling*. There is also some evidence that when competition heats up, managers spend more time in informal communication, with their work becoming more fragmented and varied (Stewart 1967:51).

Surprising in the research here is that these temporary pressures seemed prominent in only seven of the twenty-nine days.[21] Does this negate the finding of Chapter 2, that managers are real-time responders to the pressures at hand, exhibiting action orientations and quick response times in their work? I think not. The more appropriate conclusion seems to be that **the pressures of managing are often not temporary but perpetual.** The pace, as noted, can be unrelenting (as I saw in the days of Max Mintzberg, Brian Adams, and Fabienne Lavoie, etc.). In other words, pressure in this job is business as usual—as quoted in Chapter 2, managing is "one damn thing after another."[22]

- Brian Adams of Bombardier was not in a classical job of "management by exception"; his was a job of the management of exceptions. Because Brian managed development aircraft programs, not routine operations, he was there to deal with the exceptions.

---

[21] These were Paul Gilding and Charlie Zinkan under challenge, the former from the Greenpeace chairperson and the latter over that parking lot in the park; Marc in the hospital under siege from many quarters; Alan Whelan under pressure to get sign-off on that contract; Brian Adams to get that airplane up on schedule; and Abbas Gullet and Stephen Omollo intent on keeping those refugee camps stable (these last two being the only ones whose pressures were neither competitive nor political). It might be added that while Rony Brauman, as head of Doctors Without Borders, was running around Paris because of concerns about the political situation in Somalia, in good part he seemed to be doing this by choice. Being new to managing can also be considered a temporary pressure, as Linda Hill made clear in *Becoming a Manager* (2003) and will be discussed later. Gord Irwin, as Front Country Manager in the Banff National Park, was new to managing but did not seem under pressure. Paul Gilding was new to his job at Greenpeace, but the pressures seemed to be beyond that. Perhaps the pressures that Marc experienced in the hospital may have related to his short tenure on the job (to be discussed later in this chapter).

[22] This conclusion is reinforced by the finding in Chapter 2 that managerial work does not appear to differ significantly across days of the week or across weeks.

Managerial Fashion

Worth a brief mention here is fashion as a temporal factor. **Much like political correctness, there is "managerial correctness"—the fashionable way to practice management for a time** (see Brunsson 2007:52–57). Here is the flavor of the managerial month, so to speak (the expression itself having been the flavor of a few managerial months)—for example, over the years with regard to managing people: human relations, participative management, Theory Y, quality of work life, total quality management, empowerment, and so on.[23]

Such fashion can influence managerial work temporarily, at least for those managers inclined to follow the crowd (more and more, it seems). There are also fashionable managerial styles—for example, the "heroic leadership" discussed earlier (see Mintzberg 2004b:104–111). But fashion was not much in evidence in the twenty-nine days observed (perhaps because of the sample selected). Instead, we had Norm Inkster reinforcing a long-established culture at the RCMP and Bramwell Tovey conforming to an even older tradition in the field of orchestral music. The one exception pertained to fashion within the organization itself: the NHS's reforms around purchasers and providers that played a significant role in Peter Coe's day.[24]

THE PERSONAL CONTEXT

By far the greatest attention among all the factors has been accorded to managers' "style"—namely, how they approach their work, beyond the demands of the environment, the job, the organization, and the situation at hand. Style, in other words, is about how the incumbent *makes* the job, as opposed to just *doing* the job. Put two people in the same job

---

[23] McCauley et al. (1998:408) have tabulated models of leadership over very long periods of time, as have Quinn et al. (1990) for more recent times—as the rational goal model 1900–1925, which emphasized the "producer" role (controlling and doing); the human relations model 1926–1950, which emphasized the "facilitation" and "mentor" roles (leading); the open systems model 1951–1975, which emphasized the "innovation" or "broker" roles (doing and dealing); and the internal process model, from 1976 onward, which emphasizes the "coordinator" and "monitor" roles (controlling and communicating). See also Pascale (1990), who tabulated dozens of management techniques that have come and gone over the years.

[24] Similar but not particularly significant on Sandy Davis's day was her request that the word *heritage* appear in documents going to the new Heritage Department in Ottawa.

under the same circumstances, and the differences in their behavior can be attributed to their respective styles.[25] Dalton, for example, described President Truman as having "loved to make decisions," which he did quickly, while President Eisenhower was "disposed" to keep away from them (1959:163). But there is more to personal context than style. Background and tenure count, too.

Nature + Nurture   Is style the result of character or of experience, nature or nurture? The answer, of course, has to be both. How can we even separate the two? For example, is a manager who favors the *controlling* role intrinsically power-hungry, or rendered careful from some childhood experience? Who is to tell? Moreover, nature and nurture can work together; for example, we all seek out situations that go with, and so reinforce, our natural predispositions.

We shall begin by discussing nurture briefly, in the form of the manager's background and tenure—in the job, the organization, and the industry. Then we shall consider at greater length different personal styles of managing, whether influenced by nature or nurture.

Background

A manager's background can include all sorts of experiences: education, earlier positions, successes and failures, and many more.[26] McCall et al. (1988), for example, have made a strong case for developing managers by rotating them into various challenges, rather than relying on formal training (see also Ohlott 1998). Similarly, in *Managers Not MBAs* (Mintzberg 2004b), I argued that conventional MBA training encourages a rather analytical, and unbalanced, approach to managing, as compared with bringing experienced managers into a classroom to reflect on their own experience. Of course, here again nurture can reinforce nature: conventional MBA programs tend to attract young people predisposed to analysis, and then reinforce this; our programs, in contrast, attract

---

[25] Ironically, despite the massive amount of writing on managerial styles, I know of no systematic research that has attempted to make such direct comparisons, at least in organizations, if not politics, even though as soon as one person succeeds another in a managerial job, people affected inevitably make such comparisons.

[26] See Kotter (1982:44–58) for an extensive discussion of background, including childhood, education, career, and so forth.

practicing managers more oriented to the craft side of managing, and reinforce that.[27]

While background obviously influenced all twenty-nine managers of this study, it seemed significant in only six cases, all but one due to education: John Tate at the Justice Department (with his background in law, which also encourages an analytical orientation); and Ann Sheen, Fabienne Lavoie, and Drs. Thick and Webb, all with professional backgrounds, in nursing and medicine. (See the accompanying box on Doctors as Managers.) The exception was Marc, head of the hospital, whose absence of a clinical background, and experience in professional organizations in general, seemed to make a difference, especially given his early tenure in the job.

- John Tate's training and experience as a lawyer likely reinforced an analytical orientation. But that was in the nature of the Justice Department, too, which did policy analysis, also in the nature of government, which has to justify its actions formally. Hence, this was a day of informing, advising, and controlling on the information plane. John fit the job, which fit the organization, which fit its sector.

Tenure

Tenure in the job, the organization, and the industry was found to be a significant factor in nine cases.

- Abbas Gullet joined the Red Cross as a youth, attended international conferences in his teens, and worked in its central offices. And so he knew the institution intimately, which was evident

---

[27] These programs include www.impm.org for business managers; www.mcgill.ca/imhl for health care managers; www.alp-impm.com for teams of managers who work on key issues in their company; and www.CoachingOurselves.com, where teams of managers in organizations download various topics and work on them in small groups. Some polling of IMPM classes, using the instrument reproduced a few pages ahead, has indicated that these managers see themselves as oriented to craft (on the art-craft-science triangle). Only one of the managers of the twenty-nine had an MBA—Sandy Davis of the parks, where I did see a favoring of formal planning. In contrast, three of the twenty-nine managers attended our International Masters in Practicing Management: Abbas Gullet and Stephen Omollo of the Red Cross and Alan Whelan of BT. All seemed clearly oriented to the craft side of managing. (More later on the styles of art, craft, and science in managing.)

Doctors as Managers

In an article on health care (2001), Sholom Glouberman and I discussed whether doctors may be less intrinsically suited to the practice of management than, say, nurses, because of the very nature of their profession.

First, medicine is oriented more to curing than to caring. The nature of medical practice is interventionist (the French word for a surgical operation is, in fact, *intervention*). But this may not be a good model for management, which has to be about continuous and preemptive care—to steady the operations and sustain strategic positions—more than intermittent, specialized, and radical cure. (A box later in this chapter compares the yang managing of Dr. Rony Brauman of Doctors Without Borders with the yin managing of Catherine Joint-Dieterle of the Paris fashion museum.)

Second, physicians are trained to make decisions individually and decisively, whereas managers often have to ponder ambiguous issues collectively. Every time a doctor sees a patient, some kind of explicit decision is usually made, even if it is to do nothing. Sitting on committees and debating the nuances of vague issues is hardly in the nature of their work. (I once saw a cartoon that showed a group of surgeons around a patient with the line "Who opens?" In management, that is a serious question.)

Third, much of medicine is about parts, not the whole. Few physicians these days treat the entire person. Organizations need to be treated holistically.

The problem, however—once again—is that these are generalities. I have come across some doctors who were superb managers. People do vary, despite their training. Hospitals need leaders and managers in their senior positions; they do not need categories.

especially in how he served as a bridge between the operating site in Tanzania and the headquarters in Geneva. Likewise embedded in their organization's culture through long tenure were four other managers: Doug Ward of the CBC, John Tate at Justice, John Cleghorn of the Royal Bank, and Norm Inkster of the RCMP.[28] Paul Gilding of Greenpeace and Sandy Davis of the parks, both not long into their jobs, favored formal planning. Can we conclude

---

[28] Catherine Joint-Dieterle was also noted for her tenure in the fashion industry. I could have noted others here, such as Bramwell Tovey and Carol Haslam, except that I saw the nature of the industry itself as being more influential than their tenure in it. For example, would Bramwell's management behavior have been much different were he relatively new to conducting?

that managers rely on such planning to get a sense of a new job? Perhaps only sometimes, because Alan Whelan of BT, also new to his job, did not seem so inclined. I did record tenure as a factor for Gord Irwin of the Banff National Park, but for another reason: he was new to managing altogether and puzzled by it.

PERSONAL STYLE OF MANAGING

Now we turn to personal style, the predispositions of the person in the job, whether or not influenced by background and tenure. Because so much attention has been devoted to personal style, it is considered here at somewhat greater length, in this separate section.

The Many Dimensions of Managerial Style

There is no shortage of dimensions to describe aspects of managerial style. Noordegraff (1994), for example, provided a long list of "style in a narrow sense":

> task versus people orientation, "open" versus "closed" (listening versus talking), "centrifugal" versus "centripetal" (delegating versus non-delegating), formal versus informal, "patient" versus "impatient," systematic and orderly versus unsystematic and disorderly, team-oriented and cooperative versus solitary and non-cooperative, process versus result orientation, change and innovation versus status quo orientation, long term versus short term orientation, quantity versus quality orientation. (p. 21; see also Skinner and Sasse 1977:147)

To these could be added many dimensions of a more specific nature—for example, Fabienne Lavoie who managed on her feet and Carol Haslam's hard dealing and soft leading.

In the academic literature, "task versus people orientation" has received the greatest attention, much of it under the unfortunate labels of "initiating structure" versus "consideration" (e.g., Fleishman 1953a; Price 1963). Why not simply "command-and-control" versus "facilitate-and-empower" (e.g., Ezzamel et al. 1994)?

In the practitioner literature, the prize for the most popular dimension probably goes to "change and innovation versus status quo orientation," as in Miles and Snow's (1978) popular categorizing of managers as Prospectors, Defenders, Analyzers, and Reactors. Some managers create organizations (Max Mintzberg with the retail chain); others maintain them, sometimes by making adaptive changes (Sandy Davis in the parks); and then there are those who try to drive radical change (Alan Whelan at BT, Sir Duncan Nichol in the NHS). But no matter which it is, **the drive for change always requires the maintenance of some stability, just as stability cannot be had without the promotion of adaptive change** (Huy 2001:78–79).

Proactiveness   This brings up another dimension of style, which may appear similar to change but can be quite different. **If one factor stood out in these days of observation, it was _proactiveness_: the extent to which the managers used whatever degrees of freedom available for the benefit of their units or organizations, even if that was to reinforce stability** (Stewart 1982). Abbas Gullet, for example, was about as proactive as any manager in this study, but for purposes of stabilizing the refugee camps, while Alan Whelan sought to drive change in BT. (See the appendix for full descriptions of both these days.)

Thus, as noted earlier, **a manager need not have wide scope in order to be proactive.** What struck me was the propensity of a number of the twenty-nine managers to act in the face of great constraints: they sized whatever initiative they could and drove forward.

> • Peter Coe, in the difficult structure of the NHS, was a prime example. Above him was its vast hierarchy, while below, much of the activity he was supposed to manage was removed from his direct control (independent physicians, hospitals from which he was supposed to "purchase"). The frame of his job, as noted, was rather vague, and while it seemed to be imposed, thus rendering his job "passive" (in the terms used in Figure 4.1), in fact, on the day observed, Peter appeared to be profoundly proactive.

In the words of H. Edward Wrapp, **the effective manager walks "corridors of comparative indifference"** (1967:93). In the final chapter, we shall return to this dimension of proactiveness, which I see as a key determinant of managerial effectiveness.

On the Top, in the Center, or Throughout   Another dimension could be added to the literature: where the manager sees him- or herself in relation to others in the unit.

Some managers see themselves on top with regard to the hierarchy of authority, but also metaphorically: they are above those who report to them. While I cannot speak of Sir Duncan Nichol's personal feelings on this, I can ask, Where else can someone in charge of the work of almost a million people see himself?

In general, the more an organization emphasizes hierarchy, the more its managers are inclined to see themselves on top of their unit, if not necessarily on top of what goes on in that unit, and so are likely to give considerable attention to the role of *controlling*. Hence, we should expect this view of position to be especially common in machine organizations.

Other managers see themselves in the center, with activities revolving around them, outside as well as inside the unit. This seemed true for six of the managers of this study, four of them women.[29] In *The Female Advantage: Women's Wages of Leadership*, Sally Helgesen wrote that women managers "usually referred to themselves as being in the middle of things. Not on top, but in the center; not reaching down, but reaching out" (1990:45–46). The sharpest gender difference came out in two of the days I spent in Paris; the accompanying box compares the yin of Catherine Joint-Dieterle with the yang of Rony Brauman.

The Yin and Yang of Managing

Since I observed Rony Brauman of Doctors Without Borders and Catherine Joint-Dieterle nine days apart, both in Paris, it was natural to make comparisons. Both were longtime heads of visible institutions, but operating in very different domains. Both occupied tiny offices, and both commuted on two wheels, but very different wheels—a motorcycle in one case, a scooter in the other, reflecting the pace of their work. Both were deeply involved, but one was far less driven, so to speak. So despite the similarities, these were two very different days.

Doctors Without Borders runs around the world dealing with crises on an intermittent basis. It goes where the world is sick, trying to cure it, or at least palliate it, and then leaves. The fashion museum in Paris stays put, and collects heirlooms, which it may hold forever.

---

[29] Fabienne Lavoie and Ann Sheen in the hospitals, Carol Haslam in the film company, Catherine Joint-Dieterle in the museum, and Bramwell Tovey in the orchestra. (Don't be fooled by that podium.) Max Mintzberg in the retail chain was typical of the entrepreneur around whom tends to revolve everything in the company.

Managing followed suit (on these days, at least), in one case, intensive and aggressive, like yang; in the other, nurturing and infusive, like yin—short-term interventions compared with more stable engagement.

All of this works rather nicely, even as metaphors. Doctors Without Borders is not just *about* medicine but *like* medicine. It makes its decisions decisively—to treat a crisis or withdraw treatment from it—and it prefers the acute to the chronic, tending to leave when the condition stabilizes. Not coincidentally, it had a physician as its chief. On the day observed, he also practiced management like medicine—as interventionist cure. His work this day was thus largely external—networking and promoting.

The museum conserved both garments and a legacy. It was explained to me that a new garment could take from four hours to four days of full-time work to clean, and at least another four hours to arrange on a mannequin for display at an exhibition. The leader of the museum was tellingly called its "Chief Conservator," and her work this day was more internal—doing and detailing. She operated with her hands on, literally as well as figuratively. Just as she selected garments by sight and feel, so, too, was she evidentially in touch with the details of her organization. When she talked about the intimate relationship of clothes to the body, she might well have used this as a metaphor for the relationship of her organization's mission to its own body—namely, to preserve the heritage of French clothing within its carefully woven structure.

Of course, there is more to the symbolism of yin and yang. Yin may be absorbing, but it is said to be dark, obscure, and mysterious. Yang is said to be clear, light, white—maybe a little too much so. And while yang is active, yin is more passive (although Catherine hardly so, nor dark, obscure, or mysterious, for that matter).

Perhaps we can use a little more passivity in management, to enable everyone else to be more active. Above all, we are told that these two "great cosmic forces" cannot exist without each other. In the duality is found the unity: there has to be light in the shadows and shadow in the light. If harmony is achieved when yin and yang are balanced, then is there some rebalancing to be done in much of managing?

Then there are the managers who see themselves functioning, not on top of a hierarchy or at the center of some kind of hub, so much as throughout a web of activities. We talk a lot about organizations as networks these days—webs of interactive activities, with communication going every which way. Well, picture that, as in Figure 4.2, and ask yourself where the manager belongs in such a structure. On top? A manager on top of a network is *out* of it. In the center? A manager

The Manager on Top (of a hierarchy)

The Manager in the Center (of a hub)

The Manager Throughout (a web)

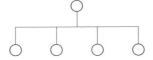

Figure 4.2 PERCEPTIONS OF THE PLACE OF THE MANAGER

who acts as if in the center of a web *centralizes* it—that is, draws its communication patterns toward him- or herself.

So to manage a network, the manager has to function *throughout*—and see him- or herself that way. In other words, the manager has to be everywhere, not drawing people into some center so much as going out to where they are.[30] This suggests a favoring of *linking* over leading, *dealing* over doing, and *convincing* over controlling—as was most evident in the project work of the adhocracy organizations, such as that of Brian Adams at Bombardier. It also suggests that the management of a network can extend beyond its manager, to others who take on managerial-type responsibilities—for example, to drive innovation (as we shall discuss in the last section of this chapter).

---

[30] Sally Helgesen used the word *web*, not *hub*, but differently in her description of the woman managers (1990:46), and she published a follow-up book called *The Web of Inclusion* (1995). She referred to a spider's web, "roughly circular in shape, with the leader at the central point, and lines radiating outward to various points": "the women who led the organizations labored continuously to being every point closer to the center" (1995:20).

The Many Styles of Managing

If the dimensions of managerial style are so numerous, imagine all the combinations of these dimensions into possible styles themselves. To cope with this, researchers, writers, and consultants have over the years developed categories of styles—typologies, so called—into whose round holes they try to fit the sometimes square pegs of managers.

Probably the most popular typology, even if not developed for managers per se, has been that of Myers-Briggs, which offers sixteen styles by combing the dimensions of Sensing (S) versus Intuition (N), Thinking (T) versus Feeling (F), Introversion (I) versus Extroversion (E), and Judging (J) versus Perceiving (P). Thus, we have managers running around calling themselves STIJs or whatever.

I have never been much of a fan of this (having never been able to get past Sensing vs. Intuition: is not Thinking, more specifically analyzing, the opposite of Intuition?). I prefer Maccoby's (1976) simpler categorization of managers as reliable *craftsmen*, power-hungry *jungle fighters*, steady *company men*, or competitive *gamesmen*; also Khandwalla's more systematic list of styles as conservative, risk taking, seat-of-the-pants, technocratic, participative, coercive, mechanistic, and organic (1977: Chapter 11).[31]

Styles as Art, Craft, Science   What has worked best for me is the art-craft-science triangle, introduced in Chapter 1, as a means to identify various styles of managing. As shown in Figure 4.3, close to science is what can be called a *cerebral* style—deliberate and analytical. It has long been influential in business (but perhaps represented best among the twenty-nine by John Tate of the Justice Department). Close to art is what can be called an *insightful* style—concerned with ideas and visions, more intuitive in nature (as perhaps best seen during the day with Alan Whelan of BT). And close to craft is what can be called an *engaging* style—hands-on and helpful, rooted in experience (as in the case of Fabienne Lavoie on the hospital ward, Doug Ward of the CBC, and many others).

But the pure practice of any one of these styles can lead to imbalanced managing—too much science, or art, or craft. So also shown on Figure 4.3

---

[31] See also Stewart (1976) for carefully derived typologies of managerial styles. In my 1973 book (pp. 127–129), I suggested eight types, based on the roles I discussed there: contact man, political manager, entrepreneur, insider, real-time manager, team manager, expert manager, and new manager.

Figure 4.3 STYLES OF MANAGING IN TERMS OF ART, CRAFT, SCIENCE

are the dysfunctional aspects of each of these styles: the cerebral style can become *calculating* (too heavy on the science), the insightful style can become *narcissistic* (art for its own sake), and the engaging style can become *tedious* (managers hesitating to venture beyond their personal experience). Even a combination of two of these styles with an absence of the third can be problematic, as shown on the three lines of the triangle: art and craft without the systematic scrutiny of science can encourage a *disorganized* style of managing; art and science without the rooted experience of craft can lead to a *disconnected* style of managing; and craft and science without the vision of art can result in a *dispirited* style of managing, careful and connected but lacking spark.

So the place to be is inside the triangle: **effective managing requires some blend of art, craft, and science, whether in the person of the manager alone, or else in a management team that works together** (see Pitcher 1995 or 1997). In other words, **management may not be a science, but it does need some of the order of science, while being rooted in the practicality of craft, with some of the zest of art.** An instrument I developed with Beverley Patwell, presented in Figure 4.4, allows you to plot your own style on this triangle. You are welcome to use it.

Consider how you manage in your job. Circle one of the three words from each row that best describes it. When you are finished, add up how many you have circled in each of the three columns. (Together they should add up to 10.)

_____

The first column represents art, the second craft, the third science.

Ideas	Experiences	Facts
Intuitive	Practical	Analytical
Heart	Hands	Head
Strategies	Processes	Outcomes
Inspiring	Engaging	Informing
Passionate	Helpful	Reliable
Novel	Realistic	Determined
Imagining	Learning	Organizing
Seeing it	Doing it	Thinking it
"The possibilities are endless!"	"Consider it done!"	"That's perfect!"

Total Scores

Figure 4.4 ASSESSING YOUR PERSONAL STYLE OF MANAGING IN TERMS OF ART, CRAFT, SCIENCE

Source: Developed by © Henry Mintzberg and Beverly Patwell, 2008.

Putting Style in Its Place

Earlier I described Carol Haslam's day as hard dealing and soft leading. Notice the distinction between the nouns and the adjectives. The nouns are about _what_ she did, the roles she performed; the adjectives are about _how_ she did it, how she performed those roles (Stewart 1982:5).

A manager is asked for help from a report. The answer can come as the what, in the form of one role or another. For example: "You can see Sally on this" (communicating); "What do _you_ think is best?" (leading); "I don't know, but you better resolve it by Friday" (controlling); or "Leave it with me" (doing). And within each of these can be the how. For example, concerning the communicating response, compare "In my experience, Sally will be skittish on this" with "Tell Sally we miss her—it will help."[32]

So how did personal style influence _what_ the twenty-nine managers did? A lot less than might be expected. While personal style influenced

[32] In their book _Real Managers_, Luthans et al. show "management by walking around" as _controlling_ (1988:90). But it could just as easily be seen as _communicating_ (getting information) or _leading_ (encouraging others), depending on what the manager has in mind as well as how he or she carries it out.

Record your three scores on the triangle. The horizontal lines marked A0 to A10 represent art. Identify the line that corresponds to your score for art. (In the example on the little triangle on the right, line A7 corresponds to a score of 7 in the first column.) Do the same for the diagonal line represented by C for craft. Mark the point where these lines meet. The score for science, on the diagonal line marked S, should fall at the same point. (Otherwise, your scores don't add up to 10.) This point represents your managerial style in this chart as you perceive it.

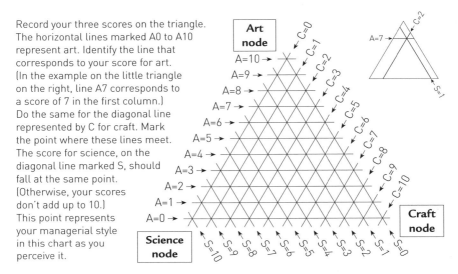

Feel free to use this for yourself and to compare your results with those of other managers you know, also to assess your perceptions of each other's styles, and to see how you come out as a team. You can also consider the prevalent managerial style in your organization, etc.

---

how all of these managers did their work, it seemed to have had surprisingly limited effect on *what* that work was.

Each of the twenty-nine managers certainly exhibited his or her own style of managing: nursing manager Ann Sheen was quick; GSI president Jacques Benz was reflective; Catherine Joint-Dieterle was more yin and Rony Brauman more yang, and so forth. All this was evident as I did my observation. But when I went back over the twenty-nine days and asked myself how much this was a major determinant of what the managers did that day, the answer was no in all but four cases.

- Rony Brauman seemed particularly enthusiastic about the lobbying he did concerning the situation in Somalia, as was Peter Coe about dealing with the higher reaches of the NHS on behalf of his unit. Dr. Stewart Webb of the NHS, intent on getting to his clinical work, sought to dispense with his managerial responsibilities quickly, which drew him into emphasizing the *controlling* role: rapid decisions directed to his assistant. And Paul Gilding tried to come to grips with his new job as head of Greenpeace by engaging in an elaborate exercise of planning. A typical example of the other twenty-five days was that of Carol Haslam of Hawkshead: her dealing may have been hard and her leading soft, but would we have expected the head of another similar film company to have concentrated on different roles? And how about Bramwell Tovey: did personal predisposition have much effect on what he did, on or off the podium?

Why should personal style, which has had so much attention in the literature of management, let alone that of leadership, seem to have so little influence on what these managers did? Because context matters: people don't usually find themselves in managerial jobs by chance, to shape them as they wish. (Or perhaps I should say, when they do, there may to be trouble ahead.) Rather, **what you do as a manager is mostly determined by what you face as a manager.** The person generally fits the job.

- Bramwell Tovey went into music, and from there to a conductorship, because of his natural disposition. Norm Inkster was no doubt attracted to the RCMP because of its culture and likely became head of it because he resonated so well with that culture. Sandy Davis fit well the regional post she had in the parks.

Of course, who you are helps determine what you get to face. Carol Haslam was not coincidentally in a job that required considerable external dealing, nor was Fabienne Lavoie in one that required intensive internal leading. (Imagine Carol and Fabienne in each other's jobs.)

Let me reiterate. **Personal style is important, no question. But that seems to be more about *how* managers do things, including the decisions they make and the strategies they shape, than *what* they do as managers.** In this regard, the literature, practitioner and academic alike, may be vastly overrating the importance of personal style. Style matters and context matters, but mostly they matter together, in a symbiotic relationship. As Kaplan put it, "the only way to think of any given [general managerial] job is the person-in-the-job" (1983:29).[33]

---

[33] McCall came to a similar conclusion, especially with regard to leadership style: "leadership models which emphasize the 'style' of a leader vis-à-vis the follower group have limited utility, even when they introduce situational contingencies. They have no explanatory power when it comes to nonsubordinate interactions, and it is difficult to understand the relationship between some global measure of a leader's style and the literally hundreds of activities that are part of the daily life of a manager" (1977:16).

Is the Manager a Chameleon?   A *Harvard Business Review* article entitled "Leadership That Gets Results" was described by its author Daniel Goleman (2000) as taking "much of the mystery out of executive leadership" (p. 78), by reducing it to six basic styles. These were coercive ("Do what I tell you," which Goleman called a "negative style"); authoritative ("Come with me . . . toward a vision," which he called "most strongly positive"); affiliative ("People come first"), democratic ("What do you think?"), and coaching ("Try this"), all three of which he called positive; and pacesetting ("Do as I do," which he considered negative (pp. 82–83; by the way, seeing style in strictly interpersonal terms, as carried out on the people plane with no reference to the planes of information or action, is common in much of this literature).

Goleman claimed that, much like "the array of clubs in a golf pro's bag," these styles can be picked and chosen "based on the demands of the shot. . . . The pro senses the challenge ahead, swiftly pulls out the right tool, and elegantly puts it to work. That's how high impact leaders operate too" (p. 80).

This assumption, that we can change our behaviors the way we change our golf clubs—a long-standing one in much of applied psychology and management development—needs to be scrutinized.

- Consider Marc, Executive Director of the hospital. As noted earlier, looking out he was an advocate for his institution, lobbying for it with apparent effectiveness. Perhaps Goleman would have called him "authoritative," even "pacesetting" (leaving aside the fact that one is supposed to be positive, the other negative). But turning around and looking in, Marc himself faced a whole host of advocates, all looking out for their own interests. So the very style that made him effective externally may have caused him problems internally, unless, of course, he could have pulled out a different club—in the more common metaphor, changed his colors like a chameleon. The tough, aggressive, advocate—"authoritative," "pacesetting," even perhaps "coercive" (really negative, though perhaps positive for the hospital)—merely had to become, say, "affiliative," "democratic," "coaching." Unfortunately for him, however, this was not a question of putting away a driver in favor of a putter so much as switching from boxing to badminton.

Bear in mind that while chameleons change colors, they do not change tails or tongues, let alone habitats. In fact, all they really do is hide—that is, use color to pretend to fit.[34] It may work for them in a very limited context, but for how long can that work for any manager? **The effective manager may more usually be the one whose natural style fits the context, rather than the one who changes style to fit context, or context to fit style (let alone being a so-called professional manager whose style is supposed to fit all contexts).**[35]

Doing the Job as Well as Making the Job   No doubt we can all adapt somewhat,[36] as did Stephen Omollo, who was more subdued at meetings in the Red Cross compound, more effusive as he walked around the refugee camps. But only within limits. Terribly destructive can be the other side of this coin, which is popular now under the guise of heroic leadership—namely, that the organization simply has to adapt to the style of its chief executive. This can ride roughshod over important aspects of the organization, such as its culture. **Expecting the incumbent to conform rigidly to the needs of the job may be bureaucracy, but no better is allowing the incumbent carte blanche to make the job whatever he or she pleases, which amounts to autocracy.**[37]

Of course, managers have to concern themselves with change, their own as well as that around them. Many of the twenty-nine managers I observed were driving change, but from positions of strength—a depth of understanding of the industry and the organization, combined with their natural fit with the needs of the job at the time.

- Alan Whelan of BT was an interesting case in point: he knew the industry, the technology, the function of selling, but he was new to BT. He was promoting ambitious change—in his organization. But that was the very reason he was put in that job.

---

[34] Wikipedia claimed (on July 5, 2008) that these changes of color are an expression of their condition and a means of communication, but they are not done to match their surroundings; chameleons are naturally colored to do that.

[35] Skinner and Sasser conclude that "nearly all managers tend to settle into a fairly rigid or limited executive style" (1977:146), but (as we shall discuss later) they see this as commonly rather close to the analytical, or professional, style.

[36] Braybrooke has referred to executives as applying "personal resources," information being an especially important one. Some (e.g., skill in bargaining) are "relatively transferable" to different jobs; others (e.g., local connections) are not (1964:544).

[37] As Vaill has commented: "One mistake the arts would never make is to presume that a part or role can be exactly specified independent of the performer, yet this is an idea that has dominated work organizations for most of the twentieth century. The part or the role in the arts defines and frames a context within which the performer is expected to operate artistically" (1989:124).

So **while every manager has to *make* the job, he or she also has to *do* the job. That is why managerial style cannot be considered out of context, independent of where it is practiced**—as does so much of the literature. And that is why, to me at least, so much of the literature on style feels sterile.[38]

So if you are a manager, be careful to understand your own style, not in general but in the context in which you practice management. And then be awfully careful about what other managerial jobs you take or put other managers into. Recently a professor of education asked me what I thought about the current American practice of appointing retired army officers to head up school systems. Good idea, I replied, and let's have schoolteachers run the army.

POSTURES OF MANAGING

As we have seen throughout this chapter, the various contexts of managing—external, organizational, job, temporal, personal—tend to be intertwined. In Max Mintzberg's case, for example, a young, small, and competitive business with an entrepreneurial form of organization allowed its chief executive somewhat wide scope to act but generated considerable pressure in the job, leading to a hectic pace with lots of doing and dealing—all of which fitted Max's nature quite well.

Such natural combinations appeared in many of the other days. But it has to be pointed out that no two managerial jobs, not even any two days of the same person in the same job, are ever exactly alike. Does this mean, as Whitley (1989) was cited in Chapter 3, that there is no consistency in managerial work?

Consistency is found only where you look for it. If you are what Charles Darwin called a "splitter," then everything is nuanced. "Lumpers," on the

---

[38] Biggart has argued that "theories or frameworks of managerial style assume that [it] is a property of the leader or manager . . . viewed as a personal capacity that somehow exists apart from its exercise in a social setting, at least for analytical purposes. Numerous theorists have, for example, frozen prototypic styles into tables and grids in an attempt to develop universal model applicable to many settings. . . . [This] has abstracted management style . . . from its exercise . . . and from the process it initiates and to which it responds; the result is theories that fail to capture the dynamic aspects of a manager's interrelationships with subordinates" (1981:292–293). To change this, of course, would require a revolution in the research: away from one-variable-at-a-time methodologies toward thick description (as Gertz [1973] called it), in order to see behavior in its full context.

other hand, look for consistencies. Splitting may be more precise, but we need lumping too, if we are to understand things—so long as we don't carry these generalizations too far.

So I proceeded as follows. First, I concluded that if we really wish to develop a robust understanding of the varieties of managing (for the purposes of selecting, developing, and assessing managers, etc.), we will get it, not by concluding that these are infinite, but by developing a coherent classification of managing—some lumping into what seem to be the prominent patterns in the job. And second, this will not come from considering one by one each of the factors that influence managing; rather, we need to combine these factors as they appear commonly in the work of managers.

Accordingly, I went over each of the twenty-nine days (as well as other days discussed in the agenda), looking for the pattern that best described it. I collected the similar patterns into groups, which I labeled *postures*—where the managers seemed to stand, so to speak, at that point in their jobs. Of course, no manager adopts any posture for a day, any more than he or she does across all days. But patterns did seem to appear for a time.

I have identified nine postures in all, plus two temporary ones. They are listed in Table 4.1 by numeral for each of the managers who adopted them. When more than one posture seemed appropriate for a manager, I chose the one that was most evident, but I also discuss the other here.

These postures range from maintaining the workflow of the organization to connecting the organization to its outside environment. Three describe how senior managers of large organizations try to penetrate their hierarchies: by remote controlling, fortifying the culture, and intervening strategically. One describes balanced managing, all around (inside and outside), while another two contrast managing *in* the middle with managing *out* of the middle. The final one describes managing as advising from the side. The two temporary ones, discussed briefly after these, are the new manager and the reluctant manager. A final section of this chapter considers another set of postures of increasing importance: managing beyond the manager.[39]

---

[39] In *Contrasts in Management*, Rosemary Stewart (1976) offers two typologies of managerial postures, one concerning contact patterns (Chapter 2), the other work patterns (Chapter 4), which comes closer to the typology presented here. See also Fondas (1992), on "creating a behavior profile" of managing and "profiling managerial jobs."

1. Maintaining the Workflow

A number of the managers of this study clearly focused on maintaining the basic workflow in one way or another: they were personally engaged in ensuring that the operations proceeded smoothly. To use the fancy word, **these managers maintained *homeostasis*—a dynamic balance—in order to keep the organization on course.**

This posture of managing is more about fine-tuning than major renewing. As Sayles put it: "For the most part, the manager [tries to] detect where the system of human relations may break down . . . [and seeks] through remedial changes to return the system to equilibrium" (1964:257; see also Thompson 1967).

This posture would seem to be most applicable to first-time managers in machine organizations, as in the case of Stephen Omollo in the refugee camps. But I also saw it in more professional organizations (Fabienne Lavoie and Ann Sheen in the hospitals, Gord Irwin in the Banff National Park, Ralph Humble in the RCMP detachment[40]) and at the middle management level (Abbas Gullet in the refugee camps), even for a chief executive or two. Certainly Bramwell Tovey maintained the basic flow of the music—its rhythm, pace, and so forth.—in rehearsals and performances alike.[41] Max Mintzberg's work as head of the retail chain could also be described as maintaining the workflow (although I put him in a later group).

A number of common expressions about managing apply to this posture: managing "on the ground" (Gord Irwin quite literally); "hands on" (Bramwell Tovey literally with regard to the baton; in Fabienne Lavoie's case, on her feet); "managing by exception" (used as the title of the report on Abbas Gullet and Stephen Omollo). All of these suggest a practice of managing rooted especially in craft, if not devoid of analysis, and likely to exhibit a pace of rather brief episodes, as was especially evident in the work of Fabienne and Max.

---

[40] But Pitner did not see it in the schools: "Principals engage predominately in service, advisory, and auditing relationships; they neither become directly involved in the work flow at the classroom level, nor do they seek change or improvement through innovative or stabilization relationships" (1982:8, citing Peterson).

[41] Three years before I observed Bramwell, I described Fabienne Lavoie in similar terms: "The remarkable thing to me about this day is how everything just flowed together in a natural rhythm." In the report on his day, as noted earlier, I described Bramwell as engaged in orchestra operating more than orchestra directing.

A key role here is *doing*, alongside either *leading* or *controlling*, depending on how the manager exercises authority (Fabienne and Stephen more leading, Abbas more controlling). And *communicating* is particularly important here: the manager needs instant information to catch anything that goes off course. As noted in Abbas's case, he dug constantly for every scrap of information he could get and exhibited a remarkable command of the detail.

There are a couple of interesting anomalies about this posture. First, although maintaining the workflow implies a clear sense of authority, managers such as Fabienne, Ann, Max, Abbas, and Stephen seemed to be more at the center of activities than hierarchically on top of them. As I concluded about Abbas, who emphasized hierarchy more than most, he was most decidedly the "nerve center" of his operation, with information flowing around him relentlessly. Second, although the frame of these jobs seemed narrow and imposed—to keep these operations humming—here we find some of the most proactive managers among the twenty-nine, including Fabienne and Abbas. It can take an awful lot of initiative just to keep an organization on course.

2. Connecting Externally

At the other extreme is a posture that connects out more than controls in. In formal terms, **these managers, maintain the boundary condition of their organization.**

Although all managers have to do some of this, we might expect more of it at the senior levels, where there are representations to be made, figurehead duties to be performed, and lobbying to be done on behalf of the entire organization. This seemed to hold true especially in the case of Rony Brauman of Doctors Without Borders, but also Carol Haslam of Hawkshead, Sir Duncan Nichol of the NHS, and Marc in the hospital.

The most apparent reason is that other managers looked after the internal operations—or else these did not require close supervision. In fact, the managers just mentioned all ran organizations of knowledge workers—three in health care (counting Doctors Without Borders) and one in filmmaking, so their people knew what they had to do and mostly just did it. That not only allowed the senior managers to focus on outside concerns but also required them to do so in order to protect and support these knowledge workers.

How they did so varied, however. Carol negotiated the deals for new film contracts, which required an intricate juggling of ideas, customers, and budgets, and then turned them over to capable crews. Sir Duncan and Marc acted more like advocates (to use Marc's own word) on behalf of their organizations, which were enmeshed in complex webs of political forces. Marc's hospital in particular could be pulled every which way by government, patients, directors, and physicians, and that required some tricky buffering. Too many pressures allowed to seep in could only aggravate an already difficult situation.

Just as the first posture was also found above the hierarchical base of the organization, so too can this one be found below its senior management. Middle managers of functions such as government relations and purchasing, for example, may have to focus on external work. I put Peter Coe, district manager of the NHS, in another posture, but he could easily have been here. Certainly on the day observed he managed out, to the NHS headquarters and other units.

The focus of this posture is clearly on the external roles of *linking* (compared with leading) and *dealing* (compared with doing). Here we find negotiators par excellence, also the most enthusiastic networkers— in effect, Maccoby's "gamesmen." Contrast Rony Brauman's external yang with Catherine Joint-Dieterle's internal yin, also Marc's advocacy with Fabienne Lavoie's dislike of "that PR stuff." While the first posture seems mostly craft, here we find more art. Note also that being externally oriented, managers adopting this posture were hardly "on top"; they are better described as functioning "throughout" the external networks as well as serving as central hubs with respect to many of the pressures exerted on their organizations.

3. Blending All Around

This third posture includes aspects of the first two, and more. The manager is close to the workflow, but also connects significantly to the outside world, and most importantly, blends them together. So this is a more balanced posture than the first two, and more integrative. (I used the word *blending* in Chapter 3 to make the point that all managers have to integrate all the roles of the model. I use it again here because this is especially important for certain managers, as we shall see.)

Note that while we might expect this to be a posture of chief executives, it did not come out that way: just two of those I put in this posture headed up their organizations (out of twelve chief executives in all— Catherine Joint-Dieterle of the museum and Max Mintzberg of the retail chain). All the rest were middle managers: Brian Adams of Bombardier, Glen Rivard of the Justice Department, Doug Ward of the CBC Ottawa radio station, and Paul Hohnen of Greenpeace. As noted several times, **middle management may be the best place in an organization to integrate its activities**.

All but one of these people (Max) were heavily involved in project work, which was carried out in organizations, or at least units, that subscribed to the adhocracy form. Two of these jobs—Brian's in the aircraft program and Glen's in the policy unit of the Justice Department—were essentially about projects, while others included some important project work: radio programming at the CBC, development of exhibitions in the museum, creation of new policies for Greenpeace. Projects are more or less self-contained and require rather complete managing—the blending of all kinds of efforts all around. For example, to create family law at the Justice Department, Glen had to oversee, review, and push along a range of legislative projects by making linkages among their social, legal, and political aspects. In Max's case, he had to blend the doing, the dealing, and the controlling, not only the strategic deals with the operating details but also internal concerns with external ones. We might describe this as *strategic maneuvering* more than strategy making per se.

Because of the importance of their lateral relationships, these managers could not afford to see themselves as being on top, or even in the center, so much as throughout. They had to reach out and work through extensive networks, as was most evident in Brian Adams's work. In fact, in this posture superiors and subordinates can get all mixed up with associates and partners. Brian was engaged in what might be called "extended controlling" with subcontractors, and I wrote of Doug Ward that he linked naturally to people one might otherwise think he would have led, while he did not hesitate to lead people who did not officially work for him.

All of this suggests that this is a posture, not of specific roles so much as of the connections among the roles. But if key roles are to be identified, certainly they would include *dealing* and *doing* alongside much *communicating*. This posture seems closest to the craft style of managing—more facilitative than directive. There were certainly signs of art, and analysis was required especially to manage the projects, but craft appeared to predominate. Most of the managers here were deeply involved in the details and highly experienced in complex industries that required much tacit knowledge.

4. Remote Controlling

The next three postures each describe a different way in which especially the senior managers of large organizations try to penetrate their hierarchies, to put their stamp on the organization.

Remote controlling describes a posture of managing internally on the information plane, that is somewhat detached and analytical—"hands-off," if you like. Managers here may see themselves on top and favor techniques that make extensive use of the *controlling* role, whether by making decisions themselves, planning formally to influence the decisions of others by the allocation of resources, or simply deeming performance. This presumably reduces the pace of managing as well as its variety and oral nature in favor of more formal order and control. This posture is closest to the science corner of the art-craft-science triangle.

I wrote in *Managers Not MBAs* (2004b: Chapter 4) that this seems to be a particularly prevalent approach to managing these days, especially among senior managers in large corporations.[42] Perhaps my concerns about this encouraged me to study managers more inclined to the craft side, because among the twenty-nine, I considered that only three of the days were inclined toward the science side of managing in this posture: Paul Gilding at Greenpeace and Drs. Thick and Webb of the NHS, all for particular reasons.

Paul Gilding was new at the helm of Greenpeace, and he seemed to be trying to use formal planning to bring things under control. Ironically (as can be seen in the appendix), while he was encouraging others to engage in more hands-on doing, Paul was consciously avoiding it himself (despite being vigorously urged by a staffer at one point in the day to do it). He never got the chance to find out if this posture would have worked, nor we if he would have changed postures.

While we might expect more remote controlling at the top of large, especially machine-like organizations, Drs. Webb and Thick worked at the base of professional organizations. Both were part-time managers, more involved with their clinical and/or research activities (where they exhibited more of a craft orientation) than their managing per se. So they did the latter rather briefly, on the day observed at least, in good part authorizing decisions in the controlling role.

I have included Sir Duncan Nichol, Sandy Davis, John Tate, and Bramwell Tovey under different postures, but their days exhibited some aspects of this one too. Sir Duncan headed a massive hierarchy, difficult

---

[42] Tengblad (2004) examined "the link between financial markets and managerial work" in the case of eight CEOs of large Swedish corporations. What he found was a good deal of remote controlling, thanks to the pressures of financial markets that were passed to other managers down the hierarchy. As noted earlier, "The exercise of controls by setting and monitoring expectations resulted in some managers working to exhaustion, and also in conformity and non-constructive communication" (p. 583; see also Tengblad 2000 for some evidence that this posture has been on the increase among corporate chief executives).

for anyone to penetrate directly, which encouraged some remote controlling. Sandy, in the middle of the parks' hierarchy, was partial to planning and the like. And the management practice of John at the Justice Department seemed more formal.

Bramwell Tovey was most interesting in regard to the posture. What I saw, in my opinion, belongs under the first posture, of maintaining the workflow. But Bramwell was also exercising control in perhaps the remotest sense of all—built into the very nature of orchestra conducting. As noted earlier, the conductor waves the baton and everyone plays, while the exercise of leadership is significantly covert. There is so much power in such a little stick—as long as it is used accordingly to the rules. Remote controlling with a vengeance!

5. Fortifying the Culture

Also especially from senior management, but very different, comes this next posture. Mostly art and craft, this posture works to enhance performance through personal engagement rather than impersonal control. **The object of this posture is to fortify the culture of the organization—its sense of community—so that people can be trusted to function appropriately.** Put differently, a strong culture can decentralize an organization extensively.

Leading is the key role here, reinforced by a good deal of *communicating*, combined with *linking* to protect the organization from external disturbances—as in Norm Inkster's policy of "no surprises" at the RCMP. Here, too, we might expect to see a relatively less hectic pace of managing, with the managers perceiving themselves to be more at the center of things than on top. Around the leader swirls the culture, much as the queen bee emits the chemical substance that holds the hive together. "One CEO defined his task mainly as 'to tell the history of the company'" (Tengblad 2000:36).

As just suggested, this posture came out most distinctly on the day I spent with Norm Inkster as superintendent of the RCMP—and its consequences were evident in the other days with Commanding Officer Allen Burchill and Detachment Commander Ralph Humble. It was as if he watered the RCMP garden and then let the flowers bloom. A combination of factors encouraged this practice in the RCMP: a noble mission, a distinguished history, a chief executive with long tenure and an absolute devotion to its culture, and a personal style that seemed to focus on the people plane.

Some managers whom I listed under other postures exhibited aspects of this one, too. John Cleghorn was certainly fortifying the Royal Bank's culture on the day I observed him, with similar effects. Doug Ward at the CBC, Fabienne Lavoie on the surgical ward, and Stephen Omollo, especially when in the camps, were also fortifying the cultures of their units, which indicates that this posture can be also found at middle and operating levels of organizations.

6. Intervening Strategically

Another posture for penetrating the hierarchy is personal intervention on an ad hoc basis to drive specific changes. Jacques Benz did this at GSI by getting involved in projects he believed would have strategic impact, while John Cleghorn at the Royal Bank immersed himself in operating issues about which he was knowledgeable. All managers do this to some extent; I call it a posture when a manager seems to be doing a good deal of it.

The favored role here is obviously *doing*, possibly reinforced by *controlling* and *communicating*. The manager's style tends to be oriented to craft, based on tangible experience, with strategies more emergent than deliberate—that is, coming out of informal learning more than formal planning. (We shall return to this point in the next chapter.) And while the manager may be seen as "on top"—driving change from "above"—he or she tends to be acting throughout, by intervening in many places, as was evident in John's day. Here the manager is inclined to circumvent hierarchy, going straight to where changes have to be made.

7. Managing in the Middle

Next we consider managers who sit squarely in the middle of the hierarchy, but who adopt one of two very different postures. Either they go with the flow, and manage in the middle, or else they resist it, and manage out of the middle.

The classic view sees the middle manager in the line hierarchy, between a senior management above that formulates strategy and more junior levels below that implement it. The middle manager does neither but rather facilitates the downward flow on the information plane, by *communicating* and *controlling*, and transmits performance information back up. So there is relatively less doing and dealing on the action plane, also perhaps less leading on the people plane. Overall, this is a posture that feels more analytical, or cerebral, dependent as it is on planning, budgeting, and other formal systems. It is thus more about maintaining stability than promoting change, with a pace of work that is perhaps less hectic than some other postures, and more formalized.

I identified three managers among the twenty-nine in this posture, all in regional positions: Allen Burchill of the RCMP, and Sandy Davis and Charlie Zinkan of the Canadian Parks.[43] Commanding Officer Burchill, for example, sat in the hierarchy between a headquarters that set much of the policy, established most of the systems, and influenced many of the norms, and the detachments of highly trained and rather empowered officers who carried out the work. When I remarked to him about how much of his time on the day observed was devoted to *communicating*, he replied "that seems to be about my job." (We shall return to the special case of regional management in the next chapter.)

All these managers were in government. Has the "downsizing" of recent years rendered this posture obsolete in business? I doubt it: the need for managers who link different levels in a hierarchy remains. I could easily have found such managers to study in BT or the Royal Bank of Canada.

8. Managing Out of the Middle

We discussed earlier that there is more to middle management than managing in the middle of a hierarchy. Here we look at middle managers who seemed to be managing their way out of the middle—which indicates how varied and interesting the job of managing can be.

Alan Whelan of BT was certainly in the middle: of an extensive hierarchy, a culture in transition, and a complicated issue and the ethical dilemma it raised. Perhaps because of the ambiguity associated with all this, he was able to manage out of the middle, spearheading change by encouraging his senior management to recognize a new world of telecommunications (see the description of the day in the appendix). It is interesting that of all twenty-nine days of observation, twelve of them with chief executives, it was on this day that I heard the most articulate expression of strategy. (But Alan wasn't "intervening strategically"; he was doing his job.)[44]

---

[43] John Tate has been included under another posture, but there were aspects of this one, too. He may have been the civil service head of the Justice Department, but being between the minister and the department also put him in the middle.

[44] To quote from my report on Alan's comments: "The days of the supplier push of services, to which clients simply subscribed, were long gone. Now business clients wanted services

Peter Coe, as a District General Manager of the NHS, was also breaking out of the middle, but differently, and from a different place—more of a straightjacket. Above Peter sat the extensive and controlling hierarchy of the NHS, which in a sense, stopped at his unit: the physicians who carried out much of the operating work did not report to it, and the operating units of the NHS were being converted to "providers" from which such districts "purchased" their services. This all seemed a bit like a surreal game, except that Peter used it to gain advantage for his unit (as will be described in the next chapter).

Managing out of the middle appears to focus on the external roles of *linking* and *dealing*, making special use of the negotiating skills of the manager. Here were the truest gamesmen of this study, who built their coalitions to influence people over whom they did not have formal authority. I did not see much controlling here or leading—at least not as central preoccupations. This posture, perhaps more than any of the others, exhibited managing closest to art.

Thus, the key contextual factors for this posture seem to be (1) the personal, proactive style of the incumbent, (2) the large, hierarchical nature of his or her organization, and (3) sometimes temporary pressures that the manager feels compelled to escape. These can be jobs of narrow scope made broader by the manager's own proactiveness.

Compare Alan Whelan and Peter Coe with Brian Adams, Abbas Gullet, and Sandy Davis. Each of the latter three have been described under a different posture, but all were also highly proactive gamesmen (or gameswoman) in their own right, leaving clear stamps on their units. But their work was about execution, not strategy—accomplishing effectively what was expected of them: Brian getting that airplane up on schedule, Abbas keeping the lid on the camps, Sandy connecting the headquarters to the parks.[45] Sandy, for example, may have been playing the political context very astutely, but on *its* terms, in *its* way. Peter, in contrast, was reversing the political process for the sake of his district, and Alan was pushing for a major reconception at BT.

---

that met their own specific needs. Power had moved to the consumer. Network services like those of BT were partial, while the client sought 'end-to-end' services through a single agreement. There was thus a need for integrators to bring together data centre, desktop, network, and other services, which required that different suppliers collaborate."

[45] Abbas came closer to this posture during the Lake Victoria crisis (described earlier), when he realized that the Tanzanian Red Cross was unable to deal with the tragedy of the overturned boat and so grabbed the initiative and went there with a team from N'gara.

9. Advising from the Side

There is another posture common enough to merit inclusion here, even if it was not fully represented in this research. This is the manager as adviser, specialist, intervener, based on expertise more than authority. **If the traditional middle manager sits in midair, then these advising managers sit off to a side, seeking to influence others, or simply responding to requests.** Hence, they are not on top, or even at any center, but can only hope to involve themselves in influential networks.

This may sound like a posture of experts, not managers. But managers can get into it in two ways. First, staff units require managers (Paul Hohnen was the manager of two in Greenpeace). In fact, these managers are sometimes the most experienced experts in their units, and have to represent them as such (Hales and Mustapha 2000:15; see also Wolf 1981, on audit managers). Second, line managers can sometimes be drawn into this advisory role. Aside from managing the Canadian Department of Justice, John Tate had to act as adviser to the minister on issues of policy and legislation. Of course, any manager can be called on for his or her knowledge (Bramwell Tovey on music, Dr. Thick on kidney transplantation, Gord Irwin on mountain rescue).

In this posture, personal style seems to be closer to science than art or craft; the roles of *linking* and *communicating* would appear to be prominent, and the organization would often be large, stable, and rather formalized—where expert advice is provided internally.

The New Manager

To complete this discussion, two other postures deserve mention, one that is temporary and the other that should be: the new manager and the reluctant manager.

I noted earlier that **the day someone becomes a manager for the first time, everything changes. Yesterday you were doing it; today you are managing it. That can be quite a shock.** Even for an experienced manager in a new job, there is a required time of adjustment. As discussed in my earlier book (1973:129), the manager in a new job has to develop a network of contacts (*linking*) in order to gain the necessary base of information in the job (*communicating*), which eventually enables him or her to take action (*doing* and *dealing*).

Most of the twenty-nine managers I observed had extensive experience, many in their current jobs, some (such as Bramwell Tovey, Abbas

Gullet, and Brian Adams) also in similar jobs. New to managing altogether was perhaps only Gord Irwin in the Banff National Park; new to the industry, or the context, was especially Marc. All sought out their space while trying to get their feet on the ground. Paul Gilding was not new to Greenpeace, but to its job of Executive Director.[46]

A thorough discussion of this posture can be found in Linda Hill's book *Becoming a Manager* (2003), whose ideas have been quoted several times in our discussion. Hill pointed out that to become a manager means maneuvering the abrupt transition from being a specialist and a doer to becoming a generalist and an agenda settler, plus often having to shift from acting individually to becoming a network builder who gets things done through others (p. 6).

In a section entitled "From Control to Commitment"—in our terms, from the role of *controlling* to that of *leading*—Hill described how many of the nineteen new managers she studied "were eager to exercise their formal authority and to implement their own ideas about how to run an effective organization." Most thus "adopted a hands-on autocratic approach to management" (p. 99), only to discover the limits of their formal authority: "very few people seemed to be following their orders" (p. 100). As one of the new managers put it:

> Becoming a manager is not about becoming a boss. It's about becoming a hostage. There are many terrorists in this organization who want to kidnap me. I used to love my job. People listened to me. People liked me. I'm the same person now, but no one listens and no one cares. (p. 261)[47]

These managers "had to learn to lead by persuasion and not by directive" (p. 100), and to discover "new ways to measure success and derive satisfaction from work. It meant evolving an entirely new professional

---

[46] See Gabarro (1985) on the experienced manager in a new job, whose "taking-charge process" can also take "a long time (2–2.5 years), through what he describes as five stages: "Taking Hold" (learning, setting the tone, taking corrective actions; p. 111); "Immersion" (more changes, with a less hectic, finer grained and "more focused learning" process; p. 113); "Reshaping" (reconfiguring some aspect[s] of the organization); "Consolidation" (dealing with leftover issues and uninterrupted problems; p. 115); and "Refinement" (little change, instead refining operations and looking for opportunities; p. 116). Gabarro concluded that success among the fourteen managers studied depended on "industry experience, clear understanding of what is expected, support for superiors, [and] good interpersonal relationships" (p. 110).

[47] Gord Irwin expressed similar frustrations. While working on his e-mail, for example, he commented that once you become a manager, it can be difficult to get meaningful work done.

identity" (p. x). Hill's prescription for this: "new managers should see themselves as engaged in strenuous self-development," by capitalizing "on their on-the-job learning" (p. 234), a point we shall return to in Chapter 6.

The Reluctant Manager

Two people were, to my mind, reluctant managers—both, in fact, part-time managers in one way or another. Most evident was Dr. Webb, who dispensed with his managerial duties quickly so that he could get on with his clinical work, which he relished and where he was transformed.

After an intense hour with his "business manager," during which she asked the questions and Dr. Webb gave quick answers, while drinking one cup of coffee after another and smoking a steady chain of cigarettes, he left for his clinical rounds. There he settled down as a calm clinician, responsive to his patients, with time for all their needs, and relaxed with the accompanying staff as well. Coffee and cigarettes were neither consumed nor mentioned during his two hours on the ward.

John Tate at Justice clearly was a manager, although more than that; as noted earlier, he was an adviser to the minister, too. But he was also reluctant about his management, and he articulated that clearly.

Some other managers also expressed reluctance—for example, Gord Irwin, although he was new to managing, and Bramwell Tovey, because of the natural conflict between being a musician and a manager of musicians. But I would not call either of them reluctant managers.

Far more numerous were those who relished the job of managing—loved the action, the influence, the pace, all of it. Sandy Davis, John Cleghorn, Ann Sheen, Peter Coe, Carol Haslam, and Abbas Gullet all come to mind, among others. None expressed any real concerns about being a manager, although everyone in this job must complain about it sometimes, even if only to a spouse. This sounds healthy to me. **Managing is no job to approach with hesitation: it simply requires too much of the total person.** Like medicine, the work of managing cannot be distracted by another focus. Both require rather full commitment. So the reluctant manager should probably be temporary—either the reluctance, or else the manager.[48]

---

[48] On this posture, see Scase and Goffee (1989) and Watson (1994:63ff.).

Postures and Purposes for All

I have associated each of the twenty-nine days of managing mainly with the one posture that seems to describe it best, sometimes accompanied by another. But it has to be appreciated that all managers adopt most of these postures, at least at some time or other. That is because **all these postures are basic purposes of managing. All managers have to connect externally (with all kinds of stakeholders), to maintain the workflow (to keep things on course, even if only in their own offices), and even to remote control (who can manage without a budget?). Most have to give attention to fortifying their culture, promoting certain strategic initiatives, and acting as experts in their own domain from time to time. And every single manager, no matter where in the hierarchy, has to manage in the middle—of a complex web of influencing forces—which also means, of course, that sometimes he or she has to manage out of that middle too.** So to function effectively, every manager not only has to combine all of these postures but also to blend them all around.

As we have seen here, managers do tilt one way or another, at least for a time, giving rise to these postures. Were these, then, the posture of the day, the month, the job? That probably varied from one manager to another. My own impression, from the days of observation as well as evidence of other days in their agendas, is that these were common, if not exclusive, postures for these managers.

Figure 4.5 shows these postures mapped on the art-craft-science triangle. That they tend to range around the node of craft, whether up toward art or over toward science, provides more evidence, either of managing being a practice rooted in context, or else of my personal bias toward craft.

MANAGING BEYOND THE MANAGER

Beyond reluctant managing, or sometimes because of it, is managing beyond the manager. Indeed, this can be the opposite of the reluctant manager: people without formal managerial responsibility embrace some of the tasks of managing.

So far we have taken managing to be rather strictly what managers do. But **always of some importance, and now increasingly so, is the managing that happens beyond what is done by the people**

Figure 4.5 POSTURES IN TERMS OF ART, CRAFT, SCIENCE

designated as managers. The job, or at least parts of it, gets diffused to other people, who carry out certain of the managerial roles (see Gray 1999; also Martin 1983).

There are perhaps two reasons for the increased attention to managing beyond the manager. One is that, as knowledge work and networks become more prevalent, power over certain kinds of decision making passes naturally to nonmanagers. In the professional form of organization, for example, strategies emerge from the venturing efforts of the professionals themselves.

The second reason, not independent of the first, is that many of us have a love-hate relationship with our managers, especially as "leaders." Some of us love them and think they are the answer to just about every problem in this world. Bring on the great leader and all will be well. Others of us hate them and believe that they are the cause of just about every one of these problems. Get rid of those people and all will be well. Most of us, I suspect, adhere to both positions, depending on our mood and our latest encounter with a manager.

Beware of both. **We can neither do without managers nor afford to idolize them.** As I hope our discussion to this point has made clear, managers have basic duties to perform in organizations: they provide a sense of unity, consolidate information for action, represent their unit to the outside world, are responsible for its performance, and so on. But I hope our discussion has also made clear that **there is much more to organizational purpose, accomplishment, and responsibility than what managers do.**

So, on the continuum shown in Figure 4.6 we should ignore the two extremes—of managers totally in charge at one end and managing entirely without managers at the other—and consider instead what are labeled maximal managing, participative managing, shared managing, distributed managing, supportive managing, and minimal managing.

Maximal Managing

In some respects, Fayol was right, roughly speaking: there are managers who plan, organize, coordinate, command, and control. Let's call theirs' *maximal managing,* to contrast it with minimal managing. It seemed most evident in the work of Max Mintzberg, a classic entrepreneur, and Abbas Gullet, running a machine organization requiring a very firm hand.

Shan Martin in *Managing without Managers* has referred to the "image of a manager as the motor of the organizational machine, or the heart, brain, and other vital organs of the organizational body, whose job it is to keep all the other parts 'going'" (1983:30). But even in machine organizations, much of the necessary coordination is achieved, not by the manager who supervises the work, so much as by the analysts who program it. This amounts to the delegation of important aspects of the controlling role to nonmanagers.

While no one is disputing the existence of entrepreneurs who manage maximally, the gurus of management have been telling us for years that machine organizations are disappearing, and with them their maximal managing. Well, look around—at the auto assembly lines, textile factories, supermarkets, call centers, and the clerks abundant in so many government offices, insurance companies, and elsewhere. Consider, too,

Figure 4.6 MANAGING BY AND BEYOND THE MANAGER

all those economists and financial analysts who continue to equate the enterprise with its chief executive. And don't forget those organizational charts, with that chief on "top." To paraphrase Mark Twain, the rumors of the death of maximal managing have been greatly exaggerated.

Participative Managing

An apparent but in fact small step away from maximal managing goes under the label of "participative management," or "empowerment," or "decentralization."

Participation occurs when senior managers pass some of their power down the hierarchy (Likert 1961, McGregor 1960, and many more). But that usually means to other managers. Moreover, the senior managers who give such power can easily take it back: the other people participate with a clear sense of where the ultimate authority is anchored.

As for "empowerment," the word may now be more fashionable, but as discussed earlier, **people who have a job to do shouldn't need to be "empowered" by their managers**, any more than worker bees need to be by their so-called queen.

Decentralization is often taken to mean a diffusion of power from a headquarters to the managers who run the business divisions. But passing power in a big organization from a few managers in the center to a few more in dispersed units hardly constitutes a serious diffusion of power.[49]

Colin Hales (2002) has captured the limited nature of this posture perfectly with his discussion of "bureacracy-lite." He challenged three popular claims: "that centralized, regulated bureaucratic organizations characterized by hierarchy and rules are inevitably giving way to decentralized and empowered post-bureaucratic organizations characterized by internal networks and an internal market"; second "that, as a consequence, the traditional managerial role of command and control is being superseded by one of facilitation and coordination"; and third, "that, in turn, managerial work as routine administration of work processes is being supplanted by the 'new managerial work' of non-routine leadership and entrepreneurship." Instead, Hales sees a "limited change to a different form of bureaucracy in which hierarchy and rules have been retained but in an attenuated and

---

[49] In fact, the most famous case of "decentralization" was actually one of centralization. In the 1920s, Alfred Sloan of General Motors reined in the power of the people running its separate businesses (Chevrolet, Buick, etc.) by creating a divisional structure that subjected them to the performance controls imposed by the headquarters (see Mintzberg 1979:405–406).

sharper form—'bureaucracy-lite'" (p. 51). As a consequence, "there is little change in the substance of managers' work activities . . . individual responsibility and a preoccupation with administration remain" (p. 64).

Shared Managing

What Hales captures less perfectly are other changes in how management is practiced. The first of these, discussed here, is fundamental if still limited in scope: one managerial job is shared among several people.

In its simplest form, which can also be called *comanagement*, two people share a single job, whether formally or informally. In an article entitled "The Co-Manager Concept," John Senger (1971) found this to be common in the U.S. Navy: in "60 percent of the [commands studied] the task and social functions were divided between the commanding officer and the second in command" (p. 79). Another version common at senior levels in business is where a CEO focuses on the external aspects of the job (linking, dealing) while a COO (Chief Operating Officer) looks after the internal aspects (controlling, leading, doing).[50]

Key to this is the sharing of information. As noted in several places, information is the glue that holds the different managerial roles together. If two people sharing the same job do not fully share their information, problems inevitably ensue.

Team management extends shared management to several people. For example, Hodgson, Levinson, and Zaleznik (1965) described an "executive role constellation" in a psychiatric hospital, involving both tasks and emotions. The chief executive related the organization to its environment (linking, dealing) and was both assertive and controlling. The clinical director managed internal clinical services (doing, controlling, leading), and was the supportive one. A third person dealt with nonroutine innovation (doing) and expressed friendship and egalitarian norms (another approach to leadership). A more elaborate example is provided by the state of Switzerland, which is governed by seven people who rotate the position of head of state on an annual basis. Switzerland works rather well as a country, even if most of its citizens reportedly have not been able to name its head of state.

---

[50] Jacques Benz was an example of the COO in my research. Likewise, Bramwell Tovey worked with the business manager of the orchestra, as did Max Mintzberg with his partner in the retail chain. This form of sharing was in fact discussed in an article in the *Harvard Business Review* almost a century ago (Robinson 1925).

Earlier in this chapter, we discussed the research of Pat Pitcher (1995, 1997), who found in her study of a financial institution that its management was balanced among what she called artists, craftsmen, and technocrats. So long as they worked together, complementing each other's strengths and correcting for each other's weaknesses, the company thrived. But when a "technocrat" took over and drove out the artists and many of the craftsmen, the company faltered. So balance in style is important alongside the sharing of information.[51]

Distributed Managing

Distributed managing, which could also be called "collective managing," diffuses responsibility for some managerial roles more widely, to various nonmanagers in the unit.[52] Compare, for example, the classic kibbutz with Switzerland. The latter has its inner circle of seven, while any member of the kibbutz may be rotated into a managerial role, if temporarily.

If this sounds strange, then look up the next time a flock of geese flies by in V formation. The leadership changes periodically, as the goose in the front gets tired and falls back. No doubt all the other geese find the one in the lead greatly empowering, perhaps even terribly charismatic— for a while. **If geese can rotate their leadership, and bees can work vigorously without having to be empowered by the queen (which is our label, not theirs), then surely we human beings can achieve such levels of sophistication.** In other words, we can treat leadership as something quite natural, with the "leader" just doing what has to be done at the appropriate time. (More on "Managing, Naturally" at the end of the book.)

Managerial duties can be distributed even more widely. For example, certain decisions can be made collectively, as in the old New England town meetings, where the members of the community met and voted together. Here, too, the bees do better than us: a key decision, to move the hive from one place to another, is taken collectively. The scout bees survey various sites and return to convey the characteristics of each through their dances. "A contest ensues. Finally the site being advertised most

---

[51] See also Kaplan (1986:30) and the various studies of "top management teams" by Hambrick and his colleagues (reviewed in Hambrick 2007).

[52] On this posture and the previous one, see Pearce and Conger's book *Shared Leadership* (2003). On this one, see Gray (1999) and Brunsson (2007:81ff.).

vigorously by the largest number of workers wins, and the entire swarm flies off to it," with the queen joining in (Wilson 1971:548).

Professionals and other experts in organizations sometimes initiate projects, whether with official sanction or in some kind of skunkworks, from which major strategies can emerge. This is common in professional organizations and adhocracies, but can happen in more conventional organizations, too. In an article entitled "Waking Up IBM: How a Gang of Unlikely Rebels Transformed Big Blue," Gary Hamel (2000) recounted how the company got into e-business. A "self-absorbed programmer" had the initial idea, and finally convinced a staff manager with hardly any resources. He stitched together a loose team of people that made it happen. When asked "To whom he reported, he simply replied, 'The Internet.'" Certain companies have made these skunkworks more formal by designating certain managers with the authority to provide budgets and time off for people with interesting ideas. In effect, the latter are granted a managerial role without having a managerial job.

The concept of emergent strategy (Mintzberg and Waters 1985) suggests that whoever takes an initiative that sets the organization on a new course is a strategist. We studied the National Film Board of Canada (Mintzberg and McHugh 1985; see also Mintzberg 2007: Chapter 4), a classic adhocracy that was focused on the making of short, documentary films. Then one film ran long and had to be marketed differently, so it ended up as a feature in theaters. Other filmmakers were impressed and followed suit; soon the organization, including its management, found themselves with an unexpected strategy of making feature films.[53]

In his 2003 book, Joe Raelin challenged the conventional view of leadership "being out in front." He called for "communities where everyone shares the experience of serving as a leader, not serially, but concurrently and collectively" (p. 50). As Raelin put it, the conventional approach holds that leadership is an office held for a fixed period of time, or else just continuously. Hence, "leadership is individual": the organization has one leader, who directs its activities, while "the subordinate role is to follow [his or her] guidance" (pp. 10–11).

In contrast, what Raelin calls *leaderful* practice is *concurrent*, meaning that "more than one leader can operate at the same time"; it is also

---

[53] What might seem like another form of distributed management, which sometimes goes by this label (Galbraith 1997), is where staff functions are shared across line divisions. For example, the Ontario sales branch looks after HR, and the Manitoba sales branch looks after IT, for all the sales branches. But this is a distribution of specialized staff functions, not managerial roles.

collective, meaning that "decisions are made by whoever has the relevant responsibility"; and it is *collaborative*, meaning that "all members of the community . . . are in control of and may speak for the entire community" (pp. 13, 14, 15).

Supportive Managing

If nonmanagers do more of the managerial roles, then managers themselves can do less. Here and in the next posture we consider a reduced job of formal managing.

If the queen bee plays no role in a key strategic decision of the hive, then what does she do? In fact, her main job is not management at all, but manufacturing: she produces great hordes of baby bees. But she does something else that is fundamentally managerial: she emits the chemical substance (discussed earlier) that holds the hive together. In human organizations, we call this *culture*, and we have described its fortification as a key aspect of the role of *leading*, as in the example of Norm Inkster of the RCMP.

Bees work largely on their own, without much supervision or even mutual adjustment among each other, much as do professors in universities and physicians in hospitals (who do not usually even report up the hospital hierarchy). We call such human work "professional," and it changes the nature of managing significantly. "I just didn't get in their way," claimed an ex–business school dean with respect to the professors. Of course, there is always some need to get in their way—for example, to ensure that budgets get set and met.

What these professionals especially need, as noted earlier, is support and protection, so that they can accomplish their work with a minimum of disturbance. Accordingly, this posture of *supportive managing* shifts to the external roles of *linking* and *dealing*: the managers work with outside stakeholders to ensure a steady flow of resources and other means of support, while buffering many of the outside pressures coming in. Robert Greenleaf has written about this under the label *Servant Leadership*: "individuals . . . are chosen as leaders because they are proven and treated as servants"; they have a "natural feeling" of wanting "to serve," to serve "first," compared with the person "who is *leader* first" (2002:24, 27).[54]

---

[54] In The *Functions of the Executive*, Chester Barnard described this approach to managing remarkably early: "The executive functions . . . are not . . . to manage a group of persons," not even "to manage the system of cooperative efforts," which is largely "managed by itself. . . [as quoted

Does the responsibility for managing remain? Of course it does, because these servants maintain responsibility for the performance of the unit, even in those cases where they lack hierarchical control over some of the people who work there. Was Carol Haslam of Hawkshead any less a manager because the filmmakers were on contract?

Consider carefully this form called supportive managing because we are going to be seeing a lot more of it.

Minimal Managing

The last feasible point on our scale is labeled *minimal managing*. Here there is hardly anything left to manage, sometimes hardly even an organization as such. But there does remain some coherent activity in need of coordination, and that requires some managing.

This may sound curious, until we realize that most of us live with it every day. Think of the World Wide Web, the Linux Operating System, Wikipedia—so-called open source systems. These are the ultimate adhocracies, which engage the full creative potential of broad communities. People come and go; they enter, make changes, and exit, but the system carries on—in fact, with remarkable coherence. These are *self-managed* organizations, almost. Someone had to get them started, and set and enforce the rules of entry, change, and exit; and someone has to keep the whole thing coherent. On a poster with one duck following a bunch of others is the inscription: "There they go. I have to follow them because I am their leader."

Here, in fact, and in the previous posture too, is where Shan Martin comes out in his book *Managing without Managers*. The title is a misnomer because near the end he acknowledges "the need for managers," minimally but evidently:

> If one accepts the concept of self-management, the question arises as to whether managers or supervisors are necessary at all. It should be clear from the preceding examples that the answer proposed is a cautious yes, although in significantly fewer numbers than now exist. (1983:165)

---

earlier]. The essential executive functions . . . are first, to provide the system of communication; second, to promote the securing of essential efforts, and third, to formulate and define purpose" (1938:216–217).

For "top management," this means less emphasis "on the prerogatives of individual managers" and more on functions such as "facilitating coordination among teams of workers" and "minding the external environment" (p. 166).

This completes our discussion of this chapter. We have seen immense varieties in the practice of managing, and some order as well. This has not been an easy chapter to write or perhaps to read. I spent far more time on it than any of the others, trying to make sense of that variety and struggling to express that order.

The next two, and last, chapters build on the first four, considering the inescapable conundrums faced by anyone who takes on the job of managing, and then what it might mean to manage effectively.

5

The Inescapable Conundrums of Managing

The centipede was happy quite
Until a toad in fun
Said, "Pray, which leg goes after which?"
That worked her mind to such a pitch,
She lay distracted in a ditch
Considering how to run.

Mrs. Edward Craster (1871)

Managing is rife with conundrums. Every way a manager turns, there seems to be some paradox or enigma lurking.

McCall et al. identified "questions about management that emerge time and time again across organizations," including these:

- Why don't our managers have a broader perspective? They seem to be firefighters, but not fire preventers?

- Why don't our managers delegate more?

- Why doesn't information pass up the hierarchy? (1978:38)

If such questions could be resolved simply, they would go away. They remain because they are rooted in a set of conundrums that are basic to managing—concerns that cannot be resolved. In the words of Chester Barnard: "It is precisely the function of the executive . . . to reconcile conflicting forces, instincts, interests, conditions, positions and ideals" (1938:21). Notice his use of the word *reconcile*, not *resolve*.[1]

Does that mean we shouldn't be addressing these conundrums, to avoid the risk of managers lying distracted in ditches considering how to manage? Managers don't need that, but they do need a better understanding of how to cope with what they cannot escape.

Thirteen conundrums in all are discussed in this chapter, under the headings (related to our model of Chapter 3) "Thinking Conundrums," "Information Conundrums," "People Conundrums," and "Action Conundrums," as well as two final "Overall Conundrums." Table 5.1 lists them in these groups.[2]

THINKING CONUNDRUMS

Three conundrums are described here, labeled the Syndrome of Superficiality, the Predicament of Planning (a variation of the first), and the Labyrinth of Decomposition.

The Syndrome of Superficiality

This is perhaps the most basic of all the conundrums of managing, the plague of every manager, although it can be especially frustrating for new managers who have come from specialized jobs as well as experienced managers who, in their souls, never left such jobs. **How to get in deep when there is so much pressure to get it done?** As I wrote in my earlier study and noted in Chapter 2:

---

[1] Charles Handy also noted in *The Age of Paradox*, "Paradox can only be 'managed' in the sense of coping with. Manage always did mean 'coping with,' until we purloined the words to mean planning and control" (1994:12).

[2] In his book *Dilemmas of Administrative Behavior*, John Aram discussed five of these conundrums in particular, but less job related than of a personal and interpersonal nature: "to be an individualist and a collectivist, a commander and a counselor, a dispassionate official and a passionate human associate, a group member and an individual conscience, a supporter of tradition and an agent of social change" (1978:119). The second of these really contrasts our roles of controlling and leading, and the fifth will be discussed under our Riddle of Change.

Table 5.1 CONUNDRUMS OF MANAGING

THINKING CONUNDRUMS

The Syndrome of Superficiality
How to get in deep when there is so much pressure to get it done?

The Predicament of Planning
How to plan, strategize, just plain think, let alone think ahead, in such a hectic job?

The Labyrinth of Decomposition
Where to find synthesis in a world so decomposed by analysis?

INFORMATION CONUNDRUMS

The Quandary of Connecting
How to keep informed when managing by its own nature removes the manager from the very things being managed?

The Dilemma of Delegating
How to delegate when so much of the relevant information is personal , oral, and often privileged?

The Mysteries of Measuring
How to manage it when you can't rely on measuring it?

PEOPLE CONUNDRUMS

The Enigma of Order
How to bring order to the work of others when the work of managing is itself so disorderly?

The Paradox of Control
How to maintain the necessary state of controlled disorder when one's own manager is imposing order?

The Clutch of Confidence
How to maintain a sufficient level of confidence without crossing over into arrogance?

ACTION CONUNDRUMS

The Ambiguity of Acting
How to act decisively in a complicated, nuanced world?

The Riddle of Change
How to manage change when there is the need to maintain continuity?

OVERALL CONUNDRUMS

The Ultimate Conundrum
How can any manager possibly cope with all these conundrums concurrently?

My Own Conundrum
How do I reconcile that fact that, while all of these conundrums can be stated apart, they all seem to be the same?

> The prime occupational hazard of the manager is superficiality. Because of the open-ended nature of [the] job and because of [the] responsibility for information processing and strategy-making, the manager is induced to take on a heavy load of work, and to do much of it superficially. Hence . . . the job of managing does not develop reflective planners; rather it breeds adaptive information manipulators who prefer a stimulus-response milieu. (Mintzberg 1973: 5)

"I don't want it good—I want it Tuesday" was the quote that opened Chapter 2. A month from Tuesday may not be acceptable, but how about Thursday? Organizations certainly need to get things done, but in recent years there has also been a growing franticness in management, thanks additionally to e-mail (as discussed in Chapter 2). For example, "speed to market" has become fashionable: get the product out, be first. But why? To recall it?[3]

How are managers to avoid such pressures, which can lead them into practicing thin management? I concluded in my earlier study (1973:35) that they have to become proficient at their superficiality—for example, dealing with complex issues by breaking them into small steps that can be taken one at a time. They also have to hone their capacity to *reflect* in their work.

Refl'action   Given the dynamic nature of their job, managers have to find time to step back and out; this has to become intrinsic to their work. Reflection without action may be passive, but action without reflection is thoughtless. As Saul Alinsky pointed out in his book *Rules for Radicals*, "most people go through life undergoing a series of happenings." These "become experiences when they are digested, when they are reflected on, related to general patterns, and synthesized" (1971:68–69).

We developed our International Masters in Practicing Management (www.impm.org) to allow managers to reflect with each other on their own experience. One of them coined the term "refl'action," which captures perfectly this need to combine reflection with action. A number of the twenty-nine managers, such as Jacques Benz at GSI and Alan Whelan at BT, seemed especially adapt at maneuvering between the two.

---

[3] Hambrick and his colleagues (2005) considered the excess job demands on executives and found that as a result they engaged in "vacillation" and "extremism": freezing up or else lashing out, taking no new initiatives or else engaging in too many of them (p. 480). See also Ganster (2005).

It has been said of great athletes such as a Wayne Gretzky in hockey that they see the game just a bit slower than the other players, and so they are able to make that last-second maneuver. Perhaps this is also characteristic of effective managers: faced with great pressure, they can cool it, sometimes just for a moment, in order to act thoughtfully.

The Predicament of Planning

A variant of the Syndrome of Superficiality—a manifestation of it that deserves discussion in its own right—is the Predicament of Planning. If the former looks in from the outside, about the pressures to be superficial, then this conundrum looks out from the inside, about **how to plan, strategize, just plain think, let alone think ahead, in such a hectic job.** More than half a century ago, Sune Carlson noted this predicament in his research:

> When asked what particular part of their duties the executives themselves regarded as neglected, they almost without exception answered the long-range planning of their business. The increasing amount of outside activities and the difficulty of getting enough time undisturbed by visitors and telephone calls were the common excuse in this connection. (1951:106)

This conundrum pits the dynamic characteristics of managerial work discussed in Chapter 2 (the hectic pace, the interruptions, the orientation to action, etc.) against the manager's responsibilities for articulating direction and overseeing decisions made in the unit. As one manager (also in our masters program) put it: "Each day I go into the office with some preplanned action and at the end of the day, I have to regret that all the various things I [did] are very different. . . . [My] work is very interesting . . . up to now, [it is] the best work I have never [done]."

This is a conundrum because managers can neither avoid these natural pressures nor fail to get beyond them, although there is no shortage of managers who have done one or the other. As noted in Chapter 2, managers adopt their pace and workload because of the inherently open-ended nature of their job. They are responsible for the success of their unit, yet so much can flare up and get in the way: a strike, a disgruntled customer, a sudden shift in currency value. So they have to keep current, and that can even mean encouraging interruptions (which Robert Kaplan has called "the lifeline to fresh and necessary information" [1983:2]).

What to Do? *Strategic* **Planning?**   So what is the harried manager to do? Shut the door? Go off to a retreat? Call a consultant? Sure—sometimes. Just so long as these are recognized as temporary alleviations more than fundamental solutions.

And then there is the most popular prescription of all: strategic planning—the ideal solution for the overburdened manager. If you are unable to think ahead and so are devoid of strategic vision, let the system do the thinking and the visioning for you. (A technique is something you can use in place of a brain.)

Unfortunately, strategic planning never worked as planned—it has never been conducive to developing strategy. Systems provide analysis; strategies require synthesis. Analysis can certainly feed into the mental processes needed for synthesis, but it can never substitute for them. When Michael Porter wrote in *The Economist* that "I favor a set of analytic techniques to develop strategy" (1987), he was dead wrong: nobody ever developed a strategy through a technique. The world of analysis is conceptual and categorical; the world of strategy is messy and mixed up. Planning unfolds on schedule; managing has to deal with strategic problems and opportunities as they arise.[4]

For example, how was anyone in the Canadian Parks supposed to reconcile "Our mission is to sustain the integrity, health, diversity, majesty and beauty of Western Canada's Cultural and National Heritages" with a knock-down, drag-out battle over the expansion of a parking lot? (Recall the Chapter 3 box about Greenpeace, whose planning seemed to reduce to scheduling.)

Crafting Strategy Instead[5]   So how then do strategies—and managerial frames in general—come into existence? In terms of the model of Chapter 3, strategic planning works from the inside out: managers think in their heads—*formulate* strategies—so that others can act—*implement* them. The process is deductive and deliberate—in effect, close to the science corner of the art-craft-science triangle.

In our own research (reported in Mintzberg 2007) that tracked the appearance, use, and demise of strategies in ten organizations across decades (in one case, 150 years), we found something else. **Strategies can *form* without being formulated: they can emerge through efforts**

---

[4] All of this is discussed at length in my book *The Rise and Fall of Strategic Planning* (1994).

[5] The following is drawn from Mintzberg (1987, 2007: Chapter 12) and Mintzberg, Ahlstrand, and Lampel (2009).

of informal learning rather than having to be created through a process of formal planning.

In the Chapter 3 model, this works from the outside-in: acting drives thinking inductively as much as thinking drives acting deductively. In fact, the two go together, back and forth, interactively.[6] It is their ability to bounce back and forth between the concrete and the conceptual—to understand the specifics and be able to generalize creatively about them— that makes for successful strategists, whether they be senior managers or anyone else: professionals venturing alone in project teams, middle managers innovating in skunkworks, and others.

Strategies are not tablets carved atop mountains, to be carried down for execution; they are learned on the ground by anyone who has the experience and capacity to see the general beyond the specifics. Remaining in the stratosphere of the conceptual is no better than having one's feet firmly planted in concrete.

Add all this up and it appears that managers who deal best with the Predicament of Planning exhibit an engaging style, by letting a thousand strategic flowers bloom in their organizations, and an insightful style, to detect the patterns of success in these gardens of strategic flowers, rather than a cerebral style that favors analytical techniques to develop strategies in a hothouse. **Thus, the strategy process is a lot closer to craft, enhanced by a good deal of art. The science enters in the form of analyses, to feed data and findings into the process, and in the form of planning, not to create strategies ("strategic planning" is an oxymoron) but to program the consequences of strategies created through venturing and learning.**

The Labyrinth of Decomposition

The world of managing is chopped into little pieces, some natural, some not. Organizations are decomposed into regions, divisions, departments, products, and services, not to mention missions, visions, objectives, programs, budgets, and systems; likewise, agendas are decomposed into issues, and strategic issues are decomposed into strengths, weaknesses,

---

[6] Isenberg (1984) described this as "thinking/acting cycles," used "to work on a problem prior to its definition." It is "similar to 'empirical treatment' in medicine, and 'empirical design' in engineering, namely, that when faced with a complicated or poorly understood disease or design problem, treatment or design is embarked upon in the absence of a complete understanding of all the causes. . . . Thus we often observe senior managers acting before they think very much, all the while using intuition to determine exactly where to begin the thinking/acting cycle" (p. 18).

threats, and opportunities. Item 4 in a meeting of Sandy Davis of the Western Canadian Parks with her staff concerned the "Strategic Plan: Program Update." A twenty-page draft was handed out, called "Defining Our Destiny—Leadership through Excellence." It included sections on the mandate, the mission, a vision statement, ten "values" (ranging from pride in heritage to respect for "strategic thinking linked to strategic action"), and eight "strategic priorities and objectives," described at some length (including "effectively managing protected areas," "commemorating and protecting cultural heritage," and "organizational excellence").

Overseeing all of this are managers, who are supposed to integrate the whole confusing mess (albeit often of their own making). Hence, we get the Labyrinth of Decomposition: **where to find synthesis in a world so decomposed by analysis?** (Sayles 1979:11–12).

Synthesis is the very essence of managing: putting things together, in the form of coherent strategies, unified organizations, and integrated systems. This is what makes managing so difficult—and so interesting. It's not that managers don't need analysis; it's that they need it as an input to synthesis.

So how can a manager see the big picture amid so many little details? It's not as if the organization is a museum with that big picture on some wall. It has to be constructed, in the minds of its people.

Picture one of those organizational charts. This is supposed to be an orderly portrayal of the components of an organization. It might instead be seen as a labyrinth through which its people have to find their way. The assumption behind the chart is that if each unit does its job correctly, the whole organization will function smoothly. In other words, **structure is supposed to take care of organization, just as planning is supposed to take care of strategy. Anyone who believes this should find a job as a hermit**.

Chunking   As noted earlier, Peters and Waterman (1982) have written enthusiastically about "chunking." Managers have to grab hold of big problems by breaking them into little pieces—"chunks"—that can be dealt with one at a time. That makes sense, indeed is often necessary (as discussed under scheduling in Chapter 3). The problem is that the broken chunks do not fit together as in some sort of jigsaw puzzle. This is more like playing with Legos, except that the pieces don't attach very well, and the manager may not even be clear what needs to be built.

In a colorful article entitled "The Magic Number Seven, Plus or Minus Two: Some Limits on Our Capacity for Processing Information," George Miller (1956) pointed out that we humans can handle only about seven chunks of information in our short- and intermediate-term memories. So how are we supposed to get that big picture into our little brains?

Painting the Big Picture   Let's look at this metaphor literally. How does the painter see the big picture? He or she, like the manager, has nowhere to go to see it—short of copying that of someone else, in which case this person will not be a great painter (any more than a manager who copies other strategies is a great strategist).

That big picture has to be painted stroke by stroke, experience by experience. The painter may start with an overall perspective, in his or her head, but from there the picture has to emerge from a host of little actions—just as a big strategy does. Few companies these days have a bigger or better strategy than IKEA, the furniture chain. *That* is one big corporate picture. It reportedly took fifteen years to paint.

Of course, managers also have to appreciate that some pictures are simply too big to paint, some chunks are too heavy to carry, and some charts are too high to climb: the organization is too big, or the managerial job is too artificial.

Natural and Unnatural Managerial Jobs   Some entities seem rather natural to manage: a company with a clear mandate, as in the case of IKEA, or a self-standing store in the IKEA chain. Others do not—for example, a conglomerate company, or two stores in the IKEA chain.

Consider Ann Sheen of the NHS. To manage nursing in a hospital seems natural enough. But what about managing nursing in two hospitals, a few miles apart, that have been magically merged on a sheet of paper? The hospitals may have needed Ann in both jobs, but what makes them one job? What is natural about managing that?

This is one example of the many managerial jobs that have been established on a geographic basis—often rather arbitrarily. Another among the twenty-nine managers was in the work of Sandy Davis, in charge of the national parks of western Canada. But what does that mean? The Banff National Park has its own space, services, tourists, and issues. But what do several such parks, which happen to be in three of Canada's ten provinces, have in common? One danger is that the manager of such combinations will feel compelled to find things in common—for example, by calling meetings of park managers to search for synergies. Another is that the manager will micromanage.

Nothing is more dangerous in an organization than a manager with little to do. Managers are usually energetic people—that is how they got to be managers in the first place, and the more senior they are, the more energetic they tend to be. Put them in such geographic positions where they have little to do, and they will find things to do. Sometimes it amounts to control, other times it is something else. The accompanying box describes an example of the latter.

An Unnatural Day?

The first time I went into the National Health Service of England, it had 175 "districts" and 14 "regions"; the 90 "areas" in between had just been eliminated, thanks to a consulting study. When I went back some years and reorganizations later, it had only "Strategic Health Authorities," twenty-eight in number (soon to be reduced to ten). In other words, now the regions and districts were gone, and some sort of areas reinstated.

But health care is not delivered by a district, or a region, or an area: it is delivered by a hospital, or a clinic, or a physician. Perhaps the NHS has kept reorganizing because it has yet to find the unfindable magic bullet.

Peter Coe was the manager of one of these districts, called North Hertfordshire. His day began in a small room, where Peter's main meeting of the day was about to begin.

Three of his reports joined Peter, one responsible for quality, another for purchasing, the third for information systems. An official from the Department of Health (I'll call him DH) had come from London to get informed about the progress the district was making in the implementation of a new NHS initiative.

The districts were becoming "purchasers," to negotiate with the "providers" (hospitals, etc., some as independent "trusts") for the provision of services. At least this was the intention at the time, but it was not well specified. North Hertfordshire was considered to be on the cutting edge of figuring all this out, so DH had traveled here to capture and diffuse the learning of Peter and his team. As for Peter, this meeting was an opportunity to gain credibility as well as to get some more hard cash for the district. Thus, the jargon of "purchasers" and "providers" was used extensively throughout the meeting, with an air of unreality, as some kind of abstraction they were trying to make real, while health care remained in the background.

After general discussion, each of the staff people described what they were doing. Comments about "quality," for example, revolved around "ten key indicators," which apparently came out of a consulting study. This seemed unrelated to the actual delivery of health care, as did the discussion of getting "consumer" input. (The person in charge of purchasing said at one point, "I'm interested in how you get in to talk to the people." And DH added at another point, "I don't think that any of us talked to consumers properly," to which the purchasing person replied, "I did . . . about ten years ago." Yet all the participants in the room were these "people" and "consumers," since the NHS serves pretty much the entire population of England.)

Central to all this discussion was control—for example, the state's control of the health care system, the system's control of its public users, and how to get other districts of the NHS to make the changes work.

After lunch, some time was devoted to risk—"two minutes on risk," as someone put it. They considered what risk meant, with one person saying, "I don't understand it," and DH replying, "I have a view of it: we need to build some kind of decision analysis process that takes into account political risks." Then they turned to information systems, which someone called the "intelligence function." The person in charge of purchasing, in reference to the changes, said that she "spent more time negotiating the ground rules than negotiating the contract." Perhaps she captured much of this discussion best with her comment that "it doesn't feel right."

Peter left the district headquarters after this long meeting and drove to the regional headquarters in London. (He pointed out a hospital along the way, which turned out to be the only one in his district.) Here he joined a meeting to make a presentation on his district's experiences in contracting to purchase care services for the elderly. At one point, as Peter displayed various statistical findings and discussed "consumer strategy" and "value for money," a siren wailed outside, reminding anyone who cared to listen that there was more to health care than this.

THE INFORMATION CONUNDRUMS

Next are the conundrums related to the manager's information, three in particular: the Quandary of Connecting, the Dilemma of Delegating, and the Mysteries of Measuring.

The Quandary of Connecting

As mentioned earlier, a major occupational hazard of managing is to know more and more about less and less until finally the manager knows nothing about everything. The Quandary of Connecting addresses what lies behind this: **how to keep informed—in contact, "in touch"— when managing by its own nature removes the manager from the**

very things being managed? In other words, how does the manager connect when he or she is intrinsically disconnected (Watson 1994:13)?

Livingston (1971) has written about the "second-handedness" of conventional management education. He should have made that third-handedness, because managing itself is second-handed. Organizations are designed so that some people do the basic work and other people, called managers, mostly oversee it in one way or another—or, even more removed, oversee managers who oversee it. Management, to repeat, means getting things done through other people—whether that be on the people plane (leading and linking) or on the information plane (controlling and communicating). Even on the action plane (doing and dealing), as described in Chapter 3 managers generally work with others to take action. And, of course, as managers rise in the hierarchy of authority, they get further and further removed from this action—to the point where, as Paul Hirsch put it, the chief executive can become "the lightning rod for not knowing what is going on" (comment at the Academy of Management Conference, Chicago, August 15, 1986).

Some people claim that detachment can make a manager more objective. Surely so. But someone else remarked that to be objective is to treat people like objects. Is that what we want of our managers? And then there are those who believe that the Internet puts everyone in touch, no matter where they may be. In touch with a keyboard, to be sure (as noted in Chapter 2), but in touch with the nuances of organizational life?

Every Manager Incompetent—or Just Frustrated?   The Peter Principle (Peter and Hull 1989) describes how managers in hierarchies rise to their level of incompetence: they keep getting promoted until they land in a job they cannot do, and there they remain—never to be promoted again. What we have in this conundrum is a Peter Principle for the field of management itself: as people rise from the action base of the specialist to the abstract planes of the generalist, they become disconnected from what they are supposed to manage. In this respect, all managers are somewhat incompetent. Yet someone has to manage. And so we have this conundrum.

If you ask the experts—not the experts on management, but the operating experts of the organizations being managed—many will sound off about the incompetence of their managers, as if no one should manage at all. One physician I know, the head of his hospital's medical executive committee no less, claimed that a physician who became director of medical services in the hospital was no longer a physician. Physicians often make such comments. I will ask the next one who does what he or she proposes instead: Fill the job with an accountant? How about an MBA? Better still, we can eliminate the job altogether and let the CEO manage the physicians' affairs.[7]

In my research, the Quandary of Connecting came out most clearly in the frustration expressed by Gord Irwin, who found himself squeezed between the tangible realities of the park he knew so well and his new responsibilities embedded in the abstractions of administration. But that frustration was hardly restricted to this new manager. Dr. Webb expressed it in his actions, as did Bramwell Tovey in his words, nostalgic about the specialized work he left behind.

It was certainly not all frustration, however. As noted in the last chapter, most of the twenty-nine managers reveled in their managing (Bramwell included). They understood this conundrum, so they did not get bogged down in it. Peter Coe of the NHS was a particularly interesting case in point. On one hand, he could not exercise direct control over the units in his own district that had autonomy. On the other hand, he delighted in doing other things instead; for example, on the day of observation, as described in the box, he was advocating up the hierarchy for more resources. He wasn't frustrated; he just used his energy elsewhere. Under the circumstances, this seemed to be eminently sensible managing.

Slabs across Silos   We talk a great deal about "silos" in organizations, vertical cleavages running up and down the hierarchy that separate functions from each other. This conundrum suggests another kind of cleavage, horizontal in nature, that separates hierarchical levels from each other. We can call them "slabs," as shown in Figure 5.1, because they are often isolated layers of managerial activity, one upon the other, ever more abstracted from the operating realities. In the NHS, for example, we had Drs. Thick and Webb, perhaps as well as Ann Sheen, on one slab, Peter Coe on another, and Sir Duncan on the top one (with other slabs in between). **When these hierarchical slabs become especially thick, often the case in machine organizations, the Quandary of Connecting can take the organization into strategic gridlock: layers of managers sit in their own no man's land, each one lacking the information or the power necessary to connect adequately to the others.**

---

[7] Many of my colleagues who teach management itself can be included here. Two principles seem basic to their appreciation of deans: (1) Anyone who wants the job is by definition suspect. (2) Good deans exist only in retrospect.

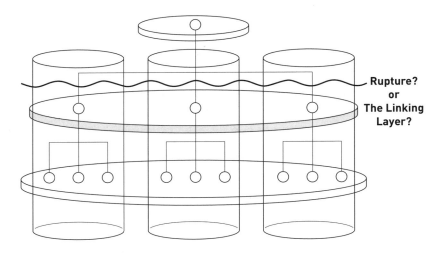

Rupture?
or
The Linking
Layer?

Figure 5.1 SILOS AND SLABS IN ORGANIZATIONS

Connecting at the Base?   This conundrum is probably least problematic for the managers on the lowest slab, who generally have ready and
natural access to the operations. This struck me especially in the time I
spent with Stephen Omollo in the refugee camps, watching him roam-
ing about, picking up information so enthusiastically. At one point, after
stopping at the food distribution area, he announced to me that there
were no problems this day because no one had come to him to complain.
Peters and Waterman (1982) have discussed "management by walking
around"; here we had management by just "being there," based on trust.

Be all this as it may, Linda Hill still found considerable frustration in
regard to this Quandary of Connecting among the new first-line managers she studied:

> As the months passed, [the new sales managers] found it more diffi-
> cult to keep their technical knowledge and skills on the cutting edge.
> They did not even have time to read through all the new product
> announcements, much less figure out the best strategies for selling
> them. They found it disconcerting that they were beginning to feel
> rusty after such a short time frame. (2003:141–142)

Accordingly, **the new managers "had to learn to handle their
ignorance"** (p. 180). As McCall et al. put it, such novice managers

could not behave as they had in previous jobs: the "responsibility for doing the job was replaced with responsibility for seeing that systems and work processes . . . got done. . . . Increasingly they had to learn to 'manage by remote control'" (1988:54). How interesting that this harks back to the posture described in the last chapter as mostly one of chief executives.

The Linking Layer or the Administrative Gap?   In contrast, a number of the other managers among the twenty-nine, at middle levels in rather large organizations—for example, Abbas Gullet, Stephen's manager, and Doug Ward of the CBC radio station—seemed quite able, not only to develop a reasonable sense of the operations, but to connect to their senior levels of management as well. I suspect that such managers are critically important. **Every large organization likely requires a layer of middle managers who can link the so-called top with the base of operations.**

It is, of course, ideal that the most senior managers be in touch all the way down the hierarchy, as I observed John Cleghorn doing in the bank branches. (See the description of his day in the appendix.) But except for entrepreneurial organizations, where the chief tends to be involved in everything, how often does this really happen? (Thanks to John, the Royal Bank had a target of its senior managers being out in the field 25 percent of their time, although he himself had attained only 16 percent in the recent period.) And so this linking layer of middle managers may be key to avoiding rupture between the concrete actions on the ground and the conceptual issues at the senior levels—a problem I find rampant in business, government, and other organizations these days.

Common these days is what can be called the **administrative gap**. Consider health care. All around the world, it seems to suffer from such a gap. **A gaping hole exists between those who administer and those who deliver the basic services.** The consequence is that above the gap, they talk abstractions (recall the NHS discussion of "quality," "consumers," and "risk"), while below it, people are confused and frustrated.[8]

How to close this gap? That's easy—in principle: (1) bring the managers down, (2) welcome the operating people up, or (3) shrink the gap.

---

[8] I discuss this in a forthcoming monograph called *Managing the Myths of Health Care* (publisher to be posted on www.Mintzberg.org in 2010 or 2011).

"Delayering"—namely, eliminating layers of middle management—shrinks the gap. It has been part of the "downsizing" discussed earlier. It can be helpful (let's start with those unnatural geographic layers just discussed), so long as it does not put an excess burden on the middle managers left behind (or, as in the case of the earlier NHS, leaves districts and regions behind after eliminating areas). Otherwise, questions have to be asked about the size of the organization, not just about the arrangements made to cope with it. Many organizations, in health care and beyond, are just too big. (Does it make sense to have one NHS for all of England? The Scottish NHS functions with about one-tenth that population.)

Getting "in Touch"   In "Managing beyond the Manager" of the previous chapter, we discussed welcoming the operating people up in order to close such a gap—for example, by encouraging the strategic initiatives of nonmanagers. But what about bringing the managers down?

The comment earlier about Stephen Omollo's "being there" suggests that a prime way to deal with the Quandary of Connecting is to get managers out of their offices, away from their meetings, and into the places where their organization serves its basic purpose—not just to "drop in" but to have personal presence, in body and spirit. One executive described how having their "feet in the mud" can make senior managers "better strategists": "My assumption is that a factory has a special character and personality when senior management understand its detailed working in their bones, and their hands; the system as a whole has a sense of integration in a way that split-off management can never achieve" (in Peters 1980:16).

Better still is the following. I was registering my car for service when the owner of the dealership said hello. We chatted, as we sometimes have, this time about management, and he said something that I should have realized but never did: "I have no office here." No wonder he's always around, on his feet, much like Fabienne Lavoie in the nursing ward.

The potency of managing standing up, or at least in easy speaking range of others, is not to be underestimated. It can promote rather holistic practice. Of course, not all managers are as lucky as these two, who have most of their contacts so close at hand. But that can be by choice, too. **Why does so much managing have to take place in isolated offices and closed meeting rooms?** Well known are Japanese companies that sit their managers in open areas, for ease of communication. One, Kao, even became known for holding management meetings in open areas;

any employee who went by was welcome to join. Such companies, like that car dealership, don't need an open-door policy.

In our International Master's in Practicing Management (www .impm.org), a manager from Fujitsu took his colleagues to see the open area where he and his colleagues worked—with no partitions, just desks. "Who's that?" asked a manager from a Canadian bank about someone she saw on his feet, talking to another person at a desk. "That's our manager," answered our host. "How can you work with your boss looking over your shoulder like that?" she replied in horror. "What's the problem?" he asked. What looked like controlling to her was facilitating to him. This wasn't micromanaging; it was keeping in touch.[9]

The big problem today is macroleading: managers who are disconnected, don't know what's going on. "Hands off" too often amounts to "brain off." Here is a comment about the *Challenger* disaster at NASA: "Top management's insistence [at a teleconference "far removed from the world of murky technology, shims, improvisation, and tacit understanding that engineers used to make the shuttle fly"] on explicit argument as a substitute for their own lack of firsthand experience silenced the tacit reservations that foreshadowed tragedy" (Weick 1997:395). Had the managers come down or, better still, had the engineers been welcomed up to close this administrative gap—had they the ear of their bosses, been part of the decision making—the tragedy might have been avoided.

The Dilemma of Delegation

Here we reverse the previous conundrum. There managers have trouble connecting because their job takes them out of touch; here managers have difficulty delegating because they are better informed than the people to whom they have to delegate.

Is this a contradiction? Not when we appreciate the kinds of information in question. The manager, as nerve center of the unit (as described in Chapter 3), should be its most broadly informed member, but not its most specifically informed. He or she has formal access to all the members, and usually to a wide array of the unit's external contacts as well, many of whom are nerve centers of their own units. But much of this

---

[9] Andy Grove of Intel used time to make a distinction between these two: "Two days a week per subordinate would probably lead to meddling; an hour a week does not provide enough opportunity for monitoring" (1983:66).

information comes secondhand, passed through others, often orally. And so the manager may lack some of the very tangible, or tacit, information.

Given, however, his or her breadth of information, what happens when it comes time for the manager to delegate, since no manager can do all that is expected of him or her? **How to delegate when so much of the relevant information is personal, oral, and often privileged?**

Consider the following incident.[10] An employee calls to ask the chief executive if a certain staff appointment should be cleared through a particular committee. The executive replies that it should not. To a second question, on another appointment, the CEO gives an affirmative reply. The employee asks about a third person and receives another negative reply. Asked later why he did not give consistent responses, the chief executive said that his knowledge of the personalities of the people in question made individual decisions necessary.

Fair enough. But what was the result? The next time such a situation arose, the chief executive would have had to be consulted again. Quite clearly, if perhaps not consciously, he chose not to delegate responsibility for this kind of decision. The obvious reason is that he believed himself to be better informed.

Consider another story, told by Charles Handy, under the heading "the paradox of delegation" (1994:93–94). He encountered a chief executive who had divided up his job neatly into the functions of planning, financial control, sales, and so forth, and put someone in charge of each, thereby freeing himself, in his words, "to act as a counselor, consultant, and arbitrator" when needed. Three months later, Handy visited the chief executive again. "The system is fine," he reported, but "the people, they're not up to it . . . can't take an overall perspective. . . . Everything I push down to them seems to come back to me as an argument to be resolved. . . . Now I'm busier than I ever was before I delegated it all so neatly." Handy replied, "But that's what you wanted, isn't it? You delegated everything except coordination, compromise, and linkage, so that remains your job." In this case, the manager delegated, but the structure impeded execution. The decisions could not be chopped up like the organization; things still had to come together at his level.

Damned If You Do, Damned If You Don't   Tasks involving only one specialized function are easily delegated to the person charged with that

---

[10] This and what follows comes from my 1973 book (pp. 74–75).

function, who likely has the necessary tacit as well as specialized information. But what about tasks that cut across specialties or that require the manager's privileged information? How to delegate these?

There would be no problem if the manager could easily disseminate the relevant information along with the delegated task. But often that is not feasible because, as noted in Chapter 2, so much of this information tends to be oral, and therefore stored only in the natural memory of this person's brain. Documented information, on paper or in a computer, can be transmitted easily and systematically; oral information in a human brain cannot. Even when some of this information can be accessed, transmission is a time-consuming and crude process. The manager has to "brief" the person orally. As Karl Weick (1974b:112) put it (in reviewing the discussion of this dilemma in my 1973 book): "delegation is a problem because the manager is a flawed and mobile data bank." (Weick speculated that "managers with poor memories delegate more," since the dilemma is less severe!)

Hence, managers seem damned by the nature of their personal information system to a life of either overwork or frustration. In the first case, they do too many tasks themselves or else spend too much time disseminating oral information. In the second case, they have to look on as delegated tasks are performed inadequately, by the uninformed (relative to them). **It is too common to witness people being blamed for failures that can be traced to their inadequate access to the information necessary to perform their delegated tasks.** Delegating by dumping is not responsible managing.

Hill concluded in her study of the new managers that, forced to choose between overworking and delegating with doubt, they largely succumbed to the latter, "mostly because circumstances forced them to [delegate]; in time, they realized their jobs were simply too big to handle alone" (2003:141). So the Syndrome of Superficiality trumped the Dilemma of Delegation.

To Hill's managers, the issue thus became not "whether . . . to delegate" but "*how* to delegate." At first, they went to extremes—"It tended to be all or nothing"—but eventually they came to understand how to treat the people reporting to them differently (p. 143).

Weick identified the Dilemma of Delegation as a problem of "information equalization," especially oral information (1974:113). And this suggests one way for managers to alleviate this conundrum: as regularly and comprehensively as possible, share the privileged information with some other people in the unit. Brief them regularly, and have them brief each other. And have a number 2 who is as fully informed as possible. Then, when it comes time to delegate, at least half the problem is solved.

Does this sharing raise the risk that confidential information will fall into the wrong hands? Sure, sometimes (although refusing to share information is often a smokescreen for political games). But contrast this with the benefits of having better-informed people all around.

The Mysteries of Measuring

It has become a popular adage in some quarters that if you can't measure it, you can't manage it. That's strange, because who has ever really measured the performance of management itself (as we shall discuss in the next chapter)? I guess this means that management cannot be managed. Indeed, who has ever even *tried* to measure the performance of measurement? Accept this adage, therefore, and you have to conclude that measurement cannot be managed either. Apparently we shall have to get rid of both management and measurement—thanks to measurement.

In fact, the only reliable conclusion to draw from this is that measurement is loaded with its own conundrums, not the least of which is, **how to manage it when you can't rely on measuring it?**

In one respect, measurement would appear to help resolve the last two conundrums. For if managers can get rzliable information from measurements, then they can sit in their offices and get fully informed. No need to spend all that time walking around, being there, communicating. And they can delegate to their heart's content: hit the send button and off goes the information alongside the delegated task. Presumably that is what has made measurement so appealing, especially for managers removed from the tangible reality of their organizations. After all, numbers don't lie, right? The data are reliable, objective, "hard."

The Soft Underbelly of "Hard Data"   What exactly is "hard data"? Rocks are hard, but data? Ink on paper or electrons in a computer are hardly hard. (Indeed, the latter are described as "soft copy.")

If you must have a metaphor, try clouds in the sky. You can see them clearly from a distance; up close they are more obscure. When you get there, you can poke your hand through them and feel nothing. "Hard" is the illusion of having turned events and their results into statistics. And these are as clear and unambiguous as clouds. Objective, too. That employee over there is not an egocentric SOB, but a 4.7 on some psychologist's scale. The company didn't do just well; it earned a 16.7 percent return on investment last year. Isn't that clear enough?

Soft data, in contrast, can be fuzzy, ambiguous, subjective. It usually requires interpretation; most of it can't even be transmitted electronically. In fact, it may be no more than gossip, hearsay, impression. How objective is that?

So the dice are loaded. Hard data win every time, at least until they hit the soft material of the human brains that generated them in the first place, and try to use them in the second. So let's consider the soft underbelly of hard data (from Mintzberg 1975a).

1. Hard data are limited in scope. They may provide the basis for description, but often not for explanation. So the profits went up. Why? Because the market was expanding? You can probably get a number on that. Because a key competitor has been doing dumb things? No numbers on that. Because your management was brilliant? No numbers on that either (so let's assume it's correct). Hence, we often require soft data to explain what's behind the hard numbers: politics in the competitor's company, the expression on a customer's face. In comparison, hard data alone can be sterile, if not impotent. "No matter what I told him," complained one of the subjects of Kinsey's famous study of sexual behavior in the human male, "he just looked at me straight in the eye and asked 'How many times?'" (in Kaplan 1964).

2. Hard data are often excessively aggregated. How are these hard data presented? Usually lots of facts are combined and then reduced to some aggregate number, such as that quintessential bottom line. Think of all the life that is lost in producing that number.

It is fine to see the forest from the trees—unless you are in the lumber business. Most managers are in the lumber business: they need to know about the trees too. Too much managing takes place as if from a helicopter, where the trees look like a green carpet. As Neustadt was quoted in Chapter 2, presidents of the United States need "not the bland amalgams . . . [but] the tangible detail that pieced together in [their] mind illuminate the underside of issues put before [them]" (1960:153, 154). It is the latter, not the former, that provides the triggers for managerial actions and that enables managers to develop the mental models needed to take those actions.

3. Much hard information arrives too late. Information takes time to "harden." Don't be fooled by the speed with which those electrons race around the Internet. Events and results first have to be documented as "facts" and then to be aggregated into reports, which may have to await some predetermined schedule (e.g., the end of the quarter). By then, competitors may have run off with the customers.

4. Finally, a surprising amount of hard data is just plain unreliable. They look good, all those definitive numbers. But where did they come from? Lift up the rock of hard data and see what you find crawling underneath:

> Public agencies are very keen on amassing statistics—they collect them, add them, raise them to the nth power, take the cube root and prepare wonderful diagrams. But what you just never forget is that every one of those figures comes in the first instance from the village watchman, who just puts down what he damn pleases. (attributed to Sir Josiah Stamp 1928, cited in Maltz 1997)

And not just public agencies. Business today is obsessed with numbers. Yet who goes back to find out what the watchmen put down? Moreover, even if the recorded facts were reliable in the first instance, something is always lost in the process of quantification. Numbers get rounded up, mistakes get made, nuances get lost. Anyone who has ever produced a quantitative measure—whether a reject count in a factory or a publication count in a university—knows just how much distortion is possible, whether or not intentional.

Ely Devons (1950), in his account of "statistics and planning" in the British Air Ministry during World War II, illustrated the potential for such distortion in sobering detail. The collection of such data was extremely difficult and subtle, demanding "a high degree of skill," yet it "was treated . . . as inferior, degrading and routine work on which the most inefficient clerical staff could best be employed" (p. 134). Errors entered the data in all kinds of ways, even just treating months as normal although all included some holiday or other. "Figures were often merely a useful way of summing up judgment and guesswork." Sometimes they were even "developed through 'statistical bargaining.'" But 'once a figure was put forward . . . no one was able by rational argument to demonstrate that it was wrong." And when those figures were called "statistics," they acquired the authority and sanctity of Holy Writ (p. 155).

All of this is not a plea for getting rid of hard information. That makes no more sense than getting rid of soft information. It means **we have to cease being mesmerized by the numbers and stop letting the hard information drive out the soft, instead combining both**

whenever possible. We all know about using hard facts to check out the soft hunches. Well, how about using soft hunches to check out the hard facts (e.g., "eyeballing" the statistics)?

The Dangers of Idiosyncratic Information   How can managers be sure that what they see with their own eyes and hear with their own ears is reliably representative of what is going on in their organization? On the day observed, John Cleghorn was visiting the Royal Bank branches he knew best, the very places in Montreal where he grew up. What if he had been in a branch in Moose Jaw, Saskatchewan? Of course, in banking one branch can be very much like another: "You seen one, you seen 'em all." Maybe. But what about the Wal-Mart executives who believed that the knowledge they gained in America was applicable in Germany?

Such information can certainly be problematic. But I think the point needs to be reversed too: what about the danger of remaining in an office and reading aggregated reports about the operations? What managers see and hear for themselves may be idiosyncratic, but it can also be direct and rich, and so counter the disconnect that is all too common in executive suites today. Think of all the information John picked up in those branches that would have been excluded, filtered, or distorted on its way to his executive suite. He needed the statistical reports too, but think of how useful was his opportunity to compare their results with his own direct observations.

Damned Again   Again with this conundrum, the managers are damned if they do and damned if they don't. They cannot avoid hard data—how else to manage a large complex organization?—yet they cannot become prisoners of it. Nor can they let themselves become prisoners of vague, idiosyncratic, soft information. The mysteries of measuring are a conundrum because, once again, there is no simple answer, no easy way out. Every manager has to find his or her own balance, not least by ensuring enough of each kind of information to check out the other.

PEOPLE CONUNDRUMS

Three of our conundrums occur mainly on the people plane of managing. They are labeled the Enigma of Order, the Paradox of Control (an extension of the previous one), and the Clutch of Confidence.

The Enigma of Order

Organizations need order. They sometimes need disorder too—shaking up—but most of the time most organizations need to concentrate on the stable delivery of their goods and services. And it is on their managers that the responsibility for ensuring much of this order falls. The people working in a unit usually look to their manager to provide definition, predictability, a sense of what is, what can be, what is to be, so that they can get on with their work of hiring people, planning operations, and producing outputs.

Here, then, is where we find the traditional equating of the word *management* with control. Much of this order comes in the form of strategies and structures—one to establish direction, the other to specify responsibilities.

Yet even while seeking to impose such order, managers often find themselves functioning in a disorderly way. That is the message of pretty much every empirical study of their work, from that of Carlson in the 1940s on, as discussed in Chapter 2. As Tom Peters put it, in managerial work "'sloppiness' is normal, probably inevitable, and usually sensible" (1979:171).

Why? Because while the organization wants to keep going, some outside forces inevitably keep changing. The organization may need predictability, but the world has this nasty habit of sometimes becoming unpredictable: customers change their minds; new technologies appear; unions call strikes. As Len Sayles noted: "All plans are incomplete. There are always unforeseen and unforeseeable defects" (1979:166). This is true even for something so orderly as organization structure itself: "Subordinates need to be given a clear understanding of their jobs and their boundaries, yet jobs inevitably overlap and boundaries are blurred" (p. 4).

Someone has to deal with what was not expected, and often that is the manager: the person whose responsibilities are broad enough and whose job is flexible enough to deal with the uncertainties and ambiguities. In a sense, **the manager is the *sink* for organizational disorder. Thus, if managing is getting order out of disorder, then the Enigma of Order reads: How to bring order to the work of others when the work of managing is itself so disorderly?** (Watson 1996:339).

This has been a widely recognized conundrum in management, well described by Andy Grove of Intel. Managers in a fast-paced world need "to develop a higher tolerance for disorder," while doing their "best to drive what's around [them] to order." They have to run things "like a well-oiled factory" yet be "mentally and emotionally ready for . . . turbulence." Grove's motto for this? "Let chaos reign, then rein in chaos" (1995:141). The perfect conundrum!

Can disorderly activities produce orderly results? Of course they can, otherwise organizations—and lots more—would not work. Think about artists, inventors, architects (writers, too, as I see my handwritten scrawls before me, trying to get my ideas into linear order for you). Some of these people are about as disorderly as you can get, yet they can come up with the most orderly of results.[11]

The Disorderly Nature of the Enigma of Order   Is what we have here really a conundrum, or just a curiosity? It would seem the latter, until we begin to appreciate how a disorderly process can contaminate its orderly results, and vice versa.

Let's go back to those painters. No few of them display their personal disorder on their canvasses—their inner turmoil, as in much of van Gogh's work or Munch's "The Scream." Yet even these canvasses are surprisingly orderly. There is, of course, no shortage of disorderly art, but most of it is soon forgotten. In art, that may not much matter; in management, it does. What makes this a conundrum is how easily disorderly managing can render an organization disorderly too. Managers simply pass on their conflicts and ambiguities.

The reverse can also happen, with negative consequences. People in the unit can force an artificial order on their manager. Hierarchies work in both directions, so what is sent down has a habit of coming back up, as when a manager imposes a nice neat plan and gets back nice neat reports—on how nicely and neatly the plan was supposedly executed. To further complicate matters, there are times when, even though a manager does not wish to impose order, people in the unit, intent on finding it, read order into whatever they are getting from their manager. In other words, they adopt a false order.[12]

---

[11] In effect, the work of these people exercises a certain control over the behavior of other people—what they see, how they live, what they think, or read. All are *designers*—of other people's order. And so too are managers (as discussed in Chapter 3). There is something about this conundrum that is intrinsic to the process of designing.

[12] "When people act, they rearrange things and impose contingencies that might not have been present before. The presence of these contingencies is what is then perceived as orderliness" (Weick 1983). So as to make this already difficult conundrum even more disorderly, Weick suggested that it is the "failure" of the manager to act at all, "rather than the nature of the external world itself, which explains the lack of order."

Letting Chaos Reign and Reining in the Chaos   So how is a manager to deal with this conundrum? Like all the others: by nuancing its two sides. He or she has to weave back and forth between, to return to Grove's phrase, letting the chaos reign and reining in the chaos.

Giving in to either side wreaks havoc on an organization. Too much order and work becomes rigid, detached. Too little order, and people can't function. We all know managers who let the chaos of their jobs and the outside world flow into their units, without providing the necessary buffering. These are the sieves discussed under the liaison role in Chapter 3. And so, too, do we all know managers who do the opposite: so protect their units that these become detached from reality. Everything seems so neat and orderly—until it blows up in everybody's face.

The Pervasive Enigma of Order   This conundrum would seem to apply to chief executives above all. As the main representative of the organization to the outside world, this person has to live with the cumulated chaos all around—changing technologies, demanding stakeholders, shifting markets, and so forth. If the chief cannot point the way through all of this—define "mission," present a coherent "vision"—who else can get their work done?

Yet this conundrum can have even more of an impact at the base of the hierarchy, because (as noted in Chapter 2) this is where the characteristics of managerial work can be the most pronounced—the pace most hectic, the brevity and fragmentation most severe, and so forth. Recall Fabienne Lavoie on the hospital ward, or the factory foremen studied by Guest (1955–1956) who averaged one activity every forty-eight seconds. As he noted, "the characteristics of a foreman's job—interruption, variety, discontinuity—are diametrically opposed to those of most hourly operator jobs, which are highly rationalized, repetitive, uninterrupted, and subject to the steady, unvarying rhythm of the moving conveyor" (p. 481).

And what about the managers in between, who may not have the same pressures as the chief executive or the same pace as the first-line managers? Does this alleviate the Enigma of Order? No, it brings on the Paradox of Control, which worsens it.

The Paradox of Control

The Enigma of Order is difficult enough. It describes the problem of dealing with disorder from without in the face of the need for order within. Add to this pressures for order from above—pile one manager upon another—and you get the Paradox of Control.

All but the smallest organizations tend to have managers neatly stacked up in hierarchies of authority, down which pass the directives emitting from "above," designed to impose order. In other words, the senior manager who works under conditions of controlled disorder expects his or her subordinate managers to work under conditions of controlled order. The problem, illustrated in Figure 5.2, is that these other managers face their own pressures from the sides—from customers, communities, and others. So this imposition of order from above can just make things worse. Managers want "control of their own circumstances" (Watson 1994:84), but their own managers, and not just outside circumstances, often impede it. As a consequence, the Enigma of Order becomes the Paradox of Control: **How to maintain the necessary state of controlled disorder when the manager above is imposing order?**

The Damage from Deeming   Here is where management by deeming can become especially destructive. It is certainly convenient for senior managers to deem, sweeping ambiguity under the rug by imposing

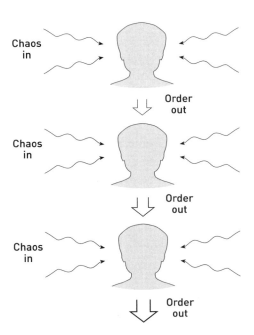

Figure 5.2 THE ENIGMA OF ORDER CASCADING INTO THE PARADOX OF CONTROL

specific performance standards on their reports. "They need order? Good. Here it is. The targets are clear. Meet them!"

But what do these targets constitute—where did these numbers come from? As we all know, they can sometimes be arbitrary, and even contradictory, picked out of the thin air of wish lists, with little regard for the difficult situations in which they have to be met. An awful lot of the ambiguity associated with such targets gets swept, not just under the rug, but into the faces of other managers. So a good deal of deeming, which is becoming increasingly prevalent in our large organizations, amounts to an executive cop-out. Tengblad studied eight chief executives of large corporations who were influenced by stock market pressures to produce "shareholder value." He found that these pressures "were passed down the hierarchy," which "resulted in some managers working to exhaustion, and also in conformity and non-constructive communication" (2004: 583).

Compounding the Conundrum   Compared with other managers, chief executives have somewhat of a free rein. Boards may be demanding, but usually not so much as these CEOs themselves. So they usually face just the Enigma of Order. It is below them in the hierarchy where the Paradox of Control begins.

As the pressures for order descend the hierarchy—as managers "prove to their bosses that they are loyal and responsible by transmitting a goodly percentage of the demands of upper management down to their subordinates" (Sayles 1979:115)—the weight of these pressures increases until finally the whole "cascade" falls on the managers at the base of the hierarchy.[13] Yet these are the ones least able to hide, for they usually have to face directly the disgruntled customers, the angry workers, the strident activists. Recall the Banff National Park, where the environmentalists battled the developers about a parking lot, while more senior managers discussed this in their polite offices in the big cities.

It is the senior managers who can hide (for a time, at least)—in their systems, that is, their abstractions. They can pretend that all that planning and controlling will take care of the ambiguities. It does, at this level at least, and for some time, until these ambiguities reemerge at lower

---

[13] See Hambrick, Finkelstein, and Mooney for a discussion of "the tendency for executives to impose demands on their subordinates in proportion to the demand they themselves face," which can "be manifested in bullying," and result in a "cascade" down the hierarchy (2005:482).

levels. President Truman was famous for a plaque on his desk that read "The buck stops here." All too often these days it is the opposite: **deeming managers pass the buck down, level by level, until it stops where the rubber hits the road**, where the environmentalists battle the developers.

Delayering, as noted, has become fashionable in recent years: thinning the hierarchy by eliminating levels of middle managers. Does that help the Paradox of Control? Again, its effect may be the opposite: the managers left behind may become more overworked while still facing the conundrum.

Fighting Back Up   So what are the pressured managers at lower levels of the large organizations to do? Morris et al. suggest that sometimes they can ignore the chain of command, at least when they have the "wisdom of knowing where and how to disobey" orders. "Sophisticated" managers develop this "into an art form" (1981:143). Moreover (as discussed in the posture of Managing Out of the Middle), they can turn the tables and promote change up the hierarchy. And managers at more senior levels can help by appreciating the consequences of passing down problems that are essentially theirs to resolve.

The Clutch of Confidence

Our last people conundrum is easier to explain if no less difficult to handle.

It takes a good deal of confidence to practice management effectively. Think about all the pressures discussed in Chapter 2, not to mention all the conundrums discussed here. As was evident in so much of the managing I observed (in the refugee camps, the NHS, Greenpeace, etc.), this is no work for the feint-hearted or the insecure. Anyone inclined to avoid problems, pass them on, or simply cover their own rear ends, can make things dreadful for everyone else.

But how about the supremely confident? They can be even worse. Bear in mind the shaky foundations on which such confidence can lie: information about which the manager is never sure; issues loaded with ambiguities; conundrums that can never be resolved, often forcing the manager to "wing it." This expression comes not from airplanes but from the stage, where actors who didn't know their lines had someone call them in from the wings. Managers have no such someones. All alone, they have to convey the impression that they know what they are doing, even when they are not sure where they are going, so that others feel safe to follow. In other words, managers often have to feign confidence. For reasonably modest managers, this can be difficult enough; for the supremely confident, it may be not difficult at all, just catastrophic.

The trouble with even reasonable confidence is that it can go over the edge and put the manager on a slippery slope—to arrogance. It does not take much for someone in this job to stop listening, become isolated, think of him- or herself as heroic.

The line between confidence and arrogance can be not only thin but also vague. A manager can cross it without being aware. And once on the way down that slope, there may be no stopping, until reaching the bottom. So the Clutch of Confidence reads: **How to maintain a sufficient level of confidence without crossing over into arrogance?**

This is not a casual conundrum. It probably undermines as much management practice, and causes as much grief for other people, as any of the other conundrums. This is especially true in this age of heroic leadership, where even modest managers, when successful, can get put on pedestals for all to revere.

In Praise of the Modest Manager   How can a manager avoid the Clutch of Confidence? Honest friends and advisers can help. When someone is getting close to that edge, as every successful person does from time to time, it is helpful to have someone to yank him or her back. But, of course, having such friends and advisers—and listening to them—requires a certain amount of confidence too, at least inner confidence, which, happily, is usually accompanied by a certain modesty. So **perhaps the key to dealing with this conundrum is to ensure that more people who are confidentially modest end up in management positions in the first place. But in this age of heroic leadership, how many truly modest people get to be managers?** (In Chapter 6, we shall discuss a simple way to change this: give voice in the selection of managers to the people who know the candidates best, namely, the ones who have experienced their management.)

But even when more modest people get into managerial jobs, this conundrum does not disappear. That is because of managers being put on that pedestal, at least in the eyes of others. Every manager, therefore, has to recognize the challenge of not taking him- or herself too seriously. And that, of course, requires a good deal of confidence, really inner confidence. So let's look for inner, not just outer, confidence in our managers.

THE ACTION CONUNDRUMS

Next come the conundrums related to managing on the action plane, one called the Ambiguity of Acting, the other the Riddle of Change.

The Ambiguity of Acting

If managing is about making sure that things get done, then managers have to be decisive. They cannot hedge too much, and they can be reflective only to a point. They have to take stands, make certain decisions, and provoke actions that move their units forward.

The problem is that much of this has to be done under difficult circumstances, full of ambiguities, not to mention the conundrums so far discussed. And this gives rise to another conundrum: **How to act decisively in a complicated, nuanced world?**

The Doubtfulness of Decision   Consider *decision* itself. The very term seems decisive. Decisions, after all, are commitments to action. But need we always commit—that is, decide—in order to act? If you think so, have someone hit you on the knee. Or visit a courtroom and listen to a second-degree murder case—that is, action without decision. Organizations sometimes get tapped on the knee, too. There was a story some years ago about the senior management of a major European automobile company hiring consultants to find out how a new model came to be.

When we do make a commitment to act, is it necessarily as clear as it appears? In the Canadian parks, they made some decisions about that parking lot. Good luck! And just because we commit, does that mean we act? A lot can happen between deciding and doing. Alan Whelan of BT decided to sign that contract. Did that commit his senior management? As Len Sayles put it in discussing one of what he referred to as "contradictions": "Managers need to be decisive, but it's difficult to know when a decision is made, and many decisions must be reconsidered and remade" (1979:11). Thus, one of Hill's new managers talked about "how disillusioning and frustrating it is to be hit with problems and conflicts all day and not be able to solve them very cleanly" (2003:181).

This conundrum takes us back to the last one, in the sense that confidence enables a manager to act decisively, yet being too decisive in the face of ambiguity can amount to arrogance—especially when the manager is distant from the issue in question (harking back to the Quandary of Connecting). Consider all those ill-conceived acquisitions in large corporations, where bold decisions were taken in remarkable ignorance of their consequences. Or how about George W. Bush's decision to go to war in 2003?

Conversely, managers who hesitate to act can bring everything to a halt. Some sort of decision, when action is truly necessary, is often better than no decision at all—at least it gets people moving (Weick 1979). But managers who act too quickly, even when well informed, may be forcing their organizations into premature action on events that are unfolding.

Of course, events are always unfolding. And major events usually unfold unpredictably. So the trick is to know when to wait, despite the costs of delay, and when to act, despite unforeseeable consequences. And for that there is no manual, no course, not even any convenient five easy steps—just good, informed judgment.

Limiting Decisiveness   Perhaps the best way to deal with this conundrum is to put some limits on decisiveness. If "the organization will tolerate only a certain number of proposals" from its management (Wrapp 1967:93), then that management has to be selective in what it gets decisive about. Moreover, if many decisions have to be remade anyway, why not make whichever possible in successive steps, with time in between for feedback? In their book *Zen and the Art of Management*, Pascale and Athos quote a manager who delayed decisions, giving himself time to understand the issues and his organization the opportunity to learn how to deal with them:

> If you are sure of the facts and are positive of the right corrective action to be taken, if you endorse any single answer, you're dead. So . . . I "juggled." . . . What I needed was time to "massage" the problem down to the level . . . where [it] occurred so that . . . the system could learn from the problem and correct itself. Yet at the same time, I had to hold the problem in "suspended animation." (1978:89)

Chapter 2 also used the metaphor of juggling, but about the many projects and issues that managers have to handle concurrently. As each comes down, it is given a boost—a new burst of energy—while the manager integrates on the run. This kind of juggling and integrating likely comes naturally to people predisposed to the calculated chaos of managerial work (Noël 1989:45). By learning about complex issues over time, the manager helps to alleviate not only the Ambiguity of Acting but also the Syndrome of Superficiality—at the expense, of course, of the Labyrinth of Decomposition.

Charles Lindblom labeled such behavior "disjointed incremental-ism," describing it as "typically a never ending process of successive steps in which continual nibbling is a substitute for a good bite" (1968:25–26). He referred to "the piecemeal remedial incrementalist" as perhaps not looking "like a heroic figure" but someone who "is, nevertheless, a shrewd, resourceful problem-solver who is wrestling broadly with a universe that he is wise enough to know is too big for him" (p. 27; see also Quinn [1980], who labeled this "logical incrementalism").

The Riddle of Change

We hear a great deal of hype about change these days. It seems that no management speech can begin without paying homage to the claim that "we live in times of great change."

Are we sure? My car uses the same basic internal combustion technology as the Ford Model T; we all dress in many of the same fabrics we've been using for decades, often even in basic styles of years gone by. (Why in the world do men wear ties? Imagine someone trying to introduce them now.) Every morning I get up and button buttons, just like my ancestors did (which may well have been sewn on a Singer sewing machine; these covered the globe a century ago, no less than the products of "global" corporations do today.) Indeed, even the claims about change haven't changed:

> Few phenomena are more remarkable yet few have been less re-marked than the degree in which material civilization, the progress of mankind in all those contrivances which oil the wheels and promote the comforts of daily life have been concentrated in the last half century. It is not too much to say that in these respects more has been done, richer and more prolific discoveries have been made, grander achievements have been realized in the course of the 50 years of our own lifetime than in all the previous lifetimes of the race.

This appeared in *Scientific American*—in 1868! *Plus ça change, plus c'est la même chose* (The more things change, the more things stay the same). My point is that **we only notice what is changing, not what isn't, which includes most of what is around us.** (This morning did you ask why, in these times of great change, you are still buttoning buttons?) Sure things change—some things, some of the time. Now it is especially information technology and the economy. We all have to deal with that.

But not to the point of blinding us to what isn't changing, because all of us, especially managers, have to deal with that too.

We hear plenty about the problems of avoiding change—organizations have to adapt, better still, lead. What we need to hear more about is that too much change leads to a perpetual and dysfunctional angst, among other problems. Thus, no manager can manage change alone—that is anarchy. Every manager has to manage continuity as well, which gives us the Riddle of Change: **How to manage change when there is the need to maintain continuity?** Once again, the trick is to get the balance right.

Chester Barnard was quoted earlier that "executive work is not that *of* the organization, but the specialized work of *maintaining* the organization in operation" (1938:215). This means keeping the organization on track and getting it back on track when it goes off, alongside improving the track when necessary, and sometimes building a new track to a different place. The manager "endeavors . . . constantly to readjust . . . behavior, marginally, in response to the ever-changing environment," while seeking "stability, holding deviations to a minimum . . . by constant change" (Sayles 1964:259; see also Aram 1976:119).

My colleague Jonathan Gosling interviewed a number of managers about how they managed change. To his surprise, mostly they talked about managing continuity. Likewise, during the twenty-nine days I saw a good deal of change totally intertwined with continuity. Abbas Gullet and Stephen Omollo in the Red Cross refugee camps were seen promoting changes to ensure stability, while John Cleghorn of the Royal Bank was seen championing changes small and large—fixing a sign, acquiring an insurance company—to keep the big bank on its course. And Fabienne Lavoie had developed a new system for better control in the nursing station.

The Dual Search for Certainty and Flexibility   In an insightful book of 1967 entitled *Organizations in Action*, James D. Thompson wrote about this conundrum as "the paradox of administration"—"the dual search for certainty and flexibility." Mostly he described how organizations function for the "reduction of uncertainty and its conversion into relative certainty" to protect its "technical core." Yet "the central characteristic of the administrative process [is a] search for flexibility" (p. 148).

Thompson believed that this paradox could be addressed by favoring certainty in the short run—for operating efficiency—and flexibility in the long run—for "freedom from commitment" (p. 150). The problem, of course, is that the long run never arrives (or, at least as John Maynard Keynes put it, we are all dead by then). So managers have to face this conundrum, like all the others, in the short run—namely, in their current behavior.

As already suggested, there is always some change amid the continuity, even if just in some hidden skunkworks, and always some continuity—some pockets of stability—amid the change. And as this itself suggests, organizations can experience some periods where change is pervasive, and other periods of relative stability. Cyert and March (1963) have written about the "sequential attention to goals" in organizations, in this case addressing these conflicting needs for change and continuity by first attending to one and then to the other, back and forth in cycles of some kind. In managing, as in the Bible, there can be a time to sow and a time to reap.

We saw this clearly in our studies that tracked strategies in different organizations over long periods of time (discussed in the Predicament of Planning). The National Film Board of Canada, for example, experienced from 1939 to 1975 surprisingly regular periods, of about six years each, in the films made: periods of much experimentation were followed by others of relative consistency, and then back. This seems to be common in adhocracies, which thrive on change, compared with the more machine-like as well as some of the entrepreneurial organizations, which seem to favor long periods of relative stability interrupted by short bursts of quantum change (Mintzberg 2007: Chapters 2–3 and 6–8).

OVERALL CONUNDRUMS

We come now to two overall conundrums, one for managers, the other for me. Here we can find some reconciliation—at least between these two.

The Ultimate Conundrum

How are managers to keep their balance when they are constantly being pressured to tilt every which way? Put differently: **How can any manager possibly manage all these conundrums concurrently?** "Realizing that the managerial role was one of balancing fundamental tensions was one of the most difficult and important insights that new managers made" (Hill 2003:80).

These are not convenient conundrums that appear on schedule or that arrive happily spaced apart. They are all mixed up in managing. So

to manage is not just to walk a tightrope, but to move through a multidimensional space on all kinds of tightropes. Managing is about nuance as much as it is about decisiveness. As Paul Hirsch was in the habit of telling his incoming MBA students at Northwestern, "Welcome to the error term!" Or in the words of Charles Handy, from his book *The Age of Paradox:*

> Paradox I now see to be inevitable, endemic, and perpetual. . . .
> We can, and should, reduce the starkness of some of the contradictions, minimize the inconsistencies, understand the puzzles in the paradoxes, but we cannot make them disappear, or solve them completely, or escape from them. Paradoxes are like the weather, something to be lived with . . . the worst aspects mitigated, the best enjoyed and used as clues to the way forward. (1994:12–13)

I have noted a few times that the trick is to get the balance right. But this is not a stable balance; rather, it is a dynamic one. Conditions cause managers to tilt much of the time (e.g., toward greater confidence when challenged, or toward more change in the face of opportunity) and later back. In its multidimensional space, managing is a balancing act of the highest order.

I have also noted repeatedly, as did Charles Handy, that such conundrums are unresolvable. There are no solutions because each has to be dealt with in context, its pressures always in a state of flux. **These paradoxes and predicaments, labyrinths and riddles, are built into managerial work—they *are* managing—and there they shall remain. They can be alleviated but never eliminated, reconciled but never resolved.** To try and escape them is to fall into the managerial dogma of which we have had more than enough already. Managers have to face them, understand them, reflect on them, play with them.

In *Management of the Absurd*, Farson wrote that what he called predicaments "require interpretive thinking . . . the ability to put a larger frame around a situation, to understand it in its many contexts, to appreciate its deeper and often paradoxical causes and consequences" (1996:42).[14] The intention of this chapter has been to encourage all this.

---

[14] To quote Farson further: "I find it disquieting to see the term *paradox* entering management literature in a way that indicates it can be managed. I suppose we should expect this because of the sense of omnipotence that plagues American management, the belief that no event or situation is too complex or too unpredictable to be brought under management control" (p. 15).

F. Scott Fitzgerald wrote, "The test of a first-rate intelligence is the ability to hold two opposed ideas in the mind at the same time and still retain the ability to function." Can we afford any other form of intelligence in the world of managing?

Of course, **all of this means that the manager's ultimate conundrum—how to deal with all these conundrums concurrently—remains.** Maybe, then, the only hope lies in my final conundrum.

My Conundrum

Finally, my own conundrum: **How do I reconcile the fact that, while all these conundrums can be stated apart, they all seem to be the same?** I have offered plenty of comments about the overlapping of these conundrums, the similarities among them, even one that seems to restate another. Maybe these are all just one great big jumbled management conundrum. In that case, you needn't be bothered by the previous, ultimate conundrum—just all the ones that preceded it.

6

Managing Effectively

Now this is not the end.

It is not even the beginning of the end.

But it is, perhaps, the end of the beginning.

Winston Churchill

Welcome to the end of the beginning.[1] This chapter considers the tricky subject of managerial effectiveness. Trying to figure out what makes a manager effective, even just trying to assess whether a manager has been effective, is difficult enough. Believing that the answers are easy only makes the questions that much more difficult. Managers, and those who work with them, in selection, assessment, and development, have to face the complexities. Helping to do so is the purpose of this chapter.

Before I scare you away, let me add that I had a good time writing this chapter. Perhaps the complexity led me into a kind of playfulness—about the inevitably flawed manager, the perils of excellence, what we can learn from happily managed families, and more. So I suspect, or at least hope, that you will have a good time reading this chapter.

We begin with the supposedly effective but in fact inevitably flawed manager. This leads us into a brief discussion of unhappily managed

---

[1] I should note at this point that all the quotes that open the six chapters of this book plus the appendix are the same ones I used to open the seven chapters of my 1973 book, *The Nature of Managerial Work* (although not in the same order, except for this one in the last chapter of both books). They seem to work again remarkably well—although I hope not too well in the case of this one.

organizational families, due to the failure of (1) the person, (2) the job, (3) the fit, or (4) success. From here it is on to healthy managed organizational families, which can be found where reflection in the abstract meets action on the ground, supported by analysis, worldliness, and collaboration, all framed by personal energy on one side and social integration on the other. This takes us to three practical issues: selecting, assessing, and developing effective managers, asking along the way. "Where has all the judgment gone?" The chapter, and the book, close with a comment on "managing naturally."

The Many Qualities of the Supposedly Effective Manager

Lists of the qualities of effective managers abound. These are usually short—who would take dozens of items seriously? For example, in a brochure to promote its EMBA program entitled "What Makes a Leader?" the University of Toronto business school answers: "The courage to challenge the status quo. To flourish in a demanding environment. To collaborate for the greater good. To set clear direction in a rapidly changing world. To be fearlessly decisive" (Rotman School, n.d., circa 2005).[2]

But this list is clearly incomplete. Where is native intelligence, or being a good listener, or just plain having energy? Surely these are important for managers, too. But fear not—they appear on other lists. So if we are to trust any of these lists, we shall have to combine all of them.

This, for the sake of a better world, I have done in Table 6.1. It lists the qualities from various lists that I have found, plus a few missing favorites of my own. This composite list contains fifty-two items. Be all fifty-two and you are bound to be an effective manager, if not a human one.

The Inevitably Flawed Manager

All of this is part of our "romance of leadership" (Meindl et al. 1985), that on one hand puts ordinary mortals on managerial pedestals ("Rudolph is the perfect person for the job—he will save us!"), and on the other hand allows us to vilify them as they come crashing down ("How

---

[2] My university, McGill, has had a long-standing rivalry with the University of Toronto, in sports and otherwise. I chose its brochure, not because of this, but because it was handy and serves the purpose well. I'm sure such lists appear in the promotional hype of most business schools, including my own, none of which is taken seriously by many on the faculty. The trouble is that too many of the students and others do.

Table 6.1 COMPOSITE LIST OF BASIC QUALITIES FOR ASSURED
MANAGERIAL SUCCESS

courageous *committed* curious confident *candid*	charismatic passionate *inspiring* visionary

reflective
insightful
open-minded/tolerant (of people,
   ambiguities, and ideas)
innovative
communicative (including being a
   good listener)
connected/informed
perceptive
	energetic/enthusiastic
	upbeat/optimistic
	ambitious
	tenacious/ persistent/zealous

	collaborative/participative/cooperative *engaging* supportive/sympathetic/empathetic
thoughtful/intelligent/*wise* analytic/objective pragmatic decisive (action-oriented) proactive	stable dependable fair accountable ethical/honest
	consistent flexible balanced integrative
	tall★

Source: Compiled from various sources; *my own favorites in italics*
★This item appeared on no list that I saw. But it might rank ahead of many of the other items
because studies have shown that managers are on average taller than other people. To quote from
a 1920 study, entitled *The Executive and his Control of Men*, based on research done a lot more
carefully than much of what we find in the great journals of today, Enoch Burton Gowin addressed the question: "Viewing it as a chemical machine, is a larger body able to supply a greater
amount of energy?" More specifically, might there be "some connection between an executive's
physique, as measured by height and weight, and the importance of the position he holds?" (1920:
22, 31). The answer, in statistic after statistic gathered by the author, is yes. Bishops, for example,
averaged greater height than the preachers of small towns; superintendents of school systems were
taller than principals of schools. Other data on railroad executives, governors, etc. supported these
findings. The "Superintendents of Street Cleaning" were actually the second tallest of all, after the
"Reformers." (The "Socialist Organizers" were just behind the "police chiefs", but well up there.)
Musicians were at the bottom of the list (p. 25).

could Rudolph have failed us so?"). Yet some managers do stay up, if not
on that silly pedestal. How so?

The answer is simple: **successful managers are flawed—we
are all flawed—but their particular flaws are not fatal, at least
under the circumstances.** (Superman was flawed, too—remember
Kryptonite?). Peter Drucker commented at a conference that "the task
of leadership is to create an alignment of strengths, so as to make peoples'
weaknesses irrelevant." He might have added "including the leader's own."

If you want to uncover someone's flaws, marry them or else work for them. Their flaws will quickly become apparent. So will something else (at least if you are a mature human being who has made a reasonably good choice): that you can usually live with these flaws. Managers and marriages do succeed. The world, as a consequence, continues to unfold in its inimitably imperfect way.[3]

Fatally flawed are those superman lists of managerial qualities, because they are utopian. Much of the time they are also wrong. For example, managers should be decisive—who can argue with that? For starters, anyone who followed the machinations of George W. Bush, who learned the importance of being decisive by reading case studies in a Harvard classroom. The University of Toronto list calls this quality "fearlessly decisive." Going into Iraq, President Bush certainly was that. As for some of the other items on that list, this president's arch enemy in Afghanistan certainly "had the courage to challenge the status quo," while Ingvar Kamprad, who built IKEA into one of the most successful retail chains ever, reportedly took fifteen years to "set clear direction in a rapidly changing world." (Actually, he succeeded because the furniture world was not rapidly changing; *he* changed it.)

So perhaps we need to proceed differently.

UNHAPPILY MANAGED ORGANIZATIONAL FAMILIES

Tolstoy began his novel *Anna Karenina* with the immortal words "Happy families are all alike; each unhappy family is unhappy in its own particular way."[4] And so it may be with managers and their organizational families: they may have an unlimited number of ways to screw up, with ever more fascinating ones being invented every day,[5] but perhaps few by which to succeed.

---

[3] Not always. Politicians seem to have become particularly adept at hiding flaws during elections until they become fatal in office. For example, the object of the political debates on television is to demonstrate that your opponent is flawed while you are not. The assumption is that the flawed candidate should lose. Perhaps this theatrical farce is one reason why people are so fed up with political leadership.

[4] An article entitled "Five Types of Marriages" (Cuber and Harroff 1986) was described in the table of contents of the book in which it was published (Skolnick and Skolnick, 1986) as finding that "happy marriages aren't all alike" (p. xi). Yet three of the types described there do not seem to be particularly happy, while the two that do—labeled "the vital" and "the total" (pp. 269–274)—sound remarkably alike.

[5] I was told the story of the chief executive of a major British company who would not let regular employees walk past the door of his office. To get by, they had to go down one set of stairs and

Tales of Two Managers

Let me bring two sets of two managers into the picture. Liz's and Larry's problems were rather normal. Both were smart, well-educated, modern managers. They worked near each other in the same company, one heading a major staff group, the other a major line operation. Liz leapt; Larry lingered. One made decisions too quickly, so that they often had to be remade; the other had difficulty making decisions at all, or else made them in ambiguous ways. The results were similar: people in their units felt excluded, confused, discouraged.

Beyond their own units, into the rest of the organization, Liz confronted while Larry connived. She often fought with her colleagues in the company—she knew better—except for the CEO, to whom she was deferential. Larry, in contrast, was careful not to upset anyone, so he hesitated to challenge when necessary.

Each, by the way, would probably recognize the other in this description. But would they recognize themselves? I need to add that although their respective managerial families were not particularly happy, these managers were not failures. None of these flaws was fatal. Things got done. They just could have been done more effectively—and happily.

The second tale comes from a study we did some years ago of a daily newspaper in a small Quebec town. It was owned, in succession, by two men of inherited wealth who went on to become quite famous as owners of Canadian media. Their approaches to managing were almost diametrically opposed. The first cared about the town, where he grew up but no longer lived, but he was passive with regard to the newspaper and so let its problems fester. The other, who followed him, was active all right; he cared about squeezing as much cost as he could out of the newspaper before selling it for a profit in a much reduced state. We concluded our study as follows:

> Our tale of two Canadian tycoons is one of sharp contrasts in leadership. One was detached administratively but involved sentimentally; the other was detached sentimentally but involved

---

up another. Those who got into that office had to sit on chairs lower than his, so that he could talk down to them. He moved to the chairmanship of an even greater company, and eventually he got knighted for his efforts. When he left that chairmanship, his advice to his successor, at board meetings, was to (1) dress properly, (2) not smoke, and (3) keep control with a clear agenda. At the latter's first board meeting, he took off his jacket, lit a cigar, and asked, "What would you like to talk about?"

administratively. One served the organization well so long as it didn't have to adapt; the other served it well only while it was forced to adapt. The failings of the first brought in the second. In that sense they complemented each other, at least over time. But we are left wondering, in conclusion, if either (or both, in sequence) is what we really want in our society. Perhaps the message of [this study] is that healthy organizations and a healthy society need leaders who both act and care. (Mintzberg, Taylor, and Waters 1984:27)

To be true to Tolstoy, I am not going to propose a definitive list of the causes of managerial failures. This book is long enough. If you wish to have such a list, let me suggest you go back to Table 6.1 and reverse all the qualities there. For example, in place of *decisive*, put *waffling*, and in place of *upbeat*, *downbeat*. Or else keep the qualities as they are, but consider overdoing each. For *decisive*, you can put *hasty*; for *upbeat*, *hyper*. Indeed, just take these qualities and apply them in the wrong context. Be decisive without understanding the situation (that war in Iraq), or upbeat in managing a funeral home. To quote Skinner and Sasser in a *Harvard Business Review* article:

> When the failure patterns [of managers] . . . are examined as a group, they are so numerous and so contradictory that they may seem frightening. . . . Managers get involved in too much detail—or too little. They are too cautious or too bold. They are too critical or too accepting. . . . They plan and analyze and procrastinate, or they blindly plunge ahead . . . without . . . analysis or plan. (1977:142)

What I offer here are some general groups of failure, within each of which reside a wide variety of possible disasters: personal failures, job failures, fit failures, and success failures. Each is discussed briefly, so that we can spend more time on the positive: healthily managed organizational families.

Person Failures

First are the failures that managers achieve all by themselves. **Some managers are just in the wrong line of work.** They may not want to manage—the reluctant ones—and so don't relish the pace, the pressures, and much else that goes with the job. Perhaps they prefer to work alone, or in peer groups without responsibility for others.

Then there are the people who are just plain *incompetent* for the job: they are thoughtless, or don't like people. These are surprisingly common, even among managers who have made it to senior positions. In a *Fortune* magazine article on "Why CEOs Fail," Choran and Colvin offered two prime answers: "bad execution" and "people problems." They commented on the former:

> Keeping track of all critical assignments, following up on them, evaluating them—isn't that kind of . . . boring? We may as well say it: Yes. It's boring. It's a grind. At least, plenty of really intelligent, accomplished, failed CEOs have found it so and you can't blame them. They just shouldn't have been CEOs. (1999:36)

Whether we call this "thin management" or macroleading (as discussed earlier), it seems to be becoming more common: managers who race down the "fast track" with the "quick fix." (You can tell these managers by their propensity to use such language—the managerial "flavor of the month," so to speak.) As CEOs in large corporations, these are the people especially inclined to diversify, merge, restructure, and downsize—all very fashionable, and often a lot easier than resolving complicated problems inside the company. Here is where we find the Syndrome of Superficiality out of control.

Beneath incompetence are managers who are *imbalanced* in their practice. In Chapter 3, I concluded that managers have to play all the roles on all the planes (information, people, action), in some sort of rough balance. As noted, too much emphasis on leading can favor style over substance, while too much acting can cause the job to explode centrifugally.[6] Likewise, in Chapter 4, we discussed the problematic styles of excessive emphasis on the art, craft, or science of managing, which were labeled narcissistic, tedious, and calculating.

Many of the common managerial imbalances can be seen in terms of the conundrums discussed in Chapter 5. As noted there, a sure way to fail is to resolve any of these conundrums, such as the Riddle of Change by

---

[6] In an article entitled "Mismanagement Styles," Ichak Adizes (1977:7–12) discussed some similar forms of managerial imbalance, which he labeled the exclusive producer (the "loner"), the exclusive administrator implementer (the "bureaucrat"), the exclusive entrepreneur (the "crisis maker"), and the exclusive integrator (the "superfollower"). (Adizes also had another category labeled "does not excel in performing any role ["deadwood," p. 12]—but that really belongs in our first group of just plain incompetencies.) He referred to these as "*the* styles of mismanagement" (p. 9, italics added), but they are but a few among the many that are possible.

promoting too much change, or too little. Similarly, with regard to the characteristics of managing discussed in Chapter 2, too hectic a pace, too much fragmentation, an excess of oral communication, and so forth, can send the job over the edge (see Hambrick et al. 2005:481–482), as seems to be happening with increasing frequency now, thanks to the Internet.

All of this is not to make the case for perfect balance in managing. That also can be a form of imbalance, with the manager exhibiting no focus, no character, no style of his or her own.[7]

Job Failures

Sometimes a person is well suited to managing and well balanced in his or her approach to the job, but that job is simply undo-able—unmanageable—and so the person fails.

In the last chapter, we discussed unnatural managerial jobs—ones that should not exist. They have been created to cut spans of control, or to impose some kind of artificial managerial oversight, often in arbitrarily designated geographic regions. To repeat an earlier comment, there is nothing so dangerous as a manager with nothing to do.

In Chapter 4, we also discussed split managerial jobs that are difficult to do, because the manager is pulled in different ways by different demands. John Tate of the Canadian Justice Department was pulled between advising the minister, serving as a policy expert, and managing the department. Marc, the hospital Executive Director, had to be the tough advocate externally yet the reconciler of the demands of other advocates internally. Can both be done by one person?

A manager can also fail because the job is embedded in an organization or an outside context that makes it impossible. Think of the officer in

---

[7] Skinner and Sasser make a similar point about "consistency," that it "causes managers to fail." But they see this happening at the extremes, not in the balanced center: "Each manager who had a problem had it at one end of the scale or the other, consistently, but never both. In other words, low accomplishers tend to develop a set style or approach, and when they err; it is always in the same particular direction. Consistency is their downfall. . . . In contrast; each outstanding achiever in our cases not only had a different executive style, but was inconsistent in personal style. . . . The paradox is revealing. The high accomplishers get into fine detail in one situation yet stay at the strategic level in another. They delegate a lot one time or a little the next time" (1977:143). While this seems to make good sense, recall our discussion in Chapter 4 about managers changing their styles like golfers change their clubs—that people may not be so flexible. As Skinner and Sasser themselves wrote, "It is a curious yet reasonable fact that nearly all managers tend to settle into a fairly rigid or limited executive style" (p. 146).

charge of rearranging the deck chairs on the *Titanic*, or the Vice President of Anything at Enron as it went down. How about being the sales manager of a company with shoddy, unsellable products? Don't blame the manager, except for taking the job, but do recognize that here, too, the possibilities for failure are endless.

Fit Failures

Next are the potentially competent, balanced managers in perfectly doable jobs, just not the jobs for them. So they *become* unbalanced and therefore incompetent—misfits quite literally.

Here, again, the stories are legion, some of them stemming from the fallacy of professional management—that any properly educated manager can manage anything. Earlier, for example, we had the question of whether school systems should be run by retired military officers, leading to the question of whether retired schoolteachers should run the army. I also recall a business school that named a dean who had been running a trucking company. He claimed that managing professors was just like managing truck drivers. So most of the competent truck driver professors left.

There is also the Peter Principle discussed in the last chapter, about managers rising to their level of incompetence. They should have been promoted once less. Managerial experience at one level in a given hierarchy does not necessarily suit someone for managing at another level.

The Quandary of Connecting, discussed in Chapter 5, suggests that the very fact of becoming a manager can render a worker incompetent in the new job. Bump this up the hierarchy and a perfectly competent junior manager can be rendered an incompetent senior manager as he or she gets promoted further and further from his or her own sphere of knowledge and competence. A fault that was tolerable before—hubris all too often these days—becomes fatal.

Fit can also became misfit when conditions change, so that positive qualities turn into serious flaws. For example, an organization in crisis may find itself being managed by someone more suitable to managing in a steady state. Or a great turnaround artist is brought into an organization that is running perfectly well in steady state. What ain't broke thus gets fixed, to paraphrase that old saying. How about the army officer trained for conventional warfare who finds himself facing guerrillas, or the manager in the public sector who finds herself running a unit that has been privatized? The situation changes; perhaps the manager cannot (Vail 1989:122–123).

But be careful here: evident matches can prove to be misfits, too. **Sometimes matches of opposites work better than matches of likes—what we might call intentional misfits.** Does a machine organization need a highly cerebral chief? Maybe it needs one who can open up its narrow tendencies, just as a wild and woolly adhocracy can *sometimes* benefit from an organized chief who keeps a lid on the madness. As Lombardo and McCall put it, "the most effective leaders we have observed seem to act in a counter-intuitive fashion, going against the grain of the environment. . . . [For example, in] the most predictable of the divisions, the effective VPs introduce a note of strategic unpredictability" (1982:58).

Success Failures

A special case of the last is the failure that derives from success. A company grows too large for its founding entrepreneur, or hubris sets into the management of a research establishment that has had too much success.

In an intriguing book called *The Icarus Paradox*,[8] which could have also been titled *The Perils of Excellence*, Danny Miller (1990) demonstrated how organizations can be changed by their own success: their strengths become weakness, their successes turn into failures. Miller described four main "trajectories" by which this happens, which in fact correspond rather closely to the four forms of organization introduced in Chapter 4. For example, "growth-driven, entrepreneurial *Builders* . . . managed by imaginative leaders . . . [become] impulsive, greedy imperialists, who . . . [expand] helter-skelter into businesses they know nothing about." Or "*Pioneers* [adhocracies] with unexcelled R&D departments, flexible think-tank operations, and state-of-the-art products, [become] utopian *Escapists*, run by cults of chaos-living scientists who squander resources in the pursuit of hopelessly grandiose and futuristic inventions" (pp. 4–5).[9] So, too, can this happen with managers themselves: the doers becoming overdoers; the linkers become gadflies; the leaders become cheerleaders.

---

[8] The book was named for the figure in Greek mythology who flew so high that the sun melted his wings and sent him tumbling to his death.

[9] The best-selling management book of its time, Peters and Waterman's *In Search of Excellence* (1992), about highly successful companies, suffered great embarrassment when *Business Week* (1984) ran a cover story titled "Oops!" about how "some of those companies aren't looking so excellent anymore." Were Peters and Waterman wrong about these companies, or had the Icarus Paradox simply come into play? Indeed, might the publicity from the book have helped to cause their problems?

Under the Icarus Paradox, a kind of *arrogance of attribution* sets in: "We [or I] must be wonderful because our organization is so successful." Maybe that *was* true, but believing your organization is wonderful can undermine its effectiveness because part of that wonderfulness may have been a certain humility, which engendered an open spirit. **Established managers who take themselves too seriously—or, perhaps more commonly, newly appointed managers who had no role in a success they associate with themselves—risk riding over the edge of confidence, into arrogance.**

Is this inevitable? Nothing is inevitable. There are plenty of managers who maintain their good sense—their own internal balance. But there are enough of the others to suggest how often success becomes a curse.

In a discussion of "failure as a natural process," Spiros Makridakis wrote: "In the biological world failure is synonymous with death and is considered a natural event. . . . Failure seems to be as natural likewise among organizational systems" (1990:207). Unfortunately, however, it is not necessarily tied to death, as we have found out about banks and automobile companies in this new millennium. Likewise, failed managers often live on, not only in life but in their jobs, there to sustain the misery.

To conclude, many evident pitfalls accompany the practice of managing. Someone once defined an expert as someone who avoids all the many pitfalls on his or her way to the grand fallacy. Not only experts, but managers too.

HEALTHILY MANAGED ORGANIZATIONAL FAMILIES

OK, enough about failure. We can dwell on that forever. What matters is success. And there is no shortage of that, more or less. As the story of Liz and Larry suggests, flawed managers can perform well enough. They avoid enough of the pitfalls without finding their way to the grand fallacy. In fact, many of the twenty-nine managers of this study were more than good enough: they managed to create or sustain healthy organizational families. How did they do that?

Wouldn't it be nice if I could now offer the answer in five easy steps? I can't, but I can offer a framework to consider it.

Lewis, Beavers, Gossett, and Phillips, in the introduction to their book *No Single Thread: Psychological Health in Family Systems*, commented:

"There is considerable literature on the pathological family types, but a 'scarcity of data' on the healthy family" (1976:xvii). There is likewise a scarcity of data, amid a plethora of speculation, about how organizations are managed effectively.

I thought initially that I could proceed here by getting clues from the literature on families, out of the fields of psychology, psychiatry, and the like. I quickly dropped that idea as futile, and settled on the framework that is presented in Figure 6.1 and discussed in this section. Then a colleague suggested I look at the Lewis et al. book just cited. I was struck by its parallels with the framework I had developed, so much so that I was able to match a quotation from that work with each of the dimensions of this framework, as you will see. Even my conclusion about managerial effectiveness having to be considered in context is paralleled by the comment of Lewis et al. that "family strengths may be understood better through the study of the total family system than a study of the individual" (p. 216). Perhaps these parallels are coincidental, although I think it more likely that different kinds of social systems (families, organizational units, etc.) share some characteristics.

A Framework for Effectiveness

What I offer here is no formula, no theory, not even a set of propositions so much as a framework by which to think about managerial effectiveness in context. As shown in Figure 6.1, at the center are five "threads," to use

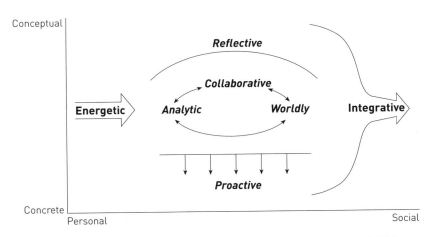

Figure 6.1 A FRAMEWORK TO CONSIDER MANAGERIAL EFFECTIVENESS IN CONTEXT

Lewis et al.'s word, or "managerial mindsets" as we call them, ranging from the more personal to the more social—labeled reflective, analytic, worldly, collaborative, and proactive. (See Gosling and Mintzberg 2003 and Mintzberg 2004b: Chapter 11. These mindsets have been used to organize the modules of our International Master's in Practicing Management [www.impm.org], as will be seen later.) Two additional threads are shown: at one end, that of being personally energetic; at the other, that of being socially integrative.

This may seem like my own short list of managerial qualities, but it goes beyond the lists discussed earlier in two ways. First, these threads are rooted more in the practice of managing rather than in the nature of the person practicing it. They were derived from the roles managers perform, as discussed in Chapter 3. For example, the analytic thread corresponds to the role of controlling on the information plane, the collaborative thread to the roles of leading and linking on the people plane, and the proactive thread to the roles of doing and dealing on the action plane.

Second, this is a framework rather than a list, in that its threads weave together. Personal energy on the left drives the five mindsets, and social integration on the right brings them together. Within the mindsets themselves, reflection above, in the abstract, and proaction below, on the ground, frame the exercise of analysis, worldliness, and collaboration.

Each thread is discussed in turn, although it is important to note that they have to be considered together, as guidelines to think about managerial effectiveness. Here, too, Lewis et al. explain it well:

> We found no single quality that optimally functioning families demonstrated and that less fortunate families somehow missed. . . . It was [the presence and interrelationship of a number of variables] that accounted for the impressive differences in style and patterning among the optimal families. . . . Health at the level of family was not a single thread . . . competence must be considered as a tapestry. (pp. 205–206)

The discussion of these threads serves also to bring together some of the key points that have come out throughout this book.

The Energetic Thread

"Although [effective] families differ in the degree of energy displayed, they all demonstrated more constructive reaching out than did patently dysfunctional families" (Lewis et al. 1976:208–209). Effective managers likewise differ in the energy they display, as do the units they manage, but we can likely expect a high degree of energy from both, and certainly a good deal of "reaching out."

If one thing is evident about the hectic pace, the orientation to action, the variety and fragmentation of the activities of managing, it is the enormous amount of energy that effective managers bring to their work. This is no job for the lazy.

Energy is a largely personal thread in our tapestry (perhaps it is the loom), anchoring one end of our framework. Of course nothing in management is ever wholly personal. As Peter Brook, legendary director of the Royal Shakespeare Company, wrote in his book *The Empty Space* (1968), the audience energizes the actor as much as the actor energizes the audience.

This thread may help us understand how managers deal with two of the conundrums. The Quandary of Connecting asks how managers can keep informed when they are fundamentally removed; the Riddle of Change asks how they can drive change while maintaining stability. This kind of energy is necessary to connect, to change, and to maintain stability.

The Reflective Thread

"In approaching problems within the family, [the healthy ones] explored numerous options; if one approach did not work, they backed off and tried another. This was in contrast to many dysfunctional families in which a dogged perseverance with a single approach was noted" (Lewis et al. 1976:208). This sounds much like the reflectiveness discussed in Chapter 5. My own observations suggest that **a remarkable number of effective managers are reflective: they know how to learn from their own experience; they explore numerous options; and they back off when one doesn't work, to try another.**

To be reflective also suggests a certain humbleness, not only about what managers know, or think they know, but also about what they don't. That is why I have been so critical of heroic management in this book.

As I discussed in *Managers Not MBAs*, reflecting means "wondering, probing, analyzing, synthesizing, connecting—'to ponder carefully and persistently [the] meaning [of an experience] to the self'" (Mintzberg 2004b:254, quoting Daudelin 1996:41). In Latin, *to reflect* "means to refold, which suggests that attention be turned inward so that it can then turn outward, to see a familiar thing in a different way" (p. 301; this metaphor is from Jonathan Gosling). Reflecting goes beyond sheer intelligence, to a deeper wisdom that enables managers to see insightfully—inside issues, beyond the usual perceptions. **Effective managers think for themselves.** (See the accompanying box on "The Best Management Book Ever.")

The Best Management Book Ever

In a family of novel programs that we have created, which focus on practicing managers learning from their own experience (to be discussed later in this chapter), each day begins with what we call "morning reflections," in three stages.

First, each manager writes quietly in his or her "Insight Book"—an empty book except for the person's name on it—about whatever seems relevant to his or her learning: ideas, thoughts overnight, concerns about a comment made on the previous day, and so on. After about ten minutes, the managers—sitting in small groups at round tables—share their insights for another fifteen minutes or so. Then it is into plenary, sometimes in a big circle, to draw out the best of the insights from the tables. This last stage is scheduled for about twenty minutes, but it often runs for over an hour. We let it go because this is the glue that bonds much of the learning together, across the entire program.

Lufthansa has sent teams of managers to one of these programs, our International Masters in Practicing Management (www.impm.org), from its inception in 1996. Each year it holds a meeting in-house, where its graduates welcome the new participants. One year Silke Lenhardt, an early graduate, held up her Insight Book and announced: "This is the best management book I ever read!" Shouldn't all managers' best management book be the one they have written from their own experience?

As noted repeatedly, much managing is hectic—"one damn thing after another." As a consequence, many managers desperately need to step back and reflect quietly on their own experience. As Saul Alinsky was quoted in Chapter 5, people cannot get the meaning of their experiences without reflection.

Reflection can be an effective antidote to a number of the conundrums: the Clutch of Confidence, the Predicament of Planning, the

Syndrome of Superficiality, the Quandary of Connecting. **Effective managers figure out how to be reflectively thoughtful in a job that naturally discourages it.** In a job that rarely allows managers uninterrupted time on complex issues, reflective managers attend to such issues intermittently and incrementally, giving themselves time to learn as they proceed. As H. Edward Wrapp put it, they "muddle with a purpose" (1967:95; see also Sayles 1964:259).

Table 6.2 reprints a set of self-study questions adapted from my earlier book on managerial work. Some of these questions may seem simple, even rhetorical, but they can help stimulate reflection. (One manager wrote to me that he "tries to re-read [the questions] every few days. Each time I seem to find a new idea to apply.")

The Analytic Thread

In discussing the art-craft-science triangle in Chapter 4, I made the point that while there has been no shortage of managers who have overemphasized the analytic dimension, inadequate attention to it can lead to a disorganized style of managing. And this brings us back to the Enigma of Order: how can the disorderliness of managing produce the necessary order for the unit being managed? **Looking for the key to effective managing in the light of analysis may be misguided, but expecting to find it in the obscurity of intuition makes no more sense.** Once again, what makes sense is a certain balance: recognizing that managing requires attention to the two fundamental ways of knowing introduced earlier, one formal and explicit, the other informal and tacit. That is why the terms "calculated chaos" and "controlled disorder" apply so well to managerial work. Interestingly, in much the same way, Lewis et al. described the most dysfunctional families as presenting "chaotic structures" and the midrange families "rigid structures," while the "most competent families presented flexible structures" (p. 209).

What does analytic mean in light of this need to be flexible? Several words can apply. One already suggested is to be *orderly*, at least in helping bring order to those who need it. Another is to be *logical*—to be clear and articulate—although *judgment*, as used later in this chapter, is probably a better word. Finally, Wrapp has described the effective manager as "skilled as an analyst, but even more talented as a *conceptualizer*" (1967:96, italics added).

The danger of overreliance on analysis came out especially in two of the conundrums: the Labyrinth of Decomposition, where so much

Table 6.2 SELF-STUDY QUESTIONS FOR MANAGERS

1. Where do I get my information, and how? Can I make greater use of my contacts? How can I get others to provide me with the information I need? Do I have sufficiently powerful mental models of those things I must understand?

2. What information do I disseminate? How can I get more information to others so they can make better decisions?

3. Do I tend to act before the information is in? Or do I wait so long for all the information that opportunities pass me by?

4. What pace of change am I asking my unit to tolerate? Is this balanced with the needed stability?

5. Am I sufficiently well informed to pass judgment on the proposals submitted to me? Can I leave final authorization for more of these proposals to others?

6. What are my intentions for my unit? Should I make them more explicit to guide better the decisions of others? Or do I need flexibility to change them at will?

7. Am I sufficiently sensitive to the influence of my actions, and my managerial style in general? Do I find an appropriate balance between encouragement and pressure? Do I stifle initiative?

8. Do I spend too much time, or too little, maintaining my external relationships? Are there certain people whom I should get to know better?

9. In scheduling, am I just reacting to the pressures of the moment? Do I find the appropriate mix of activities, or do I overconcentrate on what I find interesting? Am I more efficient with particular kinds of work at special times of the day or week?

10. Do I overwork? What effect does my workload have on my efficiency and my family? Should I force myself to take breaks or reduce the pace of my activity?

11. Am I too superficial in what I do? Can I really shift moods as quickly and frequently as my schedule requires? Should I decrease the amount of fragmentation and interruption?

12. Am I a slave to the action and excitement of my job, so that I am no longer able to concentrate on issues? Should I spend more time reading and probing deeply into certain issues?

13. Do I use the different media appropriately? Do I know how to make the most of written communication and e-mail? Am I a prisoner of the pace of e-mail? Do I rely excessively on face-to-face communication, thereby putting all but a few of my reports at an informational disadvantage? Do I spend enough time observing activities firsthand?

14. Do my obligations consume all my time? How can I free myself from them to ensure that I am taking the unit where I want it to go? How can I turn my obligations to my advantage?

Source: Adapted from Mintzberg (1973:175–177)

surrounding the manager is chopped into nice, neat, artificial categories; and the Mysteries of Measuring, where managers have to deal with that soft underbelly of hard data. As I noted in *The Rise and Fall of Strategic Planning* (1994b:386–387), there exists in organizations a "formalization

edge," over which managers can easily fall. Too much analysis or formalization and the essence of an issue can be lost. Read, for example, those
easy prescriptions about leadership and all those documents abut goals,
missions, visions, plans, and on and on.

So while Skinner and Sasser (1997) in their *Harvard Business Review* article may have had good reason to claim that effective managers
"employ the practice of analysis with great effect" and "use analytic tools
with . . . discipline and consistency," when they concluded that effective
managers are "above all else analyzers" (pp. 148, 143), in my opinion
they were just plain wrong. An overemphasis on analysis in managing has
driven out too much judgment in organizations, in the processes breeding
a good deal of dysfunction.

The Worldly Thread

"There is another complex family variable that involves respect for one's
own world view as well as that of others" (Lewis et al. 1976:207).

**We hear a great deal these days about managers having to be
global; it is far more important that they be *worldly*.** To be global
implies a certain homogeneity. The word suggests conformity, "everyone
subscribing to the same set of beliefs, style, and values. Forget your background, your origins, your roots; become modern, contemporary, part of
the emerging 'globe'" (Mintzberg and Moore 2006). Is this what we want
from our managers? It seems to me that we have too much of it already.

Reflectiveness was described earlier as very much the opposite: to
think for oneself. What may best promote this, and bring the judgment so
desperately needed back into managing, is a certain worldliness.

Worldly is identified in the *Pocket Oxford Dictionary* as "experienced
in life, sophisticated, practical." An interesting mixture of words. And
perhaps as close as a set of words can get to what many of us want from
our managers, as true leaders.

All managers function on a set of edges between their own world
and those of other people. To be worldly means to get over these edges
from time to time, into those worlds—other cultures, other organizations, other functions in their own organization, above all the thinking
of other people—so as to understand their own world more deeply. To
paraphrase a line by T. S. Eliot that has been overused for good reason,
managers should be exploring ceaselessly in order to return home and
know the place for the first time. That is the worldly mindset.

"How can you possibly drive in this traffic?" asked an American
manager of an Indian professor after she had just arrived in Bangalore to

attend the module of our IMPM program on the worldly mindset. "I just join the flow," he replied. Worldly learning had begun! There is a logic to other people's worlds—order to what may seem to us like chaos. Understand it and you will be a better manager—and more of a human being.

To appreciate other people's worlds does not mean to invade their privacy or "mind-read" them, which can be condescending. Lewis et al. found these to be "destructive characteristics," seen only in "the most severely dysfunctional families" (p. 213). In the less healthy families, they found pressures for conformity, similar to those of globalization in business. In place of these, the healthy families exhibited a characteristic they called "respectful negotiation":

> Because separateness with closeness was the family norm, differences were tolerated and conflicts were approached through negotiation, which respected the rights of others to feel, perceive, and respond differently. There was no tidal pull toward a family oneness that obliterates individual distinctions. (p. 211)

If analysis is closer to science on our triangle, then worldliness is closer to craft, rooted in tangible experience and tacit knowledge. So it is shown to the right on Figure 6.1, while analysis—based on explicit knowledge—is shown to the left, where science appeared on the triangle.

One theme that was evident in all the conundrums discussed in Chapter 5, especially the Ambiguity of Acting (how to act decisively in a complicated, nuanced world), is the need for managers to have a sense of nuance. Worldly managers who come to know their own place for the first time because they have gained insight into other places may best be able to deal with the conundrums.

The Collaborative Thread

"The trend toward an egalitarian marriage was in striking contrast to both the more distant (and disappointing) marriages of the adequate families and the marital pattern of dominance and submission that so often was seen in dysfunctional families" (Lewis et al. 1976:210).

As we move along our tapestry, the collective or social aspects of managing become more prominent. Collaboration, of course, takes us to managing the relationships with other people, in the unit and beyond.

Hiro Itami, who initially directed the IMPM module held in Japan on the collaborative mindset, told the participating managers: "Management is not to control people. Rather it is to let them collaborate." Hence, he positioned the module as "managing human networks." Kaz Mishina, who directed that module subsequently, expressed it as "leadership in the background"—namely, "letting as many ordinary people as possible lead" (in Mintzberg 2004:308).

Collaboration is not about "motivating" or "empowering" people in the unit, because as noted earlier that may just reinforce the manager's authority. It is rather about helping them, and others outside the unit, work together, in the spirit of the Lewis et al. quotation.

In the "engaging" style of managing introduced in Chapter 4, the manager engages him- or herself in order to engage others, as described in Table 6.3. There is a sense of respecting, trusting, caring, and inspiring, not to mention listening. These are the words that struck me repeatedly in my days with many of the twenty-nine managers, including Fabienne Lavoie in the nursing ward, Stephen Omollo in the refugee camps, John Cleghorn in the bank branches, and Catherine Joint-Dieterle in the museum. To draw further from the Lewis et al. book, "Healthy families were open in the expression of affect. The prevailing mood was one of warmth, and caring. There was a well developed capacity for empathy" (p. 214). **Managing seems to work especially well when it helps to bring out the energy that exists naturally within people.**

It is important to appreciate that there is nothing especially magical about this thread, no great characteristic of leadership. Like the other threads, it is perfectly natural, much as is living in a family that functions effectively.

Collaboration also extends beyond the unit, to other managers of the organization and other people outside it. Sometimes these relationships are formalized—after all, we use the word *collaboration* for joint ventures and alliances—but often they are informal, as in the networking that all managers do.

Table 6.3 ENGAGING MANAGEMENT

- Managers are important to the extent that they help other people to be important.
- An organization is an interacting network, not a vertical hierarchy. Effective managers work throughout; they do not sit on top.
- Out of this network emerge strategies as engaged people solve little problems that can grow into big initiatives; implementation, so-called, also feeds formulation.
- To manage is to help bring out the positive energy that exists naturally within people. Managing thus means engaging, based on judgment, rooted in context.
- Leadership here is a sacred trust earned from the respect of others.

Source: Compiled from various sources; adapted from Mintzberg (2004:275)

As we discussed in "Managing beyond the Manager" in Chapter 4, the past century has seen a steady shift from managing as controlling to managing as engaging. We hear more and more about knowledge workers, contract work, networked and "learning" organizations, teams and task forces, while many "subordinates" have become colleagues and many suppliers have become partners. Accompanying this has been a steady devolution of power from managers to nonmanagers, with a corresponding shift in managerial styles toward convincing from controlling, linking from leading, inspiring from empowering. But these trends are not new. Mary Parker Follett wrote in 1920 that "the test of a foreman is not how good he is at bossing, but how little bossing he has to do."

Collaboration also offers a way to deal with some of the conundrums. In particular, delegation becomes less of a dilemma when a manager naturally inclined to collaborate keeps people in the unit well informed. And connecting becomes less of a quandary when managers who collaborate get better connected, and so became more informed.

The Proactive Thread

"There was little that was passive about healthy families. The family as a unit demonstrated high levels of initiative in responding to input" (Lewis et al. 1976:208–209).

All managerial activity, as noted several times and shown in Figure 6.1, is sandwiched between reflection in the abstract and action on the ground—that refl'action mentioned earlier. **Too much reflection and nothing gets done; too much action and things get done thoughtlessly.** So here we consider action on the ground, which encompasses the managerial roles of doing and dealing.

I have saved this for last among the five mindsets because while reflectiveness is largely personal, proactiveness is fundamentally social: there can be no managerial action without the involvement of other people. Managing is a social process. Managers who try to go it alone typically end up overcontrolling—issuing orders and deeming performance in the hope that authority will ensure compliance. This may work sometimes, but it hardly taps human potential, especially among thinking people.

I use the term *proactive* here rather than *active* to designate that this thread is about managers seizing the initiative: initiating action instead of just responding to what happens, taking steps to circumvent obstacles, seeing themselves in control.[10] As I noted earlier, especially in Chapter 4, **effective managers, no matter where in the hierarchy and how seemingly constrained, grab whatever degrees of freedom they can get and run vigorously with them.** To quote Isaac Bashevis Singer in what could be a motto for the effective manager: "We have to believe in free will; we've got no choice." An additional distinction of importance here comes from Mary Parker Follett: "The leader should have the spirit of adventure, but the spirit of adventure need not mean the temperament of the gambler. It should be the pioneer spirit which blazes new trails" (1920:80; see also Mintzberg 2009b).

Effective managers thus do not act like victims. They are "agents of change," not "targets of change" (Hill 2003:xiii). **They go with the flow** (like that traffic in Bangalore), **but they also make the flow** (as, of course, do those drivers in Bangalore). Managing is for people who relish the pace, the action, and the challenges, from wherever they come, and to wherever they can take them.

The most evident conundrum here is the Ambiguity of Acting: how to act decisively in a complicated, nuanced world? Being worldly can certainly help, as can being reflective—both of them in order to appreciate the nuances. So, too, can functioning in a way that encourages learning. The word *proactive* may evoke the image of driven change from the top down—decisive, deliberate, dramatic. But I suspect that a good deal of proactive managing works in precisely the opposite direction: it is experimental, incremental, emergent, and flows from the bottom up and the middle out. Senior managers need to facilitate the proactive changes of others at least as much as initiate their own changes.

And don't forget the Riddle of Change. Effective managers may drive change, but they also have to maintain stability, which can require just as much proactiveness, as we saw in those Red Cross refugee camps.

The Integrative Thread

Let me repeat, from the outset of this discussion, what may be Lewis et al.'s most important conclusion: "health at the level of family was not a single thread . . . competence must be considered as a tapestry" (p.

---

[10] Boyatzis (1982:71ff.) presented various findings on how this related to managerial effectiveness, most as might be expected. An exception was this: "Among entry level managers, average performers demonstrated significantly more [proactivity] than did superior and poor performers" (p. 73).

206). **Managing is a tapestry woven of the threads of reflection, analysis, worldliness, collaboration, and proactiveness, all of it infused with personal energy and bonded by social integration.**

In looking "at the essentials of leadership," Follett designated "of the greatest importance . . . the ability to grasp the total situation. . . . Out of a welter of facts, experience, desires, aims, the leader must find the unifying thread. He must see a whole, not a mere kaleidoscope of pieces," in order to "organize the experience of the group" (1920:168). Moreover, the manager "must see the evolving situation, the developing situation" (p. 169); in other words, **managing means integrating on the run.** Follett, writing long ago, referred to "he," but this applies not only to "she" but also to "they"—all sorts of people, working collaboratively, managers and nonmanagers alike.

But how to integrate? There is no easy answer, but Follett provided a lovely clue:

> In business we are always passing from one significant moment to another significant moment, and the leader's task is pre-eminently to understand the moment of passing. The leader sees one situation melting into another and has learned the mastery of that moment. (p. 170)

The mastery of that moment! Kaplan described court vision that enables "a basketball player breaking down court, to see the play developing and know[s] how to position himself in relation to" others (1986:10). Wayne Gretzky, the legendary hockey player, said it more simply: "I skate to where the puck is going to be."

Integrating requires mastering *across* moments, too. Managing is about achieving a *dynamic* balance, as has been stressed throughout this book: across the information, people, and action planes of managing, while blending the various roles; reconciling the concurrent needs for art, craft, and science; juggling many issues all the time, keeping most in the air while giving each a boost as it comes down.

The word *analysis* seems clear enough; the word *synthesis*, in contrast, is characterized by its very obscurity. What does it mean to achieve synthesis, and would we even know it when we see it?[11] **A key purpose**

---

[11] Synthesis is not a mere combination of the elements. For example, to be "cross-functional" in a company or an MBA program is still to be rooted in the functions.

of managing is to strive for synthesis, continuously, without ever reaching it, or even quite knowing how close one is.

It is through the interplay of reflecting and acting—our first and last mindsets—that managers strive for synthesis. As discussed in Chapter 5, managers not only work deductively, and cerebrally, from reflection to action—formulation to implementation, the conceptual to the concrete—as is so commonly described. They also work inductively, insightfully, from action to reflection, the concrete to the conceptual, as they learn from experience. Above all, as shown in Figure 6.2, they cycle back and forth between these two, passing those moments of mastery.

Don't assume, however, that because induction and deduction proceed iteratively, reflecting and acting are necessarily separate and sequential. To return to Karl Weick's point raised in Chapter 3, thinking is not disengaged from acting in managing, but is an intrinsic part of it: managers think *while* they act; "managerial activities can be done more or less thinkingly" (1982:19).

This discussion has focused mostly on integration by the manager him- or herself. But integration goes far beyond the individual manager, as discussed at the end of Chapter 4. **Harnessing the "collective mind" is one of the great challenges facing contemporary organizations**—for example. in crafting strategies and establishing culture and community.

Of course, no matter how many people craft a strategy, it may take one particularly integrative brain to draw that learning into some sort of strategic vision. We expect this to be a senior manager, but in fact anyone

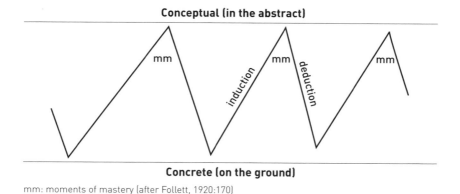

mm: moments of mastery (after Follett, 1920:170)

Figure 6.2 INTEGRATING THROUGH ITERATION

with a capacity for synthesis can be that visionary, sometimes even "the wisdom of crowds" (Surowiecki 2004).

The conundrums associated with integration seem once again to be rather obvious. The Labyrinth of Decomposition has been discussed here; the Predicament of Planning questions how a manager can think ahead—which also means to think integratively—in such a hectic job. Weick's notion of acting thinkingly offers help in this regard.

To conclude this discussion of healthily managed organizational families, it is worth repeating that these threads work only when they are woven into a coherent tapestry, whatever form that takes. There is no Holy Grail of managerial effectiveness.

SELECTING, ASSESSING, AND DEVELOPING EFFECTIVE MANAGERS

Managers as well as the people who work with them are generally concerned about how to select managers who will be effective, how to access whether they are actually being effective, and how they can be developed for greater effectiveness. The findings of this book are used to consider each of these in turn.

Selecting Effective Managers

This subject has received considerable attention, which does not need to be repeated here. I would just like to add a few thoughts of my own.

Choosing the Devil You Know   The perfect manager has yet to be born. If everyone's flaws come out sooner or later, then sooner is better. So **managers should be selected for their flaws as much as for their qualities.** The inclination has instead been to focus on people's qualities, sometimes a single one that blinds us to everything else. "Sally's a great networker" or "Joe's a visionary," especially if the failed predecessor was a lousy networker or devoid of strategic vision. No one should ever be selected for a managerial job without making every reasonable and ethical effort to identify his or her flaws—the devil in the candidate.

There is, by the way, one fatal flaw that is wholly common today, yet rather easy to ferret out. Any candidate for a chief executive position who insists on compensation far in excess of others in the company, and, worse, who insists on special protection in the event of failure or firing, should be rejected out of hand. After all, hasn't this candidate already pronounced on how important it will be to "build the team," treat "people as the company's greatest asset," take "the long view"? Imagine how instituting this would change the corporate landscape.

And then **these flaws should be carefully judged against the managerial job and situation in question**, to avoid surprises, especially from flaws that might later prove fatal. Since flaws are that in context only, performance in a previous managerial job may give no indication of a looming problem in the next one. Of course, figuring this out may be no easy matter: people's qualities are often misjudged, as are the criteria needed for success in a particular job. But there is a surprisingly simple yet rarely used way to mitigate this.

Voice to the Managed   Managing happens on the inside, within the unit (through the roles of controlling, leading, doing, and communicating), and on the outside, beyond the unit (through the roles of linking, dealing, and communicating). Yet it is usually people outside the unit who control the selection of its manager, whether that be the board in the choice of chief executive or senior managers in the case of junior ones. What sense does this make, especially when it is so much easier to impress outsiders, who have not had to live with the candidates on a daily basis? Charm may be one criterion for selection, but hardly the main one. As a consequence, too many organizations these days end up with managers who "kiss up and kick down"—overconfident, smooth-talking individuals who have never exhibited the most basic form of leadership (see Tsui 1984; also Luthans, Hodgetts, and Rosenkrantz 1988:66ff. and 160ff.).

If one simple prescription could improve the effectiveness of managing monumentally, it is giving voice in the selection processes to those people who know the candidates best—namely, the ones who have been managed by them. Some companies also have outside candidates' interviewed by members of the unit, to get their sense of the fit. This could be especially pertinent in the selection of chief executives, where blind optimism seems to be so prevalent.

Can people be trusted to assess candidates for the position of their own manager? There is no doubt about the possibility of bias. But is that worse than trusting inadequately informed outsiders? I am not calling here for the election of managers, only for a balanced assessment by insiders and outsiders together. Indeed, this is common practice in hospitals, universities, and law offices.

There is one famous company, for decades the leader in its field, whose chief executive is elected by a closed vote of its senior managers. I have asked many groups of businesspeople, all of whom know this company, to guess which it is. Rarely does anyone get it. The answer is McKinsey & Company, whose executive director is elected to a three-year term by a vote of the senior partners. This seems to have worked well for McKinsey. Has any McKinsey consultant ever proposed it to a client?

Considering an Outside Insider   There seems to be some tendency of late, at least for senior positions, to favor outsiders: the new broom that can sweep clean. Unfortunately, the sweeping may be done by the devil the selection committee does not know, while the sweeper may not know enough to distinguish the real dirt. So the danger arises, especially in this age of heroic leadership, that the new broom will sweep out the heart and soul of the enterprise. Perhaps we need a little more attention in selection processes to the devils we do know, because they know the dirt.

In fact, selection committees can get the fresh look of an outsider, unbeholden to the powers within, as well as the knowledge of an insider, by choosing both: someone who quit in disgust—an outside insider. Such a person knows the situation, voted with his or her feet against it, and so may be ideal to drive a turnaround: a new broom that knows the old dirt. Moreover, there will be insiders who can assess this person's qualities and flaws. Steve Jobs of Apple comes to mind here: he didn't quit in disgust—he was fired from the company he built. But he was able to come back and turn it around.

To return to a point near the introduction to this chapter, we make a great fuss about leadership these days But all too often we attribute leadership qualities to people we hardly know. Consider "young leaders"—to my mind an oxymoron. How can anyone be so designated before he or she has been tested in the crucible of experience? Who can know what flaws lurk below the surface? Indeed, this very designation can encourage hubris and thereby spoil what might have become real leadership. To repeat, leadership is a sacred trust earned from the respect of those people on the receiving end of it.

Assessing Managerial Effectiveness

You are a manager; you want to know how you are doing. Other people around you are even more intent on finding out how you are doing.

There are lots of easy ways to assess this. Beware of all of them. **The effectiveness of a manager can only be judged in context.** This proposition sounds easy enough, until you take it apart, which I shall do in eight subpropositions.

For starters, **(1) managers are not effective; matches are effective.** There is no such thing as a good husband or a good wife, only a good couple. And so it is with managers and their units.

There may be people who fail in all managerial jobs, but there are none who can succeed in all of them. That is because a flaw that can be tolerable in one situation—indeed, be a positive quality—can prove fatal in another. It all depends on the match between the person and the context, *at the time, for a time, so long as it lasts.* As concluded in Chapter 4, the effective manager is the one, not with the good style, but with the necessary style.[12] Thus, **(2) there are no effective managers in general**, which also means **(3) there is no such thing as a professional manager**—someone who can manage anything (see Watson 1994:220–221; Whitley 1989; Mintzberg 2004b).

Of course, managers and their units succeed and fail together. So **(4) to assess managerial effectiveness, you also have to assess the effectiveness of the unit.** The purpose of the manager is to ensure that the unit serves *its* basic purpose. As Andy Grove of Intel put it: "A manager's output = the output of his organization + the output of neighboring organizations under his influence" (1983:40; see also Whitley 1989:214).

This is a necessary condition for assessing managerial effectiveness, but it is not a sufficient one. **(5) A manager can be considered effective only to the extent that he or she has helped to make the**

---

[12] I have been quite critical of "heroic leaders" in this book, because I believe they pull down a lot of healthy organizations. Michael Maccoby (2004) called them "Narcissistic Leaders" and described them as "emotionally isolated and highly distrustful," even prone to "rage" (p. 94), plus "poor listeners who cannot tolerate dissent" (p. 97). That doesn't sound too good! "Yet narcissism can be extraordinarily useful—even necessary," Maccoby argued, because narcissists "have the audacity to push through the massive transformations that society periodically undertakes" (p. 94). Where I part company with Maccoby is in his claim that, "with the dramatic discontinuities going on in the world today, more and more large corporations are getting into bed with narcissists. They are finding that there is no substitute for narcissistic leaders in an age of innovation." I believe that the kind of narcissistic leadership we are getting now—self-serving and heroic, disconnected and deeming—is not encouraging real innovation. Maccoby does acknowledge what I find to be the pervasive problem today: "narcissistic leaders—even the most productive of them—can self-destruct and lead their organizations terribly astray" (p. 101). Perhaps what we have today is a narcissistic society. Maccoby does add that "a visionary born in the wrong time can seem like a pompous buffoon" (p. 101). So let's conclude that we need to be open to the advantages of this style but careful about its use.

unit more effective. Some units function well despite their managers, and others would function a lot worse if not for their managers. Beware of assuming that the manager is responsible for whatever succeeds or fails in the unit. History matters; culture matters; markets matter; weather matters. As for the manager, it is *personal impact* that matters, not unit or organizational performance per se.

This means that many of the numerical measures of performance (growth in sales, reductions in cost, etc.) tell us nothing directly about the manager's effectiveness. How many managers have succeeded simply by maneuvering themselves into favorable jobs, making sure they did not mess up, and then taking credit for the success (Hales 2001)?

Even if a manager can be shown to have influenced the unit for better or for worse, **(6) managerial effectiveness is always relative, not only to the situation inherited, but also in comparison with other possible people in that job** (Braybrooke 1964:542). What if someone turned down for the job would have done a lot better, perhaps because it was an easy job to do? Of course you can drive yourself crazy asking such questions. Who would ever know? But if you want to assess managerial effectiveness—truly do so—then you can't avoid this proposition any more than the others.

To further complete matters, **(7) managerial effectiveness also has to be assessed for broader impact, beyond the unit and even the organization.** What about the manager who makes the unit more effective at the expense of the broader organization? For example, the sales department sold great quantities of product, but manufacturing couldn't keep up, and so the company went into turmoil. But can you blame the sales manager? After all, he or she was only doing the job. Isn't general management responsible for these broader perspectives?

Viewed conventionally—which means bureaucratically—the answer is yes. In bureaucracies, all responsibilities are neatly apportioned. In the real world of managing, the partial answer is no. Organizations are flawed too; unexpected problems can arise anywhere and often have to be addressed wherever that is. No responsible manager can afford to put on blinders, doing the assigned job without looking left or right. A Charlie Zinkan or a Gord Irwin in the Canadian parks could not simply dismiss that fight between the developers and the environmentalists as the responsibility of the politicians. **A healthy organization is not a collection of detached human resources who simply look after their own turf; it is a community of responsible human beings who care about the entire system and its long-term survival** (Watson 1999:38).

But we cannot stop here. How about what is right for the organiza-tion being wrong for the world around it? Albert Speer was a brilliant manager, hugely effective in organizing armament production in Nazi Germany (Singer and Wooton 1976). After the war, the Allied forces put him in jail anyway. Speer might have been a lot more effective for the world, maybe also for the German people, had he been a lot less effec-tive in organizing his unit—or, better still, if he had chosen to manage something else.

We make a great fuss about holding managers responsible and accountable, but give not nearly enough attention to asking, responsible for what, accountable to whom? Imploring managers to be "socially responsible" is fine so long as we take it beyond the easy rhetoric, into the difficult conflicts that such behavior has to address. (For an illustration, see the write-up of Alan Whelan's day in the appendix.)

Some economists have an easy reply to this. Let each business look after its own business, and leave the social issues to government (Fried-man 1962, 1970). This is a neat distinction that keeps economic theory clean; unfortunately, it has made a mess of society.

Is there an economist prepared to argue that social decisions have no economic consequences? Not likely: everything costs something. Well, then, can any economist argue that there are economic decisions that have no social consequences? And what happens when managers ignore them, beyond remaining within the limits of the law? The Russian author Alek-sandr Solzhenitsyn, living in the United States at the time, had an answer:

> I have spent all my life under a communist regime, and I will tell you that a society without any objective legal scale is a terrible one indeed. But a society with no other scale but the legal one is not quite worthy of man either. A society that is based on the letter of the law and never reaches any higher is taking very scarce advantage of the high level of human possibilities. The letter of the law is too cold and formal to have a beneficial effect on society. Whenever the tissue of life is woven of legalistic relations, there is an atmosphere of moral mediocrity, paralyzing man's noblest impulses.[13]

Put together all these propositions, and you have to ask, How can anyone who needs to assess a manager possibly cope with all this? The

---

[13] See www.columbia.edu/cu/augustine/arch/solzhenitsyn/harvard1978.

answer here, too, is simple, *in principle*: use judgment. **(8) Managerial effectiveness has to be judged and not just measured.**

We can certainly get measures of effectiveness for some of these things, notably aspects of unit performance, at least in the short term. But how are we to measure the rest, and, in particular, where is the composite measure that answers the magic question? Watch someone like Fabienne Lavoie on the nursing ward for a few hours—or even, I suspect, a few months—and tell me how you are going to *measure* her effectiveness. Even in a hard-nosed business like banking, how will you measure the effectiveness of a John Cleghorn? Because the stock went up? (It did in those American banks that invested in the subprime mortgages.)

If you think that eight propositions to assess managerial effectiveness is a little excessive, not to mention academically detached, then think about the excessiveness and detachedness of the executive bonuses that ignored most of them. They relied on the simplest of measures, such as increases in the stock price in the relative short run. **Executive impact has to be assessed in the long run, and we don't know how to measure performance in the long run, at least as attributable to specific managers. So executive bonuses should be eliminated. Period.**

Where Has All the Judgment Gone?   Remember judgment? It's what used to lie beyond measurement, in the darkness—a key to managing effectively.

And then along came measurement in its dazzling light. It was fine, so long as it informed judgment. Sure, **measure what you can, but then be sure to judge the rest: don't be mesmerized by measurement. Unfortunately, we so often are, causing us to drive out judgment.**

In 1981, the Business Roundtable, a group of the chief executives of many of America's most prestigious corporations issued their "Statement on Corporate Responsibility."

> Balancing the shareholder's expectations of maximum return against other priorities is one of the fundamental problems confronting corporate management. The shareholder must receive a good return but the legitimate concerns of other constituencies (customers, employees, communities, suppliers and society at large) also must have the appropriate attention. . . . [Leading managers] believe that by giving enlightened consideration to balancing the legitimate claims of all its

constituents, a corporation will best serve the interest of its shareholders. (quoted in Mintzberg, Simons, and Basu 2002:71; since removed from the Business Roundtable site)

In 1997, the Business Roundtable issued another statement, entitled "Statement of Corporate Governance." This claimed that the paramount duty of management and of boards of directors is to the corporations' stockholders. It explained:

The notion that the board must somehow balance the interests of stockholders against the interests of other stakeholders fundamentally misconstrues the role of directors. It is, moreover, an unworkable notion because it would leave the board with no criteria for resolving conflicts between the interest of stockholders and of other stakeholders or among different groups of stakeholders. (www.businessroundtable.org)

No criteria indeed—besides judgment. Some time between 1981 and 1997, by their own account, this collection of America's most prominent corporate chief executives lost their capacity for judgment. If you want to understand what underlies the current economic crisis in America, which is really a crisis of management, here you have it, in a nutshell. (See "How Productivity Killed American Enterprise" on www.mintzberg.org.)

The message of this nonsense is that **to be effective in any managerial position, there is a need for thoughtfulness—not dogma, not greed risen to some high art, not fashionable technique, not me-too strategies, not all that "leadership" hype, just plain old judgment.** Some things are easier to measure than others, yet all but the simplest things have to get beyond the numbers.

Let's take an example right here. I write books and develop programs for managers. People sometimes ask me for measures of performance of the latter, at the limit: "How much will our share price rise if Joanne goes on your program?" I reply in terms of the former.

"Consider a book you read recently: can you quantify its costs?" Sure: so much money to purchase it, so many hours to read it. "Good. Now, please quantify the benefits. If you can do that—measure its impact on you—please let me know and I will do the same for the program." As a reader, you might be finding this book wonderful—4.9 on some 5-point scale or other—and never do anything with it. Or you may have hated every word—2.3 (some time to find this out)—yet use an idea from it a year from now without remembering its source.

Should people stop reading books because they can't measure their impact? Should they stop managing companies because they can never be sure of their long-term impact? Bear in mind that reading a book is a simple matter compared with practicing management. Stop reading books if you like, but you will not be able to get rid of management. The absence of reliable measures can certainly open the door to all sorts of games—such as phony excuses about why a manager failed, or claims of success in the light of failure—but pretending that measures are more reliable than they are can open the door to a worse set of games. And so let's bring back judgment, alongside measurement.

Developing Managers Effectively

So how should managers be developed? In 1996, we set out to rethink the world of management education and development, and as a consequence change how management is practiced—toward what is described in this book. We began in our own place, with "management" education in the business school. Some of us at McGill University in Montreal had serious reservations about MBA programs.

The conventional MBA is just that: it is about *business* administration. It does a fine job of teaching the business functions, but little to enhance the practice of managing. Indeed, by giving the impression that the students have learned management and are prepared for leadership, it encourages hubris. Moreover, it relies on learning from other people's experience, whether more directly in the discussion of cases, or less directly in the presentation of theory—the distillation of experience through research.

We teamed up with the colleagues from around the world[14] to create the International Master's in Practicing Management (www.impm.org). This set the groundwork for a series of initiatives that followed. Four are discussed briefly in the accompanying box, after laying out the premises that lie behind them. All of this can be thought of as *natural development*.

1. Managers, let alone leaders, cannot be created in a classroom. If management is a practice, then it cannot be taught as a

---

[14] At Lancaster University in England, Insead in France, the Indian Institute of Management at Bangalore, and a group of colleagues in Japan.

science or a profession. In fact, it cannot be taught at all.[15] MBA and other programs that claim to do so too often promote hubris instead, with destructive consequences. Some of the best managers/leaders have never spent a day in such a classroom, while no shortage of the worst sat there obediently for two years.[16]

2. Managing is learned on the job, enhanced by a variety of experiences and challenges.   No one gets to practice surgery or accounting without prior training in a classroom. In management, it has to be the opposite. As we have seen, the job is too nuanced, too intricate, too dynamic to be learned prior to practice. So the logical starting point is to ensure that managers get the best experience possible. As both Hill (2003:228) and McCall (1988) have pointed out, the first managerial assignment can be key, because that is when managers "are perhaps most open to experiences and learning the basics" (Hill, p. 288). Beyond that, the learning can be enhanced by a variety of challenging assignments[17] (McCall 1988; McCall et al. 1988), supported by mentors and peers (Hill, p. 227).

3. Development programs come in to help managers make meaning of their experience, by reflecting on it personally and with their colleagues.   The classroom is a wonderful place to enhance the comprehensions and competencies of people who are already practicing management, especially when it draws on their own natural experience.

It has been said of bacon and eggs that while the chicken is involved, the pig is committed. Management development has to be about commitment: to the job, the people, and the purpose, to be sure, but also to the organization, and beyond that, in a responsible way, to related communities in society.

---

[15] In a widely cited articled called "How Business Schools Lost Their Way," Bennis and O'Toole (2005) asked, "Why aren't there more scholars . . . who teach students to be generalists, to see the great connections?" The answer is because such things cannot be taught.

[16] See *Managers Not MBAs* (Mintzberg 2004b:1–194). Pages 114–119 report a study done by Joseph Lampel and me. We took a list of Harvard Business School superstars published in a book by a long-term insider in 1990, and tracked for over a decade the performance of the nineteen corporate chief executives on that list, many of them quite famous. Ten were outright failures (the company went bankrupt, the CEO was fired, a major merger backfired, etc.); another four had questionable records at best. Just five of the nineteen seemed to do fine.

[17] So long as they are substantial: taking into account the Syndrome of Superficiality, the current tendency in some companies of moving managers around every two years or so would seem to be dysfunctional.

As noted earlier, management development is about getting the meaning of experience, and that means busy managers have to slow down, step back, and reflect thoughtfully on their own experience. Accordingly, development should take place as managers go back and forth between the activities of their work and the reflections of a quieter place. This can be away at a formal program, or just getting away at work itself (e.g., an uninterrupted lunchtime). Either way, we have found that the key to this is small groups of managers sitting together at round tables and sharing experiences.

4. Intrinsic to this development should be the carrying of the learning back to the workplace, for impact on the organization.   A major problem with management development is that it usually happens in isolation. The manager is developed, perhaps even changed, only to return to an unchanged workplace. Management development should also be about organization development: teams of managers should be expected to drive change in their organization.

5. All of this needs to be organized according to the nature of managing itself—for example, in terms of the managerial mindsets. Most management education and much management development is organized around the business functions. This is fine for learning about business, but marketing + finance + accounting, etc., does not = management. Moreover, a focus on the business functions amounts to a focus on analysis. This is certainly an important mindset for managers, but only as one among others. Being the easiest one to teach should not make it the main one to learn. We have more than enough calculating managers already. We need ones who can deal with the calculated chaos of managing—its art and craft—which highlights the importance of reflection, worldliness, collaboration, and action.

All of this has been carried into a family of programs that we developed, described in the accompanying box. Linda Hill comments near the end of her book:

> This research suggests that new managers should see themselves as engaged in strenuous self-development. Their task is to learn how to capitalize on their on-the-job learning. This requires a commitment to continual learning, self-diagnosis, and self-management. The transition is daunting at best, and most organizations offer little support. (2003:234)

Development: From Management to Organization to Society to Self

In the mid-1990s, we begin to rethink the whole question of management education, which led to a family of new programs, four of which are described here.

IMPM: Adding Management Development to Management Education   We began in 1996 with the International Masters in Practicing Management (www.impm.org), designed to shift business education to management education, and combine it with management development. The IMPM was created to help managers *do* a better job in their own organization, not *get* a better job in another one.

The MBA is taught in terms of the business functions, such as marketing, finance, and human resource management. The IMPM has instead been built around the managerial mindsets, one module on each of reflection, analysis, worldliness, collaboration, and action, spread over sixteen months. These are held in England, Canada, India, Japan and Korea, and France. Practicing managers, sent by their organizations, preferably in teams, go back and forth between these modules and their work.

Sitting in small groups at round tables, the managers learn from each other through the sharing of reflections on their experience. Sometimes they engage in "competency sharing"—sharing experiences on how they practice certain competencies (such as networking, or reflecting in a busy job), to raise consciousness about their practice. They also do "managerial exchanges," pairing up to spend several days at each other's workplace, to enhance their worldliness.[18]

ALP: Combining Organization Development with Managerial Development   So-called Advanced Management Programs are often just short replicas of the conventional MBA: they use many of the same cases and much of the same theory, they are organized in terms of the business functions, and they seat managers in the same linear rows.

Our *Advanced* Leadership Program (www.alp-impm.com) has carried our learning from the IMPM further. Here companies contract for tables

---

[18] Spin-offs from this program, aside from those discussed here, include the McGill-HEC EMBA program, which follows much of this design and also has the participating managers work on business issues of concern to their organizations (www.emba/mcgillhec.ca), and EMBA Roundtables, where students from different EMBA programs around the world get together for a one-week IMPM-type experience (www.business-school.exeter.ac.uk/executive/roundtables).

instead of chairs; they send teams of six managers, each team charged with addressing a key issue in its company. In three modules of one week each, spread over six months, the teams work on one another's issues in a process we call "friendly consulting," designed for impact back home. Our experience is that managers get into this deeply, as consultants no less than as team members, to drive significant changes in their companies.

IMHL: Adding in Social Development   Our third program, the International Master's for Health Leadership (www.mcgill.ca/imhl), has been modeled after the IMPM, but for practicing managers, most with clinical backgrounds, from all aspects of health care and around the world.

This program uses the friendly consulting of the ALP, but has carried it into social development. Besides bringing in issues of concern to their work and their organization, managers in the class have been reaching out to broader health care concerns in their communities, using the class as a think tank to advance these issues. One group from Quebec, for example, arranged to make a presentation to a major public commission about conclusions they had reached on decentralizing public health services. The commissioners asked for more, and so were invited to join the class. A few weeks later they engaged in friendly consulting with the class members around the tables. Another group, from Uganda, replicated the classroom pedagogy back home in a conference for sixty health care managers from seven African countries.

Coaching Ourselves: Bringing It All to Self-Development   These earlier initiatives were carried to their natural conclusion by the Director of Engineering in a high-technology company. He needed to develop his own managers but had no budget. When he heard about what we were doing in these programs, he followed suit, on his own. The group met informally at lunch every week or two, to reflect on their experience, using some of the materials from our IMPM and ALP programs to stimulate their discussions. This continued for two years, with some of the members of the initial group creating groups of their own.

The success of this encouraged us to incorporate the initiative as www. CoachingOurselves.com, to enable groups of managers in other organizations to engage in such self-directed learning. They download various topics, such as "Dealing with the Pressures of Managing" or "Time for Dialogue," and work on them in informal sessions of about seventy-five minutes each. In the process, the groups bond into teams that enhance their sense of community and drive changes in their organization. Some organizations are now rolling this out throughout their middle management and are using it to promote transformation.

Not so daunting, it turns out, when managers realize, to repeat Hill's other words, that they can be agents of change and not just targets of change. The family of initiatives described here have been designed to do precisely what Hill calls for—to the point of managers taking responsibility for their own development.

To repeat, management is not going to be *taught* to anyone—not by any professor, not by any expert in development, not by any formal coach or even by a manager's own manager. Managers have to learn primarily through their own efforts. We have seen how this can be facilitated in a classroom, but we have also learned how much more powerful this can be when it happens spontaneously at work, as managers reflect on their experience, learn from each other, and together drive improvements in their organizations and societies. The message of our own experience is that **nothing is quite so powerful, or so natural, as engaged managers who are committed to developing themselves, their institutions, and their communities.**

MANAGING, NATURALLY

If management development can become more natural, then surely there is hope for management itself.

Which Species Is Out of Control?

As human beings, we presumably began in caves or the like, from which bands of us—communities, if you like—went out to hunt and gather, or else to fight those who were hunting and gathering in our place. We were probably organized much like geese are organized today: the strongest member took the lead and then ceded it as another became stronger. This did not mean that leadership, charisma, empowerment, management, and all the rest did not exist, only that they blended into social processes in a natural way. Luckily for them they lacked the benefit of thousands of books glorifying all this, and so they just got on with it.

We do have that benefit, and so all too often we don't get on with it. We are like that centipede quite, in the opening quotation of Chapter 5, who lay distracted in a ditch considering how to run.

Over the years, we became increasingly organized, and perhaps increasingly perverse as well. First, I suppose, came group leaders, who fought the enemies best, some of these leaders eventually turning around to intimidate their followers. Over the millennia, this evolved into chiefs, lords, priests, pharaohs, caesars, emperors, kings, queens, shoguns, czars, maharajahs, sheiks, sultans, viceroys, dictators, führers, prime ministers, and presidents, not to mention managers, directors, executives, bosses, oligarchs, CEOs, COOs, CFOs, and CLOs.

Shouldn't all these labels be telling us something—namely, that *we* are the species out of control? Earlier I mentioned the Banff National Park, where Gord Irwin mentioned a "bear jam: a traffic jam caused by a bear." One ambles down to the highway, and the tourists stop—some even get out of their cars to take pictures—while the truckers fume. In the parks, they refer to "managing the natural setting." But surely this is an oxymoron: that setting managed itself just fine for millennia without our "management." Now it has "bear management plans"!

Think about what management and leadership have become in the settings that are "natural" to us. We have taken something straightforward and made it convoluted, by putting "leaders" on pedestals, in the process undermining plain old management: by turning human beings into human resources; by fooling ourselves into believing that management is a profession and so pretending that we can create managers in a classroom; by developing bear management plans while we human beings fight with each other over our self-assumed right to "manage" the natural world.

If you really want to understand management, then you would do well to get down on the ground, where the elk graze in the towns and the truckers battle the tourists. Then maybe you can work "up" from there, to the abstractions of management that so mesmerize us—where people earn larger incomes ostensibly because their work is more important but perhaps really because they have to cope with that much more nonsense, no small measure of it imposed by their own formalized systems. Supposedly developed to deal with the complexities, perhaps all of this is really a conceptual smokescreen for a species out of control, alien to its own natural environment. The bears know full well that the real problem is "people jams."

Managing Naturally

Isn't it time to wake up to our humanity and get past our childish obsession with leadership? Can't we just be as sensible as bees in a hive? **What could be more natural than to see our organizations not as mystical hierarchies of authority so much as communities of**

engagement, where every member is respected and so returns that respect? (See "Rebuilding Companies as Communities," Mintzberg 2009c). Sure, we need people to coordinate some of our efforts, provide some sense of direction in complex social systems, and support those who just want to get useful work done. But these are managers who work with us, not rule us.

> Management is a very practical, down-to-earth activity. There are no profound truths about it to be discovered and there are no hidden secrets to be uncovered about how to do it. Management is a very simple activity which involves bringing together people and resources to produce goods or services. . . . The message is to lighten up a bit—be playful, agile and alert. (Watson 1994:215–216)

Richard Boyatzis of Case Western Reserve University has written, "There appears to be no images, metaphors, or models for management from natural life," and so "management is an unnatural act, or at least there is no guidance for being a manager" (1995:50). I have agreed from the outset that there is no guidance for being a manager, and certainly managing is an awful lot more complicated—intellectually and socially if not physically—than leading a pack of geese or emitting a chemical substance to hold together a beehive.

But I believe that managing is a perfectly natural act that we make unnatural by disconnecting it from its natural context, and then not seeing it for what it is.

If management and leadership are natural acts, then are we wasting our time trying to find, let alone create, great managers and leaders? Perhaps we should instead be appreciating that reasonably normal people, flawed but not fatally so in their positions, can simply get on with their managing and leading, and so be rather successful. To express this more forcefully, **to be a successful manager, let alone—dare I say—a great leader, maybe you don't have to be wonderful so much as more or less emotionally healthy and clearheaded.** That, at least, is what I saw in many of the twenty-nine managers I observed.

Sure, there are some rather different kinds of people—narcissists, for example—who succeed for a time, particularly under difficult circumstances. But show me one of these and I'll show you many others who failed miserably, while creating those difficult circumstances in the first place.

Imagine if we simply recognized good managers to be ordinary, natural leaders, in the right place, uncontaminated by MBA training and all that "leadership" hype. The man who put management on the map said simply, "No institution can possibly survive if it needs geniuses or supermen to manage it. It must be organized in such a way as to be able to get along under a leadership composed of average human beings" (Drucker 1946:26; see also Winnicott 1967, on the "the good-enough mother").

Consider that little boy in the Hans Christian Andersen story who announced that the emperor wore no clothes. He could have been proclaimed a great leader. Was he? Was he even particularly insightful? Or especially courageous? Maybe he just did the most natural thing of all, unlike all those people around him (including the emperor).

How to get to such natural leadership? As Peter Drucker noted, we can start by stopping to build organizations that are dependent on heroic leadership. No wonder we can't get past them: when one hero fails, we search frantically for another. Meanwhile, the organization—school, hospital, government, business—flounders. **By the excessive promotion of leadership, we demote everyone else. We create clusters of followers who have to be driven to perform, instead of leveraging the natural propensity of people to cooperate in communities. In this light, effective managing can be seen as engaging and engaged, connecting and connected, supporting and supported.**

We also make a great fuss about democracy in our societies, yet this also relies obsessively on leadership. In our organizations—where we spend so much of our time, with so much influence on the rest of our lives—we do not even have democracy, these days rarely even community. Mostly we have autocracy—and it is spilling into our governments, too.

So I like to believe that the subject of this book strikes at the heart of our lives today—our increasingly "organized" lives. We need to rethink management and organization, as well as leadership and communityship, by realizing how simple, natural, and healthy they all can be.

Eight Days of Managing

> OBSERVER: *Mr. R._____, we have discussed briefly this organization and the way it operated. Will you now please tell me what you do.*
>
> EXECUTIVE: *What I do?*
>
> OBSERVER: *Yes.*
>
> EXECUTIVE: *That's not easy.*
>
> OBSERVER: *Go ahead, anyway.*
>
> EXECUTIVE: *As president, I am naturally responsible for many things.*
>
> OBSERVER: *Yes, I realize that. But just what do you do?*
>
> EXECUTIVE: *Well, I must see that things go all right.*
>
> OBSERVER: *Can you give me an example?*
>
> EXECUTIVE: *I must see that our financial position is sound.*
>
> OBSERVER: *But just what do you do about it?*
>
> EXECUTIVE: *Now, that is hard to say.*
>
> OBSERVER: *Let's take another tack. What did you do yesterday?*
>
> (Shartle 1956:82)

As noted in the text, I observed twenty-nine different managers for a day each, writing this up in straight *descriptions* of what happened (as well as what was discussed) and conceptual *interpretations* of what I could make of these descriptions. This appendix presents the descriptions of eight of these days to anchor the use of this material in the book and to illustrate the rich and varied realities of managing. The descriptions of all twenty-nine days, as well as their conceptual interpretations, are available on www.mintzberg-managing.com, which is almost as long as the text of this book itself.

Before presenting the description of these eight days, a few words on the research behind them are in order.

Choosing the Managers to Study

I set out to vary the managers I studied, by sector, size of organization, level in the hierarchy, and location to some extent (as can be seen in Table 1.1 on p. 6). Within these criteria, I pursued the opportunities that became available to me. There are so many managers in such a wide variety of places that I made no pretense of developing a scientific sample, even if I could have figured out what that means. In any event, my intention was not to test any hypothesis or prove anything specific, so much as to gain insight into managing in its many varieties.[1]

In some cases, I approached people I knew: a banker in whose "chair" I sit at my university, a friend who ran a radio station, a relative who built up a retail chain, and so forth. In other cases, contacts helped line up managers to observe—at Greenpeace, in the National Health Service of England, in the government of Canada, and so on. I also wanted to get a sense of the people coming into our new master's program in practicing management, so I observed two of them before we began (one of whom never made it to the program, but that was compensated for by another I observed after he did the program, and then while I was at his refugee camps, another I met there and observed who later came into the program).

Did any of these personal relationships bias my observations or interpretations? With my intention of seeing managing as it is practiced, I think not. More likely I was biased by all the managers I observed, tending to look on the positive side of their practices.

Choosing the Day to Study

How to pick a typical day in the life of a manger? Forget it. For one thing, the observer may have no choice, having to settle for a day that suits two people's agendas, with no sensitive meetings or travel scheduled. In one case, for example, I wished to observe, in the Canadian Parks, a Regional Manager, a Park Manager who reported to her, and the Front Country

---

[1] My response to some comments about the sample, including the absence of Americans and the observations having taken place in the 1990s, are contained in footnote 10 in Chapter 1 and are discussed at greater length on the Web site.

Manager who reported to him. It made sense to do this on three consecu-
tive days. Where possible, however, I went over the schedule in advance
with the manager, or an assistant, to find a day that would expose me to a
reasonable variety of activities.

What is one day in the life of a manager? Not much, to be sure. Not
that one week is much more; even a year may be insufficient to get into
the mind of a strategist. That was not that I was after, nor did I set out
to describe in definitive terms the life of any of these managers. Again,
all I sought was a sense of their managing—a glimpse of some practice.
But as I hope you will agree, twenty-nine such glimpses add up to a good
deal of evidence about the practice of managing. And twenty-nine days
of managing is a good deal of time.

What I Did during the Day

Mostly I observed and wrote down what I saw, and how I saw it, as the
day unfolded. I was the fly on the wall, and off, as I followed the managers
around. This is not a very fancy research method, but it worked for the
purpose. (See Mintzberg 2005, for the shortcomings of fancy research
methods.) I did much the same thing in my first study of managerial
work, published in 1973, except that there I recorded rather precisely
times and various other factors, such as the media used and the contacts
made, in order to tabulate how managers allocated their time. In that
case, I observed five managers for a week each. (See Mintzberg 1973:
Appendix C, or Mintzberg 1970 for seven methods used to study managerial work.)

In many cases I went over the manager's agenda for a longer period
(a week or a month), to get a wider sense of the job and to identify common activities not present on the day of observation. In some cases, I did
this ahead of time with the assistant; in others, with the manager him- or
herself during pauses in the day (e.g., a lunch without any meeting, during local travel). I also used these and other pauses to ask questions, get
clarifications, probe into issues, and seek the manager's perceptions of his
or her job, and of managing in general. I had no list of questions; I just
went with what came up and seemed interesting—and this led to a good
deal of revealing discussion.

Did My Presence Influence What I Saw?   Of course it did. This was
not physics, but the Heisenberg principle applies just the same. Once
again, however, I was there for insight, not proof, so even those times

when my presence made a difference—rarely in any significant way, in my opinion—may not have interfered with my basic purpose.

Indeed, in one particular case, it helped. The assistant to John Cleghorn, CEO of the Royal Bank of Canada, set up the day well ahead of time, when the agenda was open, and arranged a mix of activities, to make it "typical." Hardly a typical day? The activities were typical, if not necessarily the combination. (But, as I note in Chapter 2, find me a day in which managerial activities follow some typical order.) In fact, I used this in my conceptual interpretation of John's day to probe into the very idea of what typical means in the work of a manager.

What I Did with the Data

As suggested earlier, I mused: I tried to use each day, however it came, as a means to consider, think, ponder, and dream about issues of managing.

During the day I took notes about all the events. In one case, that amounted to forty pages on a steno pad; many others were not much shorter. After the day, I wrote this up, in two ways, as noted at the outset. First, I described the day, chronologically, in as much detail as I could. Then I interpreted the day, or in some cases two or three days that naturally came together (as for those three managers in the Canadian parks), for what it or they revealed to me about managing. I put quite a bit of work into all this—mostly at least a week for each day of observation.

Above all, I let each day or group of days speak for itself, as clearly as I could allow this to happen. I found, for example, that plain old-fashioned management by exception may turn out to be very up-to-date in a chaotic world, and that the real politics of government may happen on the ground, where the truckers meet the tourists on a park highway, more than in the great debates of the capital. I was not after consistency, but insight, so each report came out in its own terms.

As noted, the reports on all twenty-nine days, including the conceptual interpretations, are available on www.mintzberg-managing.com. The general reader can probe into whatever days are of particular interest, while those students of the management process can use these as examples, or "cases," of what happens on managerial days, while researchers can use them as data for further research. As I read over the descriptions again, I realize how rich a database this can be—how much there is in here that I have not even begun to mine.

I have drawn on these descriptions and interpretations throughout this book to make and illustrate basic points about managing. In this appendix, I present only the descriptions of eight of the days, to give you a sense of managing itself, in many of its varieties, as well as a sense of my research.

Making the selection of these eight was not easy. Aside from a few of the early days of this research, whose descriptions were much shorter, I would have liked to include them all. But to keep the length of this appendix manageable, I selected in order to have different levels of managing, different sectors, different places, and different organizations in which managing takes place. Of course, I tried to include some of the most interesting of these days, by the setting as well as the events that occurred. Even so, some of you may find some of these minute-by-minute descriptions tiring at times (because that, too, is managing). I don't recommend reading through all this in one shot. But I do believe that many of you will be fascinated by the nature and variety of managing that these days reveal.

COVERT LEADERSHIP[2]

Bramwell Tovey, Conductor of the Winnipeg Symphony Orchestra (April 14, 1996)

Addressing the metaphor of the manager as orchestra conductor by observing a real orchestra conductor revealed all kinds of myths of managing—about control, leadership, structure, power, and hierarchy, not to mention the metaphor itself (as discussed in the text of this book).

When I heard Bramwell Tovey in an interview on CBC radio sounding very sensible and articulate, I wrote to ask if he would let me observe him for a day. He replied with enthusiasm (eight months later), and two years after that, the observation took place, followed by a public forum the next day that allowed the two of us to share our reflections on "The Music of Management," followed by an evening concert.

B ramwell picked me up at my hotel, and we drove the five minutes to the concert hall, where he was greeted with a big smile from the parking lot

---

[2] My article "Covert Leadership: Notes on Managing Professionals" in the *Harvard Business Review* (November–December 1998:146–147) presents some conclusions about this day.

attendant, reflecting the warmth he exuded throughout the day. We went into the administrative offices, which were empty and dark (although bustling a few minutes later), and down a corridor to a small windowless office at the end. "I don't actually work in this room," Bramwell said, referring to his preferred office at home.

Bramwell described his job as including the selection of the program, the choice of guest artists, the staffing of the orchestra and positioning of the players (within union constraints), and the rehearsing and conducting of the orchestra, as well as some fund-raising, marketing, and public relations.

The administrative and finance aspects of the orchestra, he explained, were handled by its Executive Director, Max Tapper, who comanaged the orchestra with Bramwell (officially titled Artistic Director). Their relationship, as Bramwell described it and as I saw it this day, seemed well balanced and constructive.

Max looked in at 9:05, commented about "Prince Charles in town for dinner" later in the month, and they discussed arrangements for a band. Max left soon after, and Bramwell continued to discuss his job. "The hard part," he said, "is the rehearsal process," not the performance. I mentioned something I had read about musicians being trained as soloists only to find themselves subordinated to the demands of a large orchestra, and he added, "You have to subordinate yourself to the composer. Being a player is just another kind of subordination."

Leadership, clearly a tricky business for Bramwell, was very much on his mind in our discussions. He pointed out the qualifications of many of the players (trained at Juilliard, Curtis, with doctorates, etc.) and expressed his discomfort at having to be a leader among ostensible equals. "I think of myself as a soccer coach who plays," referring to rehearsals as "the field of battle!" "There are moments when I have to exert my authority in a fairly robust fashion . . . although it always puzzles me why I have to." Perhaps most telling is how Bramwell summed up the whole issue of leadership: "We never talk about 'the relationship.'"

At 9:30, two women came in to discuss an evening event—the St. Boniface Hospital Awards Dinner. José Carreras, the famous tenor, was to fly in to receive an award, and Bramwell was being asked for help in making the arrangements. They discussed the layout of the hall and then the playing of three national anthems, for which Bramwell volunteered to arrange a string quartet and a choir. (He hummed a few notes of "The Stars and Stripes Forever," to which one of the women responded, "This is intimidating!")

About the music to be played, Bramwell was full of ideas and suggestions: "We should do an Andrew Lloyd Webber song called 'Friends for Life'; it would fit perfectly. . . . I could do an arrangement for you," and, on another point, "Oh, don't have canned music. Use your string quartet." After having gone through the whole sequence of events for the evening, Bramwell concluded with "Seems to me you've done everything just fine," and they laughed. "I'll talk to Tracy, I'll talk to Milly, I'll do it over the weekend, and I'll call you on Monday." They left at 9:47.

Kerry King, Bramwell's personal assistant, came in. They arranged sandwiches for lunch, since there was only a brief time between rehearsals, and discussed some scheduling. Then it was off to the rehearsal, through the office now busy with people, a number of whom greeted Bramwell. He introduced me to the Music Administrator and her assistant, "my left and right arms." We passed by the stage into what Bramwell called "my room," for changing, empty except for a couch and makeup table, plus a private bathroom. I retreated into the hall in front, taking my place in one of the 2,222 empty red velvet seats, while about seventy musicians chatted and tuned their instruments.

Bramwell arrived a few minutes later, greeting one person as he passed through. The tuning abated, except for some strings, and stopped as he mounted a high chair and took out his baton. "Good morning. I'd like to start with Hindemith," he said rather curtly, unlike his manner off the stage. (The piece was "Mathis der Maler," a symphony banned by the Nazis as subversive.)

The baton went up and seventy musicians instantly played as one. It was thrilling to see it all come together like that, so immediately—for a few seconds, at least: they were stopped just as quickly. And started and stopped again repeatedly. Anyone mesmerized with the power of management would have found his absolute control over the ensemble just as thrilling.

Bramwell conducted with great energy, and likewise performed with great affect, sounding out the notes—"ba ba," "po po pa pa pam"—as he called for changes of emphasis, accent, and so forth. Occasionally someone commented, and after about fifteen minutes, he stepped down, chatted with some of the viola players and checked their scores before continuing. The rehearsing continued, with his own comments throughout, sometimes directed at particular sections, sometimes at the whole orchestra, such as "Just give a little more B double flat— a little more crescendo." There were also occasional comments by the musicians and bits of discussion. On the whole, however, the conductor remained rather formal up there.

Bramwell had suggested that I get hold of some of the music ahead of time and listen to it, so that my ear would be attuned to it at the rehearsal. The Hindemith piece was one I had played several times at home, liking it no less as I got more used to it. But here, as the music played out and reached its climax in the empty hall, with the conductor standing up there, arms outstretched (but not theatrically), I was absolutely thrilled by it all—and not least by the beauty of Hindemith's music!

At 11:20, Bramwell announced a break of twenty-five minutes, and Max, who must have been listening in the wings, walked in. They chatted about schedules and various people, and then Bramwell retreated to his room, where we talked some more.

He can't socialize with the players at private parties, Bramwell said; there are just too many agendas. (He added that when he first took over the orchestra, at the request of the musicians, there had been hardly any personnel changes for years. He had to drop five players, which was obviously agonizing for him, and not easy, given the opposition of the powerful North American union, although its Winnipeg local supported his moves under the contract.)

Comments during rehearsals have to be directed at sections, rarely at individuals, he told me. Indeed, that was technically forbidden in certain union contracts (not Winnipeg's). But "two or three times a year, if someone doesn't get the overall message," it happened. Conducting had changed significantly since the days of the great autocrats, Bramwell said. (It should be added that this job is not very old, about a century and a half. Before that, usually one member of the orchestra simply assumed the role of "time beater" [Rubin 1974:45]. In Bramwell's view, that made for less harmony, although it provided other qualities. A symphony orchestra is obviously not a jazz quartet; with that many people, someone has to take the lead.)[3]

After more chatting in the hall, Bramwell was back in the chair in precisely twenty-five minutes (the break time specified by union contract, as was the rehearsal time overall). He announced, "Stravinsky!" ("The Fairy's Kiss: Divertimento"), and the rehearsing began again, more or less as before, but with fewer interruptions. (Bramwell said later that the beginning of the Hindemith piece is especially difficult.)

At one point something sounded awful. Everyone looked up, and Bramwell commented jokingly, as did someone else, and they continued. Later Bramwell said to the violinists in the back left, "A little more length on the top accent," and shortly after that, the concertmaster rose, turned around, and said, "You should not be able to hear anyone. I hear someone. It should be very soft and very fast."

They broke at 12:30 sharp, with "We'll be resuming this straight after lunch." But there was no lunch for Bramwell. He chatted with the concertmaster, and they were soon joined by Judith Forst, the opera soloist for the performances that were to take place the next two evenings. At 12:40, she and he went into another room, large and rather empty, except for a grand piano. He sat down and played while she rehearsed her two pieces, interspersed with discussion mostly about timing—pauses, pace, synchronization—so that Bramwell could conduct according to her preferences. They finished at 1:07 to Bramwell's "Fantastic!" and her "It's one of my favorite pieces!" and chatted for a while about people and some issues in music before Bramwell went straight into the 1:30 rehearsal. Here the two vocal pieces were repeated with the whole orchestra, pretty much straight through, with the musicians expressing their appreciation after each song by stomping their feet.

Another break followed at 2:25, with Kerry meeting Bramwell briefly to ask about scheduling. His wife and son were waiting to meet him in his room, where lunch was finally eaten, at least in part. Back at 3 o'clock, the orchestra

---

[3] Fellini did a film called *Prova d'Orchestra* in which the musicians fight the conductor, create chaos, and finally yield to him when they realize they need him to make beautiful music.

rehearsing continued, with one comment, about a half hour later, that stood out as unique during the day: "Come on guys—you're all asleep. You need to do this. It's not good enough." Later, Bramwell said that this made a huge difference. Otherwise, there would have been need for a "contrived eruption! If I had to do this all the time, it would be intrusive." Critical to all this was "gesture" and "covert leadership," Bramwell explained. The fear of censure by the conductor is very powerful: "Instruments are extensions of their souls!"

At 3:59, with a "Thanks, see you tomorrow," everyone was off. We headed back to his office, where Max dropped in to discuss various issues, including the party that evening, and at 4:30, the Toveys left for home, with me in tow, invited for tea.

There we had a chance to review his diary, to give me an idea of some of his other activities. These included, for example, seeing a player who was having difficulty with his contract, meeting someone who was to narrate "Peter and the Wolf," auditioning a violinist whose teacher wanted advice, giving a speech about Winnipeg as a cultural center in the twenty-first century, and spending seven hours listening to twenty-seven different trombonists in order to hire one.

At 7 P.M., we headed for the house of Mr. and Mrs. Bob Kozminski, the most generous supporters of the orchestra, who were hosting "The Maestro's Circle." Perhaps fifty people attended. There the "maestro" socialized with the orchestra's supporters, gave a short speech, and then entertained them at the piano while Judith Forst sang a light operatic piece.

MANAGING AS BLENDED CARE[4]

Fabienne Lavoie, Head Nurse, 4 Northwest, Jewish General Hospital (Montreal, February 24, 1993)

Everything hummed on this hospital ward as its manager blended a great deal of leading, communicating, and some linking (with little need for controlling), in short energetic bursts—all day long, on her feet.

"Through the control process, we can stop managers falling in love with their businesses," claimed the planning manager of a large British corporation (in Gould 1990). Fortunately, this person had no influence over Fabienne Lavoie, who was in love with her business—namely, nursing, her "passion not profession," as she put it. She ran 4 Northwest, a

___
[4] Published in another form by this title in the *Journal of Nursing Administration* (September 1994:29–36).

surgical unit (pre- and postoperative care) at Montreal's Jewish General Hospital.

Fabienne suggested that I come at 7:30 A.M., but she was already there when I arrived (she came in at 7:20). Around 5:10, she said she was tired and would leave soon, at which point we sat down and chatted about the day. When I left at 6, she said she was just going to review something with her assistant. The next day she told me that she left at 6:45, so she worked a total of 11½ hours on this day. But that was better than the previous day, she said, when a personal problem with a nurse kept her there until 7.

These long hours reflected her predispositions as well as her conscious choices. Thirty-one nurses who staffed the ward around the clock reported to her, as well as seven orderlies and three receptionists. Fabienne made a habit of arriving early to interact with the night shift nurses, and did the same thing with the evening shift nurses, who arrived at 3:30 P.M., saving her paperwork for after that.

Fabienne had some scheduled activity that day, but mostly she was present and seemed to pick up on what was happening around the station, filling in free time with administrative responsibilities such as the scheduling of nursing assignments. The pattern, pace, and style were evident from the moment I arrived. Fabienne stood in the middle of it all—she hovered—mostly inside the room, with people and activity swirling all around. It was hardly even possible to record all the interactions, because most, at least those in the early part of the day, lasted seconds—a comment here, a question there, a request behind. It all seemed to flow together, as questions on one side were converted to answers on the other— concerning staffing, medication for a particular patient, patient scheduling for operations and discharge, and so forth.

The room at this hour was filled mostly with nurses, their shifts overlapping, working intently, while the doctors came and went in shorter, more casual visits, to chat or get information (before or after their main work in the operating rooms). Coordination across all these groups was effected by Fabienne on the run, so to speak, with the pace energetic, to be sure, but not frenetic.

One minute Fabienne discussed a problem about a dressing with a surgeon; next minute she was putting through a patient's hospital card; then she rearranged her schedule board and looked in the pigeonholes for nurse information; after that she was out of the room to chat with someone in reception; then she went down the hall into a patient's room who "has fever," in between making several telephone calls to evening nurses to see if one could fill a staffing vacancy that day. She said, "I just want to grab Chantal" about giving some medication in 01D, and then a phone was handed to her for an outside call, and next she was chatting with a relative about special medication for a patient. All of this occurred in just a few minutes. As Fabienne put it with regard to herself, this place "needs someone who knows and can direct the traffic." Things went on more or less like this for half an hour, at which point the pace slowed (relatively).

As this happened—soon there were only five people in the room—Fabienne's movements seemed to widen a bit and to last somewhat longer. She went into the medication room to do some work there, sat down with a nurse to go over the psychological problems of a particular patient, gave advice to the receptionist who was "upset with S_____," asked a doctor if Mr. A "is still under your service," and then went to "say hello to a few patients," especially ones about to enter surgery. All the while, her style was straight, to the point, and warm without being soppy. Things happened quickly yet did not feel rushed.

At 8:30, the nurses assembled in a room—eventually nine in all—for their daily meeting, to review the different patients. This they did systematically, in turn, and rather holistically, with regard to condition, medication, particular problems, family situation, plans for discharge, and so on. Fabienne led the discussion (sometimes glancing at her own records), asking questions and occasionally giving advice, also volunteering help. ("I'll speak to her" [a patient], she said. "You speak Italian?!" asked the nurse. "Not perfect, but . . . !"). Each nurse had a sheet of paper on her lap and took the lead in discussing her own patients.[5] But there was a good deal of the sharing of information, with up to three nurses and sometimes Fabienne, too, frequently discussing a single patient.

At 9:10, the meeting ended, abruptly, with everyone leaving at once. Fabienne was supposed to attend the hospital's Pharmacy Committee meeting, as one of its nursing representatives, from 9 to 10:30, but it had been canceled, so she found herself with ninety unexpected free minutes. I was curious to see how she would fill them in. But they also seemed to pass quickly and naturally, partly by her joining the nurses at a coffee break, otherwise in all the usual happenings around the nursing station.

At 11, Fabienne slipped into the hospital's amphitheater for the "Nursing Rounds," a weekly presentation during which a nurse she knew well was discussing a new procedure. There were about fifty nurses or nursing administrators in attendance and one doctor. That ended at 11:30. After several other contacts on the floor, Fabienne did rounds with the Chief of Surgery as well as a resident and a medical student. This she did only with this chief, she said—he was a senior physician in the hospital, long used to this routine. That took about fifteen minutes, and then she turned to some paperwork in her office, explaining the budgeting procedures to me.

She did thirteen budgets a year and was responsible for costs in her unit, so that the pressures for cost control met patient care right here. She showed me procedures worked out by herself, including a form she designed and had printed, a modification of one of the hospital's major reporting forms to make it more suitable to her needs. She was also preparing a presentation for the next week's nursing rounds, on the impact of new government legislation on the hospital's nursing function.

---

[5] All the nurses I encountered that day were female, and all but one doctor were male.

I had to leave to attend a Medical Executive Committee meeting, which took me away for about three hours. Fabienne said that during this time things proceeded more or less as I had seen in the morning around the station, except that, at the request of an overwhelmed nurse, she agreed to arrange a discharge, including a call to the local community health center about home visits. She said she did this kind of thing very rarely—it was the first time in two months. After that, the day did continue in a similar fashion, with Fabienne later spending time with the nurse in charge of the evening shift to review the patients, while the nurses who were arriving listened in, on and off. The room began to fill up again, this time with more surgeons just out of the operating rooms, reaching sixteen people momentarily on two occasions.

Sometime after 4, that quieted down, and Fabienne turned to her paperwork (but this particular day, as it turned out, more to conversations with me about the work). Asked whom she had contact with outside the hospital (besides the community health center), she mentioned convalescent hospitals (also about patient discharge), patient families, Jewish aid groups, and the occasional student nurse and salesperson. But she referred to being "not crazy about the whole PR thing," describing a "good day" as one when she was not much drawn away from 4 Northwest.

I left about 6 o'clock, since Fabienne claimed she was about to leave, although she stayed for another forty-five minutes to review things with her assistant.

A "TYPICAL" DAY[6]

John E. Cleghorn, Chief Executive Officer of the Royal Bank of Canada (Montreal, August 12, 1997)

The chief executive of a large bank was surprisingly involved in the details, highly focused, and very people oriented. Feelings were blended with thinking throughout this day. Is this any way to oversee a large institution and develop its strategy? Probably yes.

John Cleghorn became CEO of the Royal Bank of Canada (RBC), Canada's largest, in 1994, having joined it in 1974. In the year of this study, the bank reported a record profit (for any company in Canadian history) of $1.7 billion. It had fifty-one thousand employees.

After two cancellations, the day was arranged the better part of a year in advance, with John's administrative assistant, Debbie McKibbon, who

---

[6] Published in different form as "A Day in the Life of John Cleghorn," *Decision* (Fall 1997:18–25).

tried to make it "typical." It was to be spent in Montreal, where the RBC maintained its official headquarters, although most of the central operations had been moved to Toronto years earlier.

John and I met at 9 A.M. at the entrance to an RBC branch inside a shopping center, near the city's center. This was one of twenty-one branches in the province of Quebec designated for full service (brokerage and trust as well as retail and business banking). John wanted to check out the signs at the front entrance, but when Bob Watson, the Area Manager, appeared, he entered the branch. He was introduced to all the managers awaiting him, and he broke away to introduce himself to the receptionist sitting nearby. "When was the last time this was renovated?" he asked someone, and after receiving an answer, he replied, "Well, I drop by, and I think it was Christmastime."

A tour began of the branch, with John asking many specific questions (e.g., about the door that had been installed to one office) and exhibiting a surprising knowledge of all sorts of details. Later he commented, "You know what looks bad—your logo, downstairs—buried. Every time I go by, I just about go nuts. Why don't you take it down?" to which Bob replied, "Redundant—it's gone!" John insisted on meeting everyone, asking many how long they had been with the bank. To a receptionist who replied seven years, he said, "It's important—you get to know the customers."

At 9:30, he and the several managers accompanying him headed upstairs, where they met the brokerage and trust people, who had been incorporated into the branch in an effort to gain synergies from recently acquired businesses. At 9:45, they and several others from the different services entered a small meeting room for a "roundtable" discussion on how things were progressing at the branch. They went around the table, with each person commenting and John again asking very specific questions. He was told about the problems of integrating the different business systems, about "sharing the numbers" among the group ("That's great!" he replied), and about job shadowing to learn about another person's work. John made some closing comments, and the meeting ended at 10:30, although he stayed to chat about some current events, including the pending acquisition of an insurance company.

We then got into Bob's car and headed to another branch, five minutes down the street. Bob asked, "Do you know Mrs. Brownlee?" an elderly customer, whom John did know. "I go once a month to pick up her bank book."

Almost as soon as he walked in, a woman came up to him. "Margo! How are you?" he asked her, explaining to me that she has been Branch Manager for ten years. Then he chatted with a teller of thirty-three years, after which John went upstairs to meet the people concerned with mutual funds, personal banking, and brokerage, followed by another "roundtable."

At 11:55 we headed downtown. John and I chatted about other days in his schedule, including the previous week with investors and clients in New York and a recent international monetary conference he attended in London. Then he mentioned that Debbie kept a detailed record of his time allocation, according to what was in his agenda plus what he told her about his weekend work. (I later consulted her and found that it showed 16 percent of his time spent with customers and field staff—nine percentage points below his own 25 percent target—12 percent at his desk, including at home, 18 percent on travel, 7 percent with the Group Office executives, 8 percent with the board and its committees, and so on. Forty-two percent of John's time was spent in Toronto, 14 percent in Montreal, 24 percent in the rest of Canada, and 20 percent abroad.)

From the car, John called Debbie to check in. "It's good to see it live," he said. "The enthusiasm is contagious." We arrived at noon at Montreal's most prominent office tower, Place Ville Marie, where the bank was officially headquartered, and entered the elegant forty-first floor reception facilities where John chatted informally with the dozen or so institutional investors who had been invited, before all sat down to lunch at 12:30.

Monique Leroux, General Manager for the Quebec Region, did much of the early briefing after John opened the discussion and later took questions, mostly about the integration of the different businesses.

As John got involved, he drew at times on the experiences of the morning—for example, recounting a story he had just heard about a receptionist who thought to refer a client to the brokerage upstairs, resulting in a $200,000 T-bill placement. He then reviewed a thirty-three page document that had been circulated here, with information on shareholding, performance, economic indicators, and the like.

Again, John was not rushed and took time to answer all the inquiries. Questions were raised about the bank's approach to global competition ("If we let foreigners come in, it's because they're doing a better job than we are"); about the pending life insurance acquisition ("because of a need for a mobile sales force"; "unimaginable a year ago"); about employee stock ownership (90 percent of employees owned stock; the CEO had to own at least three times his salary in stock, other senior executives, two). The meeting ended at 2:20.

From here, it was into his small office on the third floor, where John looked at the mail and made a few calls, including one to Don Wells, Executive Vice President in Charge of Strategic Investments, on a potential acquisition in the United States.

Just before 3, it was up to the tenth floor for a meeting with thirteen people on knowledge-based industries (KBI) in Quebec. "We set up a 'typical day,'" John said in reference to my presence, and added, "It's overdue that I spend some time with the commercial business side."

The manager of KBI began a formal presentation, about information technology companies, particularly in biotechnology and media and entertainment, and what the bank was doing in these areas. After discussion, the meeting ended at 3:45.

Five minutes later another meeting began in the same room, on strategies for Quebec business banking, with many of the same senior Quebec managers plus others from retail banking, finance and planning, and additional areas. Monique introduced the meeting, followed by a presentation and then questions from John.

Competition came up, in comments on competitors' virtual banks, which John said he was "watching very carefully." He referred to some of this as "educating the market," which he described as "good for us." The presentation ended at 4:40, which John described as "good . . . very clear," congratulating the presenter, jokingly, on "getting better: I notice you do not refer to the notes as often!"

After a short go-around on regional business markets, there began at 4:50 a presentation on personal financial services in Quebec. At one point there was a mention of FTEs (full-time equivalent employees), a term they thought John did not like. "No," he said, "it's the reference to 'bodies' I don't like. It's dehumanizing." The session ended at 5:40. "Excellent!" John said, and "One hour late." The reply was "John, we ran on your time." To Monique, he said, "It was overdue," and to me, "Thank you for giving me the excuse."

Then it was back to the office, looking at telephone messages, playing telephone tag with Don Wells, and walking over to chat with the Vice Chairman.

At this point, we had a chance to talk. "I don't think of it as a big company," John said. Asked about the question periods during the roundtables, he said, "Nobody can ask a question that upsets me." They might be asking it on the behalf of somebody. "Seventy-five to 80 percent of complaints are justified," he added. Concerning the afternoon sessions, John pointed out that Monique was new, and he wanted to see how she was doing—see her operating in what was to be her own milieu. I asked about the morning site visits, whether he also went to the problem places. He said he did, sometimes for longer periods of time. "It's amazing the patterns you get when you do so many." As for the afternoon, John said these kinds of meetings happened frequently.

At 7 o'clock, John's wife Pattie picked him up at the entrance to the building in their Subaru station wagon. As they dropped me off at my office, after John said "Thank you for the typical day," Pattie had the last word: "If it was a really typical day, something would have happened and he would have had to cancel his meetings and go somewhere else!"

SUSTAINING THE INSTITUTIONAL ENVIRONMENT[7]

Paul Gilding, Executive Director, Greenpeace International (Amsterdam, November 1, 1993)

A day each with the Executive Director (described here) and a Program Director of Greenpeace carries consideration of managerial work beyond the obvious doing, planning, thinking, and politicking,

---

[7] This report was published by this title in *Organizational Studies* (2000:71–94), coauthored with Frances Westley, who contributed especially to the conceptual interpretation.

to the question of how an institution intent on sustaining the physical environment can sustain itself.

Greenpeace needs no introduction. It is certainly the most visible and perhaps the most effective environmental NGO. It may also be the only truly "global" organization, since it has activities on all seven continents as well as on the high seas. In fact, Greenpeace is a multinational organization with a vengeance, experiencing in great degree the most common problems of such organizations: global versus local conflicts and broad mission interest that clash with more focused country concerns. Paul Gilding had become the Executive Director of Greenpeace International one year earlier, having previously headed up Greenpeace in Australia.

I arrived at 9 A.M., as arranged, to find Paul sitting at the table, beside his small desk, chatting with someone. "Criminal charges haven't been laid yet?" was the first thing I recorded, concerning news that a Greenpeace ship, out to protest oil drilling, had been seized by the Norwegian authorities. The other person soon left, and Steve, who had headed up Greenpeace in the United States before becoming Assistant Executive Director here, came in, at 9:10. They chatted about the "strategic plan," a reorganization, and whether this should go to the board. Becky, Paul's assistant, slipped in, listening to the conversation, and having been asked her opinion about the reorganization, she suggested the material be circulated to the directors.

At 9:13, there was a heavy knock at the door, and Mara came in, visiting on her way back to the Australian office from the Annual General Meeting (AGM) that had taken place in Crete the previous week. They gossiped a bit about the AGM, and Steve left while Paul asked Mara how she was doing, gave some advice on connecting with the international office and some information on a "mover and shaker," and requested information about someone in finance.

Mara left soon after, and Paul chatted with me for a few minutes. "I'm pushing for more 'hands-on'" activity, he said, citing the upcoming trip by Paul Hohnen (a director) to British Columbia for action on the clear-cutting of forests—to connect the analyses at headquarters to the actions in the field. The problem, as he saw it, was how to knit the system together without creating a big control structure at the center. He added, about structure, that he "used to be a boxes man" but now realized the key was in knitting people together in how they worked.

Then Becky came back in, and they discussed what they had to do that day. She conveyed the "good news" that the U.S. government had announced a ban on some substance. Paul said they had to call Richard, the head of the Communications Unit, stationed in London, right away.

Bouwe, the acting Finance Director, entered at 9:50 and talked about a good meeting he had had that morning with his people, to clear the air and open up communication in the unit. Bouwe discussed the complaints of the finance people—their "insecurity" and "underlying frustration"—and about the hand-over to a permanent Finance Director. Paul referred to the situation as "very tough," but told Bouwe, "I think you're handling it right" as he left at 10, commenting to me after that there had been some serious problems in finance.

Paul reminded Becky about the call to Richard. Asked if he would like to join someone lunching with an environment minister, Paul felt he had to concentrate his attention on the structural plan. He made another brief call, looked at the e-mail and then asked Becky again about the call to Richard, who said she missed him at home but that "he's desperate to speak with you." At 10:12, Paul tried Richard at work but had to leave a message. Then he worked on his PC, and wrote up some notes on a flip chart about what to do for the AGM next year. "Most of our job is to monitor what everyone else does," he said, adding, "I'm trying to avoid doing hands-on work myself." Another call came, informing Paul of a donation, and they discussed whether to "make it public."

At that point, Annelieke, the other Assistant Executive Director, opened the door and came in with a big pile of flip charts, as well as some cookies and apples. Paul hung up moments later, and Steve appeared, too. While they chatted, about a Danish documentary soon to be released that was critical of Greenpeace and how to react to it, Annelieke put up the charts, the first titled "Basic Planning Exercise," with the four of them (Becky included) assembling for the meeting (all, incidentally in their mid thirties, and all in jeans, but Paul with a dark blue shirt and bright tie).

Annelieke began explaining the charts, but Paul asked, "Before we start, what's the aim of the whole exercise?" "To have a work plan for the whole organization—who does what," Annelieke answered, and Paul then asked about the time frame and was told six to nine months. Annelieke continued to explain the nine charts she had put up on the wall, so that they could discuss what needed to be done in each (e.g., about "Fleet and Fundraising," "Political Structure") as a result of the strategic plan. "The discussion, however, revolved most evidently around organizational structure.

As they discussed the issue of planning, Paul commented, "We need to think through the strategic plan before implementation," and "We should have performance targets for the strategic plan." Then Annelieke listed on the board, "1. Objectives/mission; 2. Break down targets; 3. Communication," and they discussed how to proceed, with Annelieke taking the lead. "Are we brainstorming or just going through it systematically?" she asked at one point, clearly favoring the latter, while Steve favored the former. At one point, Annelieke said, "I think we should move on; we can discuss [Campaigns, the first chart] for two days, I'm sure. Resource Allocation [the second chart] . . ." she announced. So they discussed this, continuing to seek "action" programs.

Then the phone rang (it was 11:13), and Becky handed it over to Paul—it was Richard, finally. While the others continued with the charts, Paul and

Richard discussed the Danish documentary, Paul mostly listening, and commenting occasionally on who might be able to do what. Then they discussed the ship seizure by Norway and how to get the right press angle. The call ended after twenty-five minutes, at 11:38.

The conversation continued much as before, but it moved soon into a discussion of a conflict at the Crete meeting between the full-time Board Chair, Uta, in London, and Paul as the Executive Director in Amsterdam, and how to deal with it. Paul said he would give her a call. With an "OK" from Annelieke, they all rose, at 12:07, and soon left.

Then Paul put in the call to Uta, telling her what he was working on that week, including "prioritizing" things to get to the board. "I'm working on a draft [of the strategic plan, "to ensure a consistent line"], will get it to you later today, but it won't have details of the implementation. You should get it back to me by tomorrow at the latest." That call took six minutes.

Like everything at Greenpeace, it's a question of "personalities," Paul said, adding that the "problem is structure," stemming from "political decisions," to have a full-time Board Chair alongside an Executive Director. Concerning the relationship with Becky, Paul said they had started to work together three or four months ago (she had been with Greenpeace for several years), and that it had been working well for about a month now, "a flowing, chaotic relationship."

At 12:30, Paul called Uta again, about dealing with the Danish documentary: "I think you should do it," he said, adding later, "Honesty always works." Paul said after the brief conversation that normally he would do the external media interview, but he felt Uta had been around longer and knew Greenpeace better, also that it might be preferable for him to defer to her, given the tension.

Paul placed another call to Annelieke, while continuing to type (thanks to a headphone), asking about budgeting and a mission statement, and then Iris put her head in for Paul to sign a cash advance for Paul Hohnen's trip to Canada.

At 1:03, Ann de Wachter, the Chair of Greenpeace Australia, came in (she was Chair when Paul was Executive Director there), also on her way home from Crete, and they headed downstairs for lunch (in an environmentally friendly, freezing environment).

Ann briefed Paul on how things were going in Australia and New Zealand, mostly concerning people and personalities. She also handed him a proposal from an ex–board member in Australia who was about to parachute out of a balloon into the stratosphere and wanted Greenpeace's help, not necessarily financial. They also discussed the conflict between Paul and Uta and how Ann was trying to help in her discussions with Uta, which led these two into discussion about board activities in general. After Becky appeared with a gentle reminder that he had a meeting starting, they left the cafeteria at 2:05.

Paul joined the meeting in progress—Annelieke was talking—to review the AGM for those who had attended, eleven people in all. After her review, Steve took the chair and they went around the table to share impressions, with Paul commenting afterward.

That meeting ended at 3:07, and another meeting began in the same room with seven of the same people. Paul was discussing the "next steps" concerning the implementation of the strategic plan, especially with regard to structural redesign, when Ulrich, a director whose responsibilities included the Climate, Nuclear Industry, Disarmament, and Marine Services Units, intervened rather aggressively: "You have to make your choices soon, not wait to February or March. . . . People trust you, but you have a year—then you could be in trouble. . . . Don't misread support for you as support for your plan." He was referring to a number of related issues, including staff appointments that Paul had to make and the direction Greenpeace was headed with regard to the radicalness of its campaigns. Paul agreed but argued that the key was not to clarify structure but to do things. After more back and forth, the meeting ended at 3:50.

Afterward, Paul commented to me on the difficulties of managing an organization like Greenpeace. The people reject systems, yet without systems, the finances and other matters get messed up. So there is conflict between the activists and the systems people. If the activists run Greenpeace, they drive everybody crazy; but if the systems people run it, they drive everyone out! Paul felt the leader had to be someone who could do both. Plus there was the need for vision and professionalization of the work. He said he was appointed because Greenpeace was becoming slow and bureaucratic after not being organized enough. He referred to himself as an activist who could also be a bureaucrat—he liked structure and planning. But he had been backing off structure—realizing the need for loose structuring—and he was coming toward the same conclusion about planning, saying he was uncomfortable about the morning exercise but not quite against it yet.

Then Becky came in on scheduling matters, and Steve appeared, wanting "to discuss that meeting with you." Paul asked, "With or without Henry?" and since Steve had no problem with my presence, Paul said, "Then now." Steve was sympathetic but straight with Paul. He basically agreed with Ulrich, said there was "something real" in what he had said, that Paul did need to show decisiveness. Pointing to the charts on the wall from the morning meeting, he said, "In a sense, this stuff worries me." I asked if they thought it sped them up or slowed them down, and Steve said, "I was wondering what we were doing this morning; I suspect it slows us down," and Paul added, "But it helps me, too," providing a sense of "order and what has to be done."

Steve left at 4:15, and Paul went back to work on the memo from Uta and himself to the staff about the AGM, but complained to me that, as a joint memo, there was "no oomph to it." At 4:21, Paul called his wife to discuss Mara coming to dinner and Ann coming for drinks beforehand, and then turned back to his PC, as before typing like mad, fully concentrating between the interruptions, the next one from Becky about scheduling.

Then he went into his e-mail: about the seized ship in Norway, requests for follow-up on the strategic plan, a letter to be signed about an issue in Australia, four messages in a row about the Danish documentary (and later a fifth), two messages on the role of council chairs at the AGM, a note on a campaign victory concerning nuclear dumping, and a request about raising money in Japan.

At 4:56, Paul went out to see Pail Hohnen on the latter's "personal career development" and came back shortly after to find Steve and Annelieke back to continue their morning meeting.

"Can I say something?" Steve said. "I think we are confusing the establishment of the structure with this project [nodding to the planning sheets on the wall]. See what I'm saying?" Paul answered with a vague "Yeah," and Annelieke with an "I do," so Steve clarified: "People may have responsibility on projects, but that's not the structure." Paul argued for an interim structure that would offer people some security. At that point, ignoring the Heizenberg principle, I introduced the idea of the organigraph (showing the workflows in an organization [Mintzberg and Van der Hyden 1999, 2000]). Paul turned to an empty sheet on the flip chart and we began to develop one, with Paul commenting at one point, "What's gone wrong [referring to the conventional organigram] is that we have had this nice neat system," instead of a looser, more flexible one. When Mara opened the door at 5:30 and waved, that discussion and Paul's day ended.

Postscript   Six months later, Uta won the battle and Paul was gone as Executive Director of Greenpeace International. *Time* magazine wrote (on June 12, 1995:42) that the board "faulted [Paul Gilding] for moving too quickly on cooperation with business and government," characterizing this as a fight between the new "modernizers" and the old "confrontationalists." After pressure was brought to bear on the international board by some of the national offices, Uta Bellion resigned, and Paul's position was finally filled, after having been vacant for more than a year, by Thilo Bode, a "modernizer from the German office."[8]

MANAGING OUT OF THE MIDDLE

Alan Whelan, Sales Manager, Global Computing and Electronics Sector, BT (Bracknell, England, March 15, 1996)

A day of drama, with an insightful sales manager working out of the middle in various respects, concerned selling internally in order to sell externally.

---

[8] He wrote to me on August 27, 1996, describing my report on Paul as "fascinating to read but terrible to contemplate." He described his "challenge" as "how to transfer the job so that it is

As British Telecom became BT, in the process "downsizing" by almost a half (from 225,000 to 125,000 employees), it sought to expand its horizons, beyond both Britain and the provision of a simple telephone network. Alan Whelan's job was to lead a group he had created to sell complex communications systems to multinational companies in the computing and electronics sector.

We both arrived at Alan's office at 8:55, housed in a small building outside London. A meeting of Alan's Management Team was scheduled for the entire morning, to do the end-of-year review and discuss the plans for the next fiscal year.

As people began arriving, Alan turned to one. "We've got a problem. He won't sign off." "What? Again?" was the response.

The meeting was chaired by Alan S., who was to take over while Alan W. was away from work for the next two weeks.[9] Nine people sat around the table in a conference room, including Carol, Alan's secretary, and Peter, Alan's boss, all on the younger side, some established BT people, others new recruits. Alan himself had come in from ICL only eighteen months earlier.

The meeting began with Peter's report. "We'll start with the numbers," he said, and he put up a series of charts on sales figures, budgets, and year-end forecasts. They had done well, and there was hand stomping on the table to show it. Some specific contracts were discussed; concerns were expressed about some of the trends—cost increases, for example. A discussion ensued about "how to grow the business 20 percent." Peter put up a "Scorecard," with four items to measure: financial perspective, customer perspective— "we get into the woolly areas when we have to struggle"—organizational learning, and internal processes. There was plenty of general discussion and sharing, but when Peter left just after 10, the atmosphere relaxed a bit.

Alan S. put up a series of charts about mission, revenue, projections—the charts becoming heavier as the meeting became lighter. A list of key prospects then brought the discussion down to a more pragmatic level. Finally, Alan briefly summarized the discussion, expressing his views on the needs for the next year and then called a break at 11 o'clock.

Alan, still worried about that sign-off, went looking for Peter, whom he found eventually. "Any news?" No. They chatted about the meeting.

One month after joining the company in September 1994, Alan had been working on a huge contract, part of a bid to the Post Office for a major system

---

closer to political reality and therefore more exciting. I am not so concerned about the structure of the organization; my philosophy is to try to change behavior and to define objectives, and somehow the real structure will develop." Thilo Bode remained in office until 2001.

[9] Alan was going to the first class of our International Masters in Practicing Management (www.impm.org). I was observing him to get a sense of someone coming to the program.

to stop fraud associated with welfare benefits. One of Alan's clients was the main bidder, with BT as a subcontractor. BT called its part Project Dryden. Two other consortia had bid on the contract, one with another part of BT as a subcontractor. Alan estimated the entire contract to be in the £500 million range; BT's part, £100 million. Because of the size and unusual nature of the proposal, the BT's Group Finance Director had to sign off on it but was hesitant. They needed that approval quickly.

The meeting resumed at 11:10, with each participant presenting results, formal plans, and informal intentions for his or her own area (e.g., voice communication, data, and mobile). The level of discussion remained mostly rather general, with occasional reference to specific accounts, customers, and orders. Alan's involvement was more informational than directive, sometimes conveying vision (e.g., "In general, the more focused we can get on the account, the better—I prefer it"). There was a brief report by Elaine, representing marketing, a staff function, that was qualitative, on "Team Structure" and about people, followed by some closing comments by Alan, mostly praising the team's performance but also pointing out weaknesses in recruiting, public relations, and cautiousness on budgeting. The meeting ended just before 1 o'clock.

Alan shot straight up to Peter's office for some news, but he was not there, nor was Carol back at her office, so Alan checked his voice mail. A late afternoon meeting was scheduled with the client, and the first message was about possibly holding it there. Alan left a message with Richard, the Executive Director who looked after the client's account, asking for "Any update? . . . I desperately need it." Another attempt to reach Peter, this time on the phone, succeeded. "Any news?" Alan asked, and then listened for a while. His first comment was "Very dangerous." Then, "Why was he talking to [X], not you? . . . What time was this? . . . Oh, damn . . . I specifically asked [Y] if he needed any more briefing," and so on. At 1:14, Alan hung up, dismayed.

The sign-off had to happen this day, Alan told me; otherwise, the contractor would be left with only a week to find a replacement for BT. Peter had been to see the Chief Executive about it, whom they believed to be sympathetic, but since he had only recently joined the firm he was hesitant to intervene with the Group Financial Director. Alan was not sure how to proceed. While he wanted to wait as long as possible in the hope of getting the approval, he felt obligated to his customer, too. So the deadline was set in his mind for this day.

After several other calls, with no answer and a few minutes free before his next meeting, Alan began to describe to me his role and its impact on the larger BT, in rather strategic terms.

The days of the supplier push of services, to which clients simply subscribed, were long gone, he said. Now business clients wanted services that met their own specific needs. Power had moved to the consumer. Network services, like those of BT, were partial, while the client sought "end-to-end" services through a single agreement. There was thus a need for integrators to bring together data center, desktop, network, and other services, which required that different suppliers collaborate.

BT, with its "subscriber" past, was not used to this way of working, Alan said. It was still learning how to cope with intermediation, which to some people inside the company implied a lack of control. This uncertainty was exacerbated by regulatory constraints that allowed the clients to switch to other networks. Alan saw a role for himself as challenging this thinking—challenging, in effect, the traditional BT culture.

The early afternoon meeting was in fact to be a review about Project Dryden—what to be done if they got the contract. Four of them sat around a table in Alan's office, beginning just before 2 P.M. Alan explained who was to do what and then briefed them on the unfolding events. "So we're still in the lap of the gods, and I made it clear to everyone that today's the day."

Their discussion continued, interrupted by the occasional phone call, including one about the later meeting, which was arranged to be held in Alan's office after all. "I don't particularly want to go to the client if I'm not ready to give them an answer," he said. The meeting ended just before 3 o'clock.

At that point, we chatted briefly. I asked how typical it was for a Sales Manager like Alan to spend so much of a day on internal matters. "I create the environment to do business," he said, estimating that about 80 percent of his time was spent internally. Linking with outsiders was something he did less here than he did at ICL, except on the major projects (as in the one that was creating so much trouble this day).

Alan saw his job as involving individual creativity but a good dose of teamwork as well. He described the structure of his unit as a matrix, with some people having client responsibility and others project responsibility. He said he preferred not to emphasize the control side of his job.

From 3:05, a series of his people dropped in, one to discuss the contract for a new employee, which Alan read carefully and signed, another to mention some concerns about the Dryden contract. Alan said he was supposed to spend a half hour learning Windows 95 this day but that he would not get there. And then a call was placed to Peter: "Is no news good news?" No, he was told, no news was no news!

Fiona and Mike came in at 3:18 to discuss Dryden. Fiona had some new information suggesting that the lack of a sign-off was "not a show stopper." This was discussed, as well as what Fiona might do while Alan was away, but mostly there was a sense of limbo. At 3:31, the phone rang. Alan was informed that the Dryden meeting, to put together the client with someone from BT, due to start shortly, was canceled. Fiona and Mike left at 3:34.

Alan worked at his desk, between people dropping in, including one to receive an apology about how long his promotion had been taking, with Alan making some supportive comments.

At 4:07, Alan was informed that the BT fellow who was supposed to meet the client was at reception. Alan went to get him and they returned to his office, as Peter rang: "Just about to have a fifteen-minute meeting," he said, "then I'll come right down." With Fiona joining in, Alan briefed the fellow on the Dryden situation, and he in turn explained his "neutrality": he had been included in an earlier, unsuccessful BT bid for the work. They continued to discuss the issues until 4:33, interrupted by another call from Peter, who wanted to close the day with a half-hour meeting with Alan and Fiona.

Alan and Fiona then headed to Peter's office. The news was not good. The product line financial director had seen the Group Financial Director, without success. Peter suggested the decision might spill over to Monday.

Essentially the issue went to the heart of what the company was then struggling with: the existing BT, an institution that moved carefully in a massive, established industry, and the BT envisaged by people like Alan and Peter—leaner, quicker, more inclined to take risks to develop new markets. It was all coming down to this one contract, supported by one faction at the most senior management level and resisted by another.

"We're trying to find someone to make a decision," Alan pleaded, to which Peter replied, "We found someone to make a decision. We just don't like it!" "It's wrong," Alan said, but Peter said he didn't think the man would change his mind.

So there they sat on the horns of their dilemma. They could wait until Monday on the chance that the Group Finance Director would change his mind, or at least be convinced to. Or else they could inform the client that they were having trouble getting signed off but would keep trying, knowing that the client would have no choice but to arrange a backup subcontractor, in which case they might lose the contract, even if they did get the sign off.

Peter suggested they had to do "the right thing," and there was never any doubt that Alan felt he had to do just that. But first he had to agonize over the possibility of giving up what he had worked so hard to achieve: he had to rationalize the decision to himself.

Peter: "Do you think it's incumbent upon us to tell them something today?"

Alan (pensive throughout this discussion): "I won't want us to be the reason" they lost the contract.

Fiona: "They will have another deal [with a subcontractor] by Sunday night."

Gradually they were converging on the decision, having discussed first whether to make the call and now how to make it. The call was put in (it was by now 5 o'clock) and a message was left.

The atmosphere eased up. "All right," Peter asked, "do you know how to work it?" Alan was finally getting his Windows 95 lesson on his new computer, with "the least computer-literate person in the company teaching me!" Peter just then took another call, informing him that the Group Financial Director had been visited again, to no avail, and that another approach could be made on Monday. So now nothing could change before Monday.

With a "It is a far, far better thing I do . . . ," followed by "Oh, shit," Alan made his call. "Good afternoon. I'm trying to contact. . . ." His contact was still at the meeting that forced him to cancel the earlier meeting, so a message was left.

Fiona departed and Peter and Alan turned back to Windows 95. At 5:30 the machine was closed with "That's it, really." They discussed briefly a pay raise allocation, which Peter promised to sort out in Alan's absence.

At 5:43, Alan returned to his office, where a message told him how to reach the ICL person on his mobile phone, "to discuss the confirmation that you are really going to give us the supply you arranged with us. We really need to know by the end of today." Alan sat momentarily and then called the number, but only got voice mail. He left no message. "I don't want to go to the guy who works for him," preferring to speak to the man directly, Alan told me.

"So what do you think of a day in the life of a Sales Manager?" Alan asked me. "Well, if it's always like this, you don't get bored," I said. He agreed, reiterating the point, as he gathered his papers for his departure, that "very much like sales jobs, it's mostly internal."

Fiona stuck her head in to say good-bye. "It's all over," Alan told her as she left. Then Alan S. came in and they reviewed briefly what he had to do in Alan's absence—the pay raises, budget preparation for next year, and so forth. Alan S. asked, "Were you happy with today?" meaning the morning, and Alan said he "wants it to be more forward looking than backward looking. Rather than hearing things like 'work smarter', I want to hear ideas." After collecting the rest of his papers and trying the number again, Alan departed his office at 6:24.

Postscript   It was not "all over," not by a long shot. Alan reached the client that evening and conveyed his news. He persuaded the client not to seek an alternative partner, as he was confident the sign-off would be had on Monday. It was, and BT remained the partner for the final bid. That was successful, and the winning consortium was announced in the British House of Commons in May 1996. In July, Alan signed a supply contract for £100,000 with his client for Europe's largest ISDN (digital) network, and BT's largest single contract under Her Majesty's Government's Private Finance Initiative.

But it was still not over. The U.K. telecommunication regulator, OF-TEL, had announced ISDN price cuts from BT to take effect in September of that year. BT's competitors lodged many complaints, and in an unprecedented move, OFTEL withdrew BT's proposed price cuts. A few months later, Alan and his client terminated their contract by mutual consent. BT was now to supply this network through another intermediator, a competitive network operator.

LATERAL MANAGEMENT
(WITH A VENGEANCE)

Brian A. Adams, Director, Global Express,
Bombardier Aerospace (Montreal, March 8, 1996)

*This day took place in the realm of program management, concerning
the development of a new airplane, in a structure that could be
labeled "extended adhocracy." Management here was lateral instead of
hierarchical, to link and deal especially with partners in the program.*

With the acquisition of Canadair in Montreal, de Havilland in Toronto,
Lear Jet in the United States, and the Shorts Group in Northern Ireland,
the Bombardier Aerospace Group had become the third-largest manufacturer of civil aircraft in the world.

Brian Adams was responsible for the development of its new Global
Express airplane, including procurement and its complex relationships
with subcontractors, as well as with manufacturing, finance, and marketing. The airplane was designed to have the largest cabin and the longest
range of any corporate jet yet built.

After studying Quality Engineering, Brian joined Canadair as a
young man in 1980. The Global Express was conceived in early 1991;
in mid-1995, nine months before this day, Brain was put in charge of its
development because the head of the division felt the program needed
stronger management—a harder push.

B rian came to get me at 8:30 at the entrance to the building, a gigantic facility
in suburban Montreal. We headed for his office—small with a desk and a
meeting table. His job was to pull a vast group together, including not only the
four Bombardier producers but also Mitsubishi in Japan for the wing and center fuselage, Lucas in the United Kingdom for the electrical system, Honeywell
in the United States for avionics, a joint venture of BMW/Rolls-Royce for the
power plants, and eight other international partners.

Brian described his work as more liaison than authority, having to coordinate with peers. Yet ultimate authority rested with him: as expressed in a meeting
later in the day, "What we have to do is get a basic airplane in the air and go from
there." The date was set as September 1996. Brian said he had to watch over
the entire program and draw his immediate technical team (the "engineering
gurus") into the nontechnical issues. Each of these people currently had responsibility for one part of the aircraft, including liaison with the partner that was
designing and building it.

Brian was especially concerned about delays in the delivery of the engines. Gulfstream was ahead of Bombardier on a competing plane, a stretch version of an existing one, and so having that test flight in September was crucial—to show customers tangible results.

There were various brief telephone calls and people dropping in, about plans for a meeting and specifications for a "reduced vertical separation minimum," and so forth. Then Stephane, Brian's "right-hand man" (who would be with him much of this day), and just back from Toronto, came in to go over charts on the "dry-run corporate review." They discussed who had delivered, who was late, and what to emphasize in the presentation. Brian asked, "So, is there a way of doing the testing faster?" and Stephane replied, "There is a problem with one part: it blew up. We have to redesign it." Brian showed Stephane a letter, pointing to a list of "all the problems, all the problems!"

At 9:20 Brian took a short drive to the headquarters of the Aerospace Division, where he had a meeting with two of its senior financial people, on that dry run for the upcoming meeting with Bombardier's corporate committee, including the Chairman and President.

After discussing briefly some problems with space and small tensions with de Havilland in Toronto, they went into the finances, with Brian proposing who could present what at the meeting. As they wound down, Brian asked, "Anything shocking?" "Nothing" was the reply, as well as "We're on schedule, on budget!"

At 10 o'clock, it was downstairs and into the project offices, with many people milling about. A staff meeting had just broken up, and the next one was about to begin, at a long table with about a dozen people, including Brian and Stephane. A thick pile of papers, thirty-four pages in all, was circulated, full of detailed charts, graphs, and tables, concerning "Key Engineering Planning and Control Issues" on Global Express, "Week Ending March 21, 1996."

This was an informal group, a bit rambunctious, mostly engineers in their forties, continuously coming and going. They were obviously used to working with each other in this weekly meeting, held to coordinate the work of the different engineering teams. Here they reviewed different technical aspects of the project, some concerning specific parts of the airplane, in all cases to flag problems and ensure that the schedule was maintained. Specific people piped in on specific issues—for example, "Who needs to be there?" or "Does anyone here see the need for a mock-up of the floor panels?" Unlike everyone else, Brian sat back, away from the table. Mostly he listened; occasionally he became directive (e.g., "The priority is to get [a particular test] built as quickly as possible").

At one point, David, a participant, sitting in the back of the room, who had been quiet to this point (working on his PC, in fact), commented with some drama, "All the Gulfstream planes are on the ground. There is, right at this moment, not one engine flying . . . or ready to fly." (A Bombardier engineer stationed at the engine manufacturer had heard this in a pub and informed David the day before.) This suggested that not only was Gulfstream having a problem, but so, too, might Bombardier, since it was using the same engines, and the longer it took to supply the first ones to Gulfstream, the longer it could take to supply them to Bombardier. This hit the group hard. "What it amounts to," David added, "is that we have a disaster on our hands." Everything could be pushed back, he claimed, but he said he didn't know for how long.

They discussed the "need to monitor everything *now*" and to send a team over to the engine plant as soon as it would be allowed in. Someone made a comment about this "Black Friday."

It was now almost 12:30, and a secretary came in to announce that it was time to vacate the room for another meeting. The person in the chair reacted by locking the door after she left. The meeting did terminate soon after, at 12:43.

After a quick lunch, Brian, with Stephane, headed back to the other building, where at 1:30 he opened another meeting with about twenty people, including some from de Havilland, responsible in one way or another for the work that was to follow. Most were from production, some from promotion and marketing. (The only one in the room who reported to Brian was Stephane.) The specific intention was different from the earlier meeting (here a briefing on what was to come), as were the functions represented and the way they were organized. But the broader purpose—to coordinate their efforts—and the complexity of what had to be done, seemed similar.

Brian began by explaining the Global Express program and then showed a short marketing video about it, which ended with "First Flight, September 1996." The meeting was called, he explained, so that they could all work together to make it happen, also to make sure they all knew what was coming. He then turned the chair over to the person in charge of Experimental Shops, who listed the steps in testing, beginning with "(1) Complete the frame static test," and ending with "(10) Dynamic testing." He then passed the chair over to someone else who presented more overheads, largely checklists for organizing the discussion. All kinds of questions followed, some quite aggressive, such as about having "a structure [that] we should be modifying—today."

We were back in Brian's office at 3:12. A brief call came soon after—it's "my boss," Brian said—and Brian did most of the talking: we "just had a good meeting," he said, "everybody in manufacturing now realizes the extensive workload. Monday we're going to sit down in a smaller group to do the detailed [manpower] planning." Mostly they discussed specific problems, about subcontractors, the union, and "eleven thousand hours of outstanding work."

Then Stephane dropped in and they chatted briefly about the afternoon meeting, which Stephane referred to as "kosher but cool." At about 3:30, the manager of Quality Assurance joined as scheduled, handing out a nine-page "action plan" that specified "key milestones," challenges, and responsibilities about quality, which were reviewed and corrected as they went along. Brian and Stephane were rather directive, repeatedly asking for "commitment dates" in place of "current dates." The meeting ended at 4:06.

Several calls and drop-ins followed, and then things began to slow down, for the first time since early morning. Brian explained to me how, when he took over the program, he and the team went to a retreat off-site and realized that they needed better structure, not clearer mandates. "So we split the plane up," with different people taking responsibility for the different parts and liaisons with the partners producing them.

At 4:30, a call came from Los Angeles, from a "problem supplier"—actually a sub-subcontractor, Brian explained. Earlier, fearing a crisis, and concerned that the subcontractor was not on top of it, he had set aside niceties (as well as the decision about who would pay the costs) and dispatched one of his people to Los Angeles, who had since been there five weeks. The call was to request an extension of his mandate. Brian promised he would help to make it happen: "I'll give you all my support to keep the engineering guy there." The call ended after five minutes, with Brian explaining to me that all three of his current problems were with sub-subcontractors, not partners. Earlier, in this case, after he had met with the partner, he smelled a problem and flew to Los Angeles himself. In an hour he knew he was right—they had leveled with him, but not with the partner—which suggested that a "partner" could sometimes be not much more than a subcontractor.

Stephane dropped in for a moment to discuss scheduling for his trip the next week to Toronto, and then, at 4:50, Brian suggested a "short shop floor tour," which actually took almost half an hour. The facility there was immense: two million square feet—big enough to assemble a good-sized airplane, as well as to have its own rainstorms!

As we returned, about 5:15, Brian was ready to leave, off to have a beer with Stephane to discuss some personal issues. "What a day!" I said as we walked to his office, and he replied, "It's not so bad; I just had to sit and listen. Some days . . . ." We were back in the office when Stephane, on the phone, was saying, "Ah, he's just back now."

Postscript   On July 31 1998, the Global Express obtained the Canadian Department of Transport Certification, within two months of the target date set five years earlier.

MANAGING ON THE EDGES

Charlie Zinkan, Superintendent of the Banff National Park (Banff, Alberta, August 13, 1993)

If you really want to see politics in action, you would do well to leave the lofty debates of the capital and come down on the ground, where the environmentalists fight the developers.

Charlie Zinkan headed up the Banff National Park, perhaps the best known of Canada's parks internationally and the origin of the whole Canadian parks system. The burning issue at the time was a proposed new parking lot for a ski hill in Banff National Park. Its owner was a rather aggressive businessman, well connected to the ruling Progressive Conservative Party as well as the sitting member of Parliament from this area, herself also with a reputation for aggressiveness. The parking lot was being hotly contested by environmental groups that claimed it would block a major traverse used by several species of animals and add to the accumulating loss of old-growth forest.

The headquarters of the Banff National Park sits just beyond and above the heart of the town of Banff, Alberta, in an impressive building originally created as a spa and recently restored. Charlie Zinkan occupied a large office that looked down onto the main street. But belying that image was the low-key atmosphere inside—easy, friendly, and very much giving the impression that one was now in the park. In fact, Charlie was in a park's uniform (he spent his career in the Parks Service).

Charlie suggested I come in at 8 A.M., when his daily one-hour French class began. Since it was required for his bilingual position, he thought it could be considered part of his managerial work!

The class ended at 9:05, and we continued to chat (in English). He expected a light load this day, although "Some days it is almost impossible to escape this place." There used to be seven layers of management in the park, he said, but now, with a budget of $10 million, including 270 people full-time and another 500 in the summer, and about 30 to 50 managers, it was down to three, sometimes four. There were a set of units dealing with central administration (finance, human resources, planning, communication), and others with the park services (leases, roads, campgrounds, law enforcement and public safety, conservation, and the front and back country services).

At 9:20, in the midst of going over the chart, the man in charge of program services came in for about five minutes. He talked of conflict (with a developer), referred to "licking our wounds," and "just wanted to let you know" what was done, with which Charlie agreed, commenting that "better we did it than you." They also discussed a problem with the accounting system.

Then came a call from the manager of a power company, concerned with environmentalist efforts to stop an energy supply project, and requesting a meeting. Charles explained some of the concerns of the environmental groups and suggested that early September might be best for the meeting. The manager continued, referring to the role of his company as not trying to involve itself in the management of the park but rather as providing services within the park. He also referred to a colleague's tendency of saber rattling, intervening politically at the federal level. The call lasted twenty-one minutes, during most of which Charlie listened politely.

In between other calls (scheduling, mostly), we chatted. Before the reorganization, morale was a serious problem in the park, Charlie said. It was a struggle to get the managers to be less directive, especially given political pressures to centralize decision making and the fact that the science was not really up to the ecological questions that got raised. Charlie believed that classic top-down control in government was incompatible with the highly educated people attracted to work in the parks, even those doing simple jobs with the hope of moving on to more interesting ones. You "have to be careful when talking 'empowerment'" to these people, Charlie said. "We have mechanics reading the *Harvard Business Review!*" The people in the field are committed to their own values: "these are the Lone Rangers in the organization."

Charlie described Banff Park as especially sensitive, given its history and visibility. Here, particularly, is where everything came together (tourists, developers, a transcontinental highway, etc.). He described three parks, two in the United States—Yellowstone, Yosemite, and Banff—as "lightning rods" for these concerns, the ones that have most influenced world development policies. "There will be weeks and weeks when issues drive my life." The ecological interests of the Bow Valley (of the Banff Park) may be impossible to manage, he suggested, referring specifically to the conflicts between the Alberta Members of Parliament, all from the Progressive Conservative Party, and the ENGOs (environmental nongovernmental organizations), especially concerning that parking lot but also proposals to "twin" the Trans-Canada Highway so that it could carry more traffic.

At 10:30, Charlie began to sign leasehold documents, a required formality. Sandy Davis, to whom he reported, called at 10:40 about a conversation she had with the local member of Parliament, asking Charlie to speak to that person, too, which he did immediately. "I'm just following up," he said, telling the woman about a consulting firm that had been hired by Ottawa and a meeting with the ski hill owner and their "very positive working relationship." That call ended just before 11 o'clock, followed by another, also of about fifteen minutes, from the head of operations at the ski center who expressed concerns about the environmental report and the alignment for the road.

Charlie then met with the head of a bungalow camping ground about Indian land claims near the facility. The tone of this encounter was quite different, with the visitor mostly listening quietly as Charlie explained carefully the claim and the government's position, trying to alleviate the man's anxieties. Twenty-six years earlier, a lawyer had told him about the claim and that he could eventually be ousted, but no one had ever come back to discuss it, nor had he sought anyone out. He was grateful to Charlie for taking the initiative to explain it.

He raised one final issue. The railroad crossed the continental divide near his camping ground, and the engineers tended to blow their whistles as they did, even during the night. "We're supposed to be providing a wilderness experience, and here we have this noise pollution!" Could Charlie do anything about this? Charlie talked about having to discuss it with the railroad people. "Maybe I'll find out who the Vice President for Public Relations is and offer a gift certificate of a free night to listen to the whistles," he joked.

After a brief lunch, we headed off to the park's ranch at the far end of town so that Charlie could arrange some riding to get into shape, as he was to go on a five-day trip into the back country. Charlie wanted to have a look at that part of the park and to be visible there. But this was not just "management by riding around"; he was taking along some wardens, two RCMP people, and a businessman, as an opportunity to exchange ideas.

Back at the office just after 3, the regional specialist in public safety came in, to talk about cost recovery for emergency services (search and rescue). He had spoken with other groups (e.g., the Coast Guard) about this, and had some ideas—for example, to impose a surcharge on all the vehicles entering the park. He wanted Charlie's approval to "pitch" the idea to others.

After another brief meeting on space for equipment storage, we took a break in the schedule to look at Charlie's schedule in a broader sense, first his agenda of scheduled meetings for the rest of that week (this was Friday). Every day began with French. Monday there was a briefing on training and a team-building session, plus discussion of a problem a manager was having with some of his people. A Japanese attaché at the Washington embassy came in to discuss some issues (including Japanese commercial ownership in Banff village), which Charlie saw as a kind of VIP visit. Charlie also met with the owner of the ski hill, and with his own managers on property management. On Tuesday there was a conference call on the future of "hot pools," a "zero-based budgeting" review exercise, more attention to that parking lot, a telephone interview on a survey with the Auditor-General's Office in Ottawa, a meeting with a local organization about a space exchange, and, in the evening, a meeting of the Heritage Department (to which the Parks Service reported in Ottawa). Wednesday included PC training and lunch with Sandy in Calgary (a ninety-minute drive) about the parking lot, and another evening concerning the Heritage Department. Thursday saw a conference call with Sandy on the parking lot ("You can see how one issue can dominate chunks of my time"), and meetings in Lake Louise (almost an hour drive the other way) on union issues, and with a hotel owner concerned about pedestrians crossing his property.

The next week's scheduled meetings included an "agenda-driven" executive meeting on planning; a meeting with the ski hill owner and a consultant hired to look at different possible alignments of the parking lot; a visit by Sandy with a reception at the Banff Cultural Centre; plus a follow-up call from the Auditor-General's Office in Ottawa, lunch with a U.S. congressman on national parks conservation, and a parade at a cadet camp, where Charlie had a ceremonial role to play.

We then chatted about his job, and the positive reaction with regard to some of the projects initiated by the developers and also the park's people themselves. As a consequence of delayering, Charlie found that his job had become heavier, with many more people reporting to him. As he put it in comments to me later, "Perhaps the problem is empowerment down to some managers who lack skills and confidence and consequently try to delegate upwards." At 4:45, a consultant to the region came in. They chatted about management in the service until 5:25, when Charlie's day ended.

MANAGING EXCEPTIONALLY[10]

Abbas Gullet, Head of Subdelegation
(N'gara, Tanzania, October 8, 1996)

This report is about a manager of Red Cross refugee camps in Tanzania whose activities concentrated on communicating and controlling, in order to hold a potentially chaotic situation in steady state, at least temporarily. This is entitled "Managing Exceptionally" for three reasons. First, it is about the classic view of management by exception. Second, it is about managing in exceptional circumstances. And third, it is about exceptional people in an exceptional institution.

The International Federation of Red Cross and Red Crescent Societies (IFRC, or the Federation) brought together about 175 national societies for purposes of development and disaster relief. This report is about one of its "delegates," who ran its two refugee camps in N'gara, Tanzania. Its inhabitants had escaped the chaos that was Rwanda and Burundi in the aftermath of the slaughter of Tutsis by Hutus, followed by the Tutsis having regained power. Benaco housed 175,000 Rwandans; Lukole, 29,000 Burundians.

Running a camp meant running a municipality and more—including food distribution, sanitation, road construction and maintenance, housing, and health care. The operation under Abbas Gullet's responsibility included 17 Federation delegates from eight countries, including himself (a Kenyan), plus 516 full-time people from the Tanzanian Red Cross Society (some of them acting as

---

[10] Published in similar form under this title in *Organizational Science, 12* (November–December 2001):759–771.

"counterparts" to the 17 Federation delegates), and 1,500 paid part-time work-ers from the camps themselves.

Delegates turned over rapidly. (At eleven months, Abbas was the longest standing.) They lived in a "compound" that was pleasantly but modestly ap-pointed: fenced and guarded, but without firearms. One part of the compound contained the administrative area, where the offices (plus telecommunication equipment) were laid out in a quadrangle.

Abbas had spent most of his life in the Red Cross, including as a youth volunteer who had made trips to Germany, Britain, and later Canada. He had been with the Federation for six years, including a recent stint at the Geneva headquarters.

The day began with breakfast at 7:25, then a short walk to the office, where Abbas looked through the new "pactors" on his desk—printed correspondence, much like telex. These concerned an invoice, a shipment of material, and a re-port to be sent. He then turned to his computer to prepare his weekly news report to the Desk Office in the Geneva headquarters. At 7:45, several people came in for the daily meeting of his key direct reports: Gier, a Norwegian in charge of Health; Georges, a Canadian in charge of Finance and Administration; Sasha, a Russian in Logistics; and Stephen, from Northern Ireland (originally Africa), on Relief.

They went around the table, with Sasha talking about the supply and de-mand of the SUV vehicles (a carefully guarded resource in N'gara), and Georges mentioning that the budget was completed. The discussion revolved mainly around Abbas, who had to explain many of the details ("Who to sign?" "Where does this form go?"). Gier and Georges were relatively new, while Sasha and Stephen were sitting in for their bosses, who were away.

When his turn came, Abbas briefed the others on a "camp management" workshop taking place in the Tanzanian compound, to share experiences among various East African Red Cross Societies. An American named Bill and a Mex-ican named Juan were also attending on behalf of the Federation. Abbas ex-plained why he was reluctant to release his staff to attend for the three days, due to work pressure; he was also concerned that Sasha be careful about excessive demands on the vehicles. He gave staffing news, including replacements who had been approved. There was, however, no news yet about the replacements for himself, Stephen, and Frank (Stephen's boss, in Relief), whose assignments were coming to an end. Abbas also explained the "tougher stance" of the Tanzanian government concerning the four-kilometer ring it had recently placed around the camps. (The refugees were free to move about—for example, to work the land assigned to them, trade in the local markets, and forage for cooking firewood, but now only within four kilometers, although how this was to be enforced was not clear.) Then Abbas turned to Stephen and said, "You just need to put your ear to the ground, Stephen, and find out more about what the feelings are among the refugees."

The meeting ended at 8:13, and Abbas went back to work on his report for Geneva, with many people coming and going. That report was sent by 8:30, and then Abbas walked over to the much larger Tanzanian compound next door for the opening of the workshop. He formally welcomed the participants to the area and explained a bit of the recent history. After the huge movement, things had settled down, but with renewed tensions in Burundi, the Red Cross was ready to act quickly again. After about ten minutes, Abbas turned the meeting over to Juan, and with a "We go back to business" to me, headed out.

Business was in Benaco. Abbas's vehicle was waiting outside the hall, and we arrived in the food distribution area at 9:55. Refugee porters were milling about, awaiting the arrival of UNWFP (United Nations World Food Program) trucks, which were apparently late. Abbas went into the "stores"—large plastic sheet buildings, which were almost empty (except for "balances")—where he inquired about the "rat problem" ("Still a problem," he was told), and other details.

As the trucks arrived, the food, in fifty-kilogram sacks, was carried directly to the "chutes"—flat-covered areas, nineteen in all. Through them the food passed for weekly distribution to "team leaders," who in turn distributed it to their "family group" waiting behind a fence. But today Abbas found the system *too* efficient, because the food was supposed to go into the stores first, for purposes of counting and control. So he raised a number of questions about this with the person who managed the food distribution, also about the fact that the staff was not wearing Red Cross bibs. They had to be clearly identified, Abbas insisted, and he encouraged her to have regular meetings with her staff.

Abbas also chatted with a woman from the UNWFP about the food distribution and problems they were having with a contractor. At her request ("Maybe they will listen to you"), he promised to speak to the UN people. We then walked past one of the chutes and through a gate, where the many people milling about, awaiting the food, opened up a space for us to pass, into an open area of the camp. (This was obviously the most animated area of the camp, followed perhaps by the market area, where fresh food, grown or bartered beyond the gates, was sold alongside a surprising array of other things.)

After walking around, we returned to the car and drove to another area of the camp, where Abbas pointed out the living arrangements: rows of small houses, off a large central road, with latrines on one side and cooking facilities (two to a household) on the other. Earlier, seen from a distance, this camp had looked vast, but close up, away from the food distribution gates, it did not seem crowded. We left the camp, and after a brief visit to the water treatment facility that served the compound, we returned to Abbas's office at 12:30.

There was the usual chatting with people going past and a look at a few pactors that had arrived, one from someone needing a new passport, another concerning hotel bookings, a third about the possibility of getting some oil tanks from a departing Italian company—if Abbas moved fast. Sasha happened to drop by just then, and Abbas charged him with checking out the tanks.

A succession of people and pactors followed (about flight bookings, budgets, pay rates, and a broken machine part), and then Abbas joined several people at lunch, at about 1. Hans, from the workshops, asked Abbas if he could help him secure some needed generators, and Bill went over the plans for the workshop, seeking Abbas's approval on the participation of his people. "It's OK with me. Just tell them to talk slowly, clearly." At 1:30, he took a break to rest and then returned to the office at 2.

Gier came in then with "a number of small concerns and a few big ones": Do refugees working for the Red Cross have five-day weeks? Are there evacuation plans for Benaco? Did Abbas plan a salary increase for "the professor" (a Rwandan refugee academic who was working on software for health monitoring)? What about drainage and the installation of night lighting for the "Gulf Hotel" (their nickname for the hospital)? Abbas explained various things carefully to Gier, who had only been there one month. He took a stand on a few of these issues, especially concerning expenditures, but mostly sought Gier's opinion and encouraged him to decide.

The biggest issue concerned the Matron (Head Nurse) at the hospital. She had upset the Tanzanian staff for a variety of reasons, and they wanted her out. Gier also reported an apparent lack of Tanzanian "counterpart-ism" in the hospital. He offered a short list of candidates, none of whom was the Assistant Matron, whom Gier said was also apparently on his way out. Abbas told Gier what he knew of the situation (which seemed to be considerable), including the fact that it had been a problem since he had arrived eleven months earlier. He suggested that since the Matron had been in her job for eighteen months, they could simply view this as a normal rotation, and she could keep her job as a nurse.

At 2:34, with "OK, now for my side," Abbas raised several other issues. There was the question of the production of concrete slabs for the latrines in Benaco, which had fallen behind plan, and they discussed how to increase the rate. Gier commented on the state of sanitation in the camp, which he called remarkable: "There is a lack of smell, a lack of flies, a lack of garbage all over." Diarrhea was not a major problem, but more water would have helped, at which point Abbas discussed difficulties in dealing with the United Nations people. They noted an increase in skin disease in one camp, and Abbas wondered if soap was being pilfered and sold.

Then they came back to the Gulf Hotel, touching briefly on medical staffing, including whether to hire an anesthetist. (Nurses were doing that job.) They discussed costs, especially the large expenditures on drugs and the possibilities of pilferage, and a problem with a driver for the hospital who apparently had tried to bribe a security officer. Abbas told Gier that the wrong person had been fired in this circumstance, and the decision had to be reversed. Gier left at 3:18.

Sasha was waiting outside and came in, concerning several issues: vehicles arriving from Doctors Without Borders Holland, stocking fuel where it could not be pilfered, and "not so good news—an engine [on one of the vehicles] went kaput." Abbas asked him to check if the engine had been overhauled. Sasha went out at 3:42 to find a memo, and Abbas, seeing some people walk by carrying pillows, went out quickly and spoke to them. He was concerned about pilfering, but it turned out they were acting at the request of the workshop people. Then Sasha reappeared with the memo, about a request for vehicles for the workshops, to which Abbas replied, "No way." He also explained how to charge the fuel costs to the workshop. Sasha left at 3:47.

From here, with no more scheduled meetings for the day, pactors and other messages were reviewed (concerning chlorine tablets not available in the desired size, flight arrangements for outgoing personnel, a visit from a Bonn desk officer, a note from the TRCS office in Dar-es-Salaam advising of a physician who would be flying in for a job interview, etc.). At 4:17, Gier walked by and Abbas asked him about the physician's visit: had Gier or anyone else proposed this? The writer of that message had apparently not even checked with Abbas's direct report in Dar-es-Salaam. "I will be nasty with him—hope I won't get into trouble!"

At 4:25, Abbas began work on a "midterm" written evaluation of a delegate, but with the comings and goings picking up in frequency as well as intensity, he was not going to finish this today. Felicitus, who ran the Gulf Hospital on behalf of the German Red Cross, dropped off a memo stapled closed, which Abbas, luckily, happened to open and read immediately. He discovered that a new Assistant Matron, as well as a new Matron, were to be selected. He called her and Gier back into his office.

"Why do you want to move the Assistant Matron out of the hospital?" he asked Felicitus. Gier, unaware of what Felicitus had written, replied, "No, there's no rush on this one," but Felicitus said, "He will not be accepted as the Matron." Apparently there was some sort of misunderstanding between them. Then Abbas, in his most forceful tone of the day, said he knew the man, also named Stephen, well, that he was an excellent person, and that "I will protect him as long as I am here." Felicitus left, looking dejected, so Abbas added, "Unless you have already told him." Felicitus was back in a flash. "I have." She had apparently misinterpreted something Gier had said earlier as meaning she should remove him.

Abbas offered to speak to the Assistant Matron to help resolve the confusion, and Felicitus, obviously relieved (and stating that she, too, appreciated his talent), said, "I wish you could do that." So it was agreed that Abbas would try to work it all out the next day. Indeed, they ended up agreeing that Stephen would be promoted to "Acting Matron." "Why not Matron?" Felicitus asked, and Abbas said, "One step at a time." He wanted to speak to his own counterpart (who was away) first.

Then Abbas, commenting on how he liked this quiet time at the end of the day to get some work done, turned back to his computer and the midterm report. He hit barely one key when the telephone rang from Nairobi, about flight arrangements. That call lasted twenty minutes, after which Sasha poked his head in to report on the trucks that had been offered. They started to discuss this when, at 6 o'clock, Felicitus put her head in with "Stephen is here!"

So Abbas sat down at his table with Stephen, the Assistant Matron, who looked concerned. "How is your hospital these days?" Abbas asked, and they discussed a small outbreak of meningitis, among other things. "Is there any special reason to say you are exhausted, overworked?" Abbas asked, and Stephen said no. He did express concern about Felicitus's upcoming departure and the absence of a replacement, and Abbas urged "you guys" to be more proactive. He continued to probe on administrative arrangements at the hospital and the role of the Tanzanian staff.

Then Abbas turned to the issue at hand, to clarify Stephen's letter of appointment and understand exactly what Felicitus had told him. Stephen said that he understood he would no longer be Assistant Matron, but not that he would lose his job; he hoped to go back to his old nursing position. Meanwhile, Stephen said, he had helped Felicitus draw up the list of names for possible new Matron and Assistant Matron. They reviewed the names. When Abbas asked about the problem of management in the hospital, Stephen looked very uncomfortable, Abbas proposed they talk in Swahili (the common language of both Kenya and Tanzania, followed by English). Even so, as Abbas reported to me afterward, Stephen was hesitant to discuss his concerns about the Matron, although later (back in English), Abbas urged him to be more forthcoming with Felicitus on these issues. "If you're not giving her the information, what's she to do?"

After clarifying what Stephen had been told and who else had been told what, Abbas said, "I'll suggest that you keep your old post as Assistant Matron and prepare for you to act as Matron. . . . But you need to be up front with Felicitus. We know stuff is going on at the hospital—the driver who tried to bribe someone is being fired." Stephen said he understood. Abbas asked, "What else do you have?" With an "Actually, nothing," a very relieved Stephen left a very relieved Abbas at 6:44, whose day, aside from an evening party for one of the departing delegates, then ended.

Bibliography

Adizes, I. (1976). Mismanagement Styles. *California Management Review, 19*(2), 5–20.

Alexander, L. D. (1979). The Effect Level in the Hierarchy and Functional Area Have on the Extent Mintzberg's Roles Are Required by Managerial Jobs. *Academy of Management Proceedings*, pp. 186–189.

Alinsky, S. D. (1971). *Rules for Radicals: A Pragmatic Primer for Realistic Radicals.* New York: Random House.

Allan, P. (1981). Managers at Work: A Large-Scale Study of the Managerial Job in New York City Government (in Research Notes). *Academy of Management Journal, 24*(3), 613–619.

Alvesson, M., & Sveningsson, S. (2003). Managers Doing Leadership: The Extra-Ordinarization of the Mundane. *Human Relations, 56*(12), 1435–1459.

Andrews, F. (1976). Management: How a Boss Works in Calculated Chaos. *New York Times*, October 29.

Andrews, K. (1987). *The Concept of Corporate Strategy.* Homewood, IL: Dow-Jones-Irwin.

Aram, J. D. (1976). *Dilemmas of Administrative Behavior.* Englewood Cliffs, NJ: Prentice Hall.

Augier, M. (2004). James March on Leadership, Education, and Don Quixote: Introduction and Interview. *Academy of Management Learning and Education, 3*(2), 169–177.

Barnard, C. I. (1938). *The Functions of the Executive.* Cambridge, MA: Harvard University Press.

Barney, D. D. (2004). The Vanishing Table, or Community in a World That Is No World. In A. Feenberg & D. D. Barney (Eds.), *Community in the Digital Age: Philosophy and Practice* (pp. 31–52). Lanham, MD: Rowman & Littlefield.

Barry, D., Cramton, C. D., & Carroll, S. J. (1997). Navigating the Garbage Can: How Agendas Help Managers Cope with Job Realities. *Academy of Management Executives, 11*(2), 26–42.

Beaudry, A., & Pinsonneault, A. (2005). Understanding User Responses to Information Technology: A Coping Model of User Adaptation. *MIS Quarterly, 29*(3), 493–534.

Bennis, W. G. (1989). *On Becoming a Leader.* Reading, MA: Addison-Wesley.

Bennis, W. G., & O'Toole, J. (2005). How Business Schools Lost Their Way. *Harvard Business Review, 83*(5), 96–104.

Biggart, N. W. (1981). Management Style as Strategic Interaction: The Case of Governor Ronald Reagan. *Journal of Applied Behavioral Science, 17*(3), 291–308.

Boase, J., & Wellman, B. (2006). Personal Relationships: On and off the Internet. In A. L. Vangelisti & D. Perlman (Eds.), *The Cambridge Handbook of Personal Relationships* (pp. 709–725). Cambridge: Cambridge University Press.

Boettinger, H. M. (1975). Is Management Really an Art? *Harvard Business Review,* January–February, pp. 54–60.

Boisot, M., & Liang, X. G. (1992). The Nature of Managerial Work in the Chinese Enterprise Reforms: A Study of Six Directors. *Organization Studies, 13*(2), 161–184.

Bolman, L. G., & Deal, T. E. (1991). *Reframing Organizations: Artistry, Choice, and Leadership.* San Francisco: Jossey-Bass.

Bower, J. L., & Weinberg, M. W. (1988). Statecraft, Strategy and Corporate Leadership. *California Management Review, 30* (Winter), 39–56.

Bowman, E. H. (1986). Concerns of the CEO. *Human Resource Management, 25*(2), 267–285.

Bowman, E. H., & Bussard, D. T. (1991). Managerial Agenda Setting: An Exploratory Study. In P. Shrivastava, A. Huff, & J. Dutton (Eds.), *Advances in Strategic Management* (Vol. 7, pp. 61–93). Greenwich, CT: JAI Press.

Boyatzis, R. E. (1982). *The Competent Manager.* New York: Wiley

Boyatzis, R. E. (1995). Cornerstones of Change: Building the Path for Self-Directed Learning. In R. E. Boyatzis, S. S. Cowen, & D. A. Kolb (Eds.), *Innovation in Professional Education: Steps on a Journey from Teaching to Learning* (pp. 50–91). San Francisco: Jossey-Bass.

Braybrooke, D. (1964). The Mystery of Executive Success Re-Examined. *Administrative Science Quarterly, 8*(4), 533–560.

Brooke, P. (1968). *The Empty Space.* New York: Atheneum.

Brunsson, K. (2007). *The Notion of General Management.* Malmö: Liber, Copenhagen Business School Press, and Universitetsforlaget.

Buckingham, M. (2005). What Great Managers Do. *Harvard Business Review, 83*(3), 70–79.

Burns, T. (1957). Management in Action. *Operational Research Quarterly, 8,* 45–60.

Business Week. (1984). Oops! Who's Excellent Now? November 5, pp. 76–88.

Canada Parks. (1993). *Defining Our Destiny: Leadership through Excellence.* Unpublished manuscript, Parks Canada, Western Region.

Carlson, S. (1951). *Executive Behaviour: A Study of the Work Load and the Working Methods of Managing Directors.* Stockholm: Strombergs. Reprinted by Uppsala University in 1991 with comments by H. Mintzberg and R. Stewart. Uppsala: Uppsala University.

Carroll, G. R., & Teo, A. C. (1996). On the Social Network of Managers. *Academy of Management Journal, 39*(2), 421–440.

Carroll, S. J., & Gillen, D. A. (1987). Are the Classical Management Functions Useful in Describing Managerial Work? *Academy of Management Review, 12*(1), 38–51.

Chandler, M. K., & Sayles, L. R. (1971). *Managing Large Systems.* New York: Harper & Row.

Choran, R., & Colvin, G. (1999). Why CEOs Fail. *Fortune*, 21, pp. 69–82.

Clifford, P., & Friesen, S. L. (1993). A Curious Plan: Managing on the Twelfth. *Harvard Educational Review, 63*(3), 339–358.

Cohen, M. D., & March, J. G. (1974). *Leadership and Ambiguity: The American College President.* Hightstown, NJ: McGraw-Hill.

Cohen, M. D., & March, J. G. (1986). *Leadership and Ambiguity: The American College President* (2nd ed.). Boston: Harvard Business School Press.

Compton, J. A., & Rule, E. G. (1991). *Comparative Advantage in Canadian Leadership Styles.* Montreal: Coopers & Lybrand.

Craster, E. (1871). Pinafore Poems. *Cassell's Weekly.*

Cuber, J., & Harroff, P. (1986). Five Types of Marriage. In A. S. Skolnick & J. H. Skolnick (Eds.), *Family in Transition: Rethinking Marriage, Sexuality, Child Rearing, and Family Organization* (5th ed., pp. 263–274). Boston: Little, Brown.

Cyert, R. M., & March, J. G. (1963). *A Behavioral Theory of the Firm.* Englewood Cliffs, NJ: Prentice Hall.

Dalton, M. (1959). *Men Who Manage: Fusions of Feeling and Theory in Administration.* New York: Wiley.

Daudelin, M. W. (1996). Learning from Experience through Reflection. *Organizational Dynamics*, 24(3), 36–48.

Delbecq, A. L. (1992). Telling It Like It Is: A Diary of a CEO within a Professional Organization. *Journal of Management Inquiry, 1*(1), 9–11.

DePree, M. (1990). Today's Leaders Look to Tomorrow's Managing. *Fortune*, March 26, p. 30.

Devons, E. (1950). *Planning in Practice Essays in Aircraft Planning in War-time.* Cambridge: Cambridge University Press

DiPietro, R. A., & Milutinovich, J. S. (1973). Marketing and Finance Managers: A Review of the Literature and Comparative Analysis. *Quarterly Journal of Management Development,* November.

Dodgson, R. C., Levinson, D. J., & Zaleznik, A. (1965). *The Executive Role Constellation: An Analysis of Personality and Role Relations in Management.* Boston: Harvard Business School, Research Division.

Doktor, R. H. (1990). Asian and American CEOs: A Comparative Study. *Organizational Dynamics, 18* (Winter), 46–58.

Drucker, P. F. (1946). *Concept of the Corporation.* New York: Day.

Drucker, P. F. (1954). *Practice of Management.* New York: Harper & Row.

Drucker, P. F. (1963). Managing for Business Effectiveness. *Harvard Business Review*, 41 (May–June), 53–60.

Drucker, P. F. (1974). *Management: Tasks, Responsibilities, Practices.* New York: Harper & Row.

Drucker, P. F. (1992). There's More Than One Kind of Team. *Wall Street Journal*, February 11, p. 16.

Duncan, W. J., Ginter, P. M., & Capper, S. A. (1994). General and Functional Level Health Care Managers: Neither "Manage" Very Much. *Health Services Management Research*, 7(2), 91–100.

Dutton, J. E., & Ashford, S. J. (1993). Selling Issues to Top Management. *Academy of Management Review*, 18(3), 397–428.

Dutton, J. E., Ashford, S. J., O'Neill, R. M., Hayes, E., & Wierba, E. E. (1997). Reading the Wind: How Middle Managers Assess the Context for Selling Issues to Top Managers. *Strategic Management Journal*, 18(5), 407–425.

Eastlack Jr., J., & McDonald, P. R. (1970). CEO's Role in Corporate Growth. *Harvard Business Review*, May–June, pp. 150–163.

Ezzamel, M., Lilley, S., & Willmott, H. (1994). The "New Organization" and the "New Managerial Work." *European Management Journal*, 12(4), 454–461.

Farson, R. E. (1996). *Management of the Absurd: Paradoxes in Leadership*. New York: Simon & Schuster.

Fayol, Henri. (1916). Administration industrielle et générale. *Bulletin de la Société de l'Industrie Minérale, 10*, 5–164.

Fayol, H. (1949). *General and Industrial Management*. London: Pitman.

Fine, S. A. (1973). *Functional Job Analysis Scales: A Desk Aid*. Kalamazoo, MI: W. E. Upjohn Institute for Employment Research.

Fleishman E. A. (1953). The Description of Supervisory Behavior. *Journal of Applied Psychology, 37*, 1–6.

Floyd, S. W., & Wooldridge, B. (1994). Dinosaurs or Dynamos? Recognizing Middle Management's Strategic Role. *Academy of Management Executive*, 8(4), 47–57.

Floyd, S. W., & Wooldridge, B. (1996). *The Strategic Middle Manager: How to Create and Sustain Competitive Advantage*. San Francisco: Jossey-Bass.

Follett, M. P. (1920). *The New State: Group Organization the Solution of Popular Governments*. New York: Longmans Green.

Follett, M. P. (1949). *Freedom & Co-ordination: Lectures in Business Organization*. London: Management Publications Trust.

Follett, M. P. (1995). The Essentials of Leadership. In P. Graham (Ed.), *Mary Parker Follett—Prophet of Management: A Celebration of Writings from the 1920s* (pp. 163–181). Boston: Harvard Business School Press.

Fondas, N. (1992). A Behavioral Job Description for Managers. *Organizational Dynamics*, Summer, pp. 47–58.

Fondas, N., & Stewart, R. (1992). Understanding Differences in General Management Jobs. *Journal of General Management*, 17(4), 1–12.

Friedman, M. (1962). *Capitalism and Freedom*. Chicago: University of Chicago Press.

Friedman, M. (1970). A Friedman Doctrine: *New York Times Magazine*, September 13, pp. 32ff.

Gabarro, J. J. (1985). When a New Manager Takes Charge. *Harvard Business Review*, May–June, pp. 110–123.

Ganster, D. C. (2005). Executive Job Demands: Suggestions from a Stress and Decision-Making Perspective. *Academy of Management Review*, 30(3), 492–502.

Garratt, B. (1990). *Creating a Learning Organisation: A Guide to Leadership, Learning and Development*. Hemel Hempstead: Director Books.

Geertz, C. (1973). Thick Description: Toward an Interpretive Theory of Culture. In *The Interpretation of Cultures: Selected Essays* (pp. 3–30). New York: Basic Books.

Gimpl, M. L., & Dakin, S. R. (1984). Management and Magic. *California Management Review*, 27(1), 125–136.

Glouberman, S., & Mintzberg, H. 2001. Managing the Care of Health and the Cure of Disease: Part I. Differentiation and Part II. Integration. *Health Care Management Review*, 26 (Winter), 56–84.

Goffman, E. (1961). The Characteristics of Total Institutions. In A. Etzioni (Ed.), *Complex Organizations: A Sociological Reader* (pp. 312–340). New York: Holt, Rinehart & Winston.

Goleman, D. (2000). Leadership That Gets Results. *Harvard Business Review*, March–April, pp. 78–90.

González, V. M., & Mark, G. (2004). *Constant, Constant, Multi-tasking Craziness: Managing Multiple Working Spheres*. Paper presented at the Proceedings of the SIGCHI conference on Human Factors in Computing Systems.

Goodsell, C. T. (1989). Administration as Ritual. *Public Administration Review*, 49(2), 161–166.

Gosling, J., & Mintzberg, H. (2003). Five Minds of a Manager. *Harvard Business Review*, 81(11), 54–63.

Gould, M. (1990). *Strategic Control Processes*. Working paper, Strategic Management Centre, London.

Gouldner, A. W. (1957). Cosmopolitans and Locals: Toward an Analysis of Latent Social Roles. *Administrative Science Quarterly*, 2(3), 281–306.

Gowin, E. B. (1920). *The Executive and His Control of Men: A Study in Personal Efficiency*. New York: Macmillan.

Granovetter, M. S. (1973). The Strength of Weak Ties. *American Journal of Sociology*, 78(6), 1360–1380.

Greenleaf, R. K. (2002). *Servant Leadership: A Journey into the Nature of Legitimate Power and Greatness* (25th anniversary ed.). New York: Paulist Press.

Grey, C. (1999). We Are All Managers Now; We Always Were: On the Development and Demise of Management. *Journal of Management Studies*, 36(5), 562–585.

Grint, K. (2005). Problems, Problems, Problems: The Social Construction of Leadership. *Human Relations*, 58(11), 1467–1494.

Gronn, P. C. (1982). Methodological Perspective: Neo-Taylorism in Educational Administration. *Educational Administration Quarterly*, 18(4), 17–35.

Grove, A. S. (1983). *High Output Management*. New York: Random House.

Grove, A. S. (1995). A High-Tech CEO Updates His Views on Managing and Careers. *Fortune*, 123(6), 229.

Guest, R. H. (1955–1956). Of Time and the Foreman. *Personnel*, 32, 478–486.

Gulick, L., & Urwick, L. (1937). *Papers on the Science of Administration*. New York: Institute of Public Administration.

Hales, C. (1986). What Do Managers Do? A Critical Review of the Evidence. *Journal of Management Studies*, 23(1), 88–115.

Hales, C. (1989). Management Processes, Management Divisions of Labour and Managerial Work: Towards a Synthesis. *International Journal of Sociology and Social Policy*, 9(5/6), 9–38.

Hales, C. (1999). Why Do Managers Do What They Do? Reconciling Evidence and Theory in Accounts of Managerial Work. *British Journal of Management*, 10, 335–350.

Hales, C. (2000). Management and Empowerment Programs. *Work, Employment & Society*, 14(3), 501–519.

Hales, C. (2001). Does It Matter What Managers Do? *Business Strategy Review*, 12(2), 50–58.

Hales, C. (2002). Bureaucracy-lite and Continuities in Managerial Work. *British Journal of Management*, 13, 51–66.

Hales, C. (2005). Rooted in Supervision, Branching into Management: Continuity and Change in the Role of First-Line Manager. *Journal of Management Studies*, 42(3), 471–506.

Hales, C., & Mustapha, N. A. (2000). Commonalities and Variations in Managerial Work: A Study of Middle Managers in Malaysia. *Asia Pacific Journal of Human Resources*, 38(1), 1–25.

Hales, C., & Tamangani, Z. (1996). An Investigation of the Relationship between Organizational Structure, Managerial Role Expectations and Managers' Work Activities. *Journal of Management Studies*, 33(6), 731–756.

Hamblin, R. L. (1958). Leadership and Crises. *Sociometry*, 21, 322–335.

Hambrick, D. C. (2007). Upper Echelons Theory: An Update. *Academy of Management Review*, 32(2), 334–343.

Hambrick, D. C., Finkelstein, S., & Mooney, A. C. (2005a). Executive Job Demands: New Insights for Explaining Strategic Decisions and Leader Behaviors. *Academy of Management Review*, 30(3), 472–491.

Hambrick, D. C., Finkelstein, S., & Mooney, A. C. (2005b). Reply: Executives Sometimes Lose It, Just Like the Rest of Us. *Academy of Management Review*, 30(3), 503–508.

Hamel, G. (2000). Waking Up IBM: How a Gang of Unlikely Rebels Transformed Big Blue. *Harvard Business Review*, 78 (July–August), 37–144.

Handy, C. B. (1985). *Gods of Management: The Changing Work of Organisations* (Rev. ed.). London: Pan.

Handy, C. B. (1994). *The Age of Paradox*. Boston: Harvard Business School Press.

Hannaway, J. (1989). *Managers Managing: The Workings of an Administrative System*. New York: Oxford University Press.

Harrison, M. T., & Beyer, J. M. (1991). Cultural Leadership in Organizations. *Organization Science*, 2(2), 149–169.

Hart, S. L., & Quinn, R. E. (1993). Roles Executives Play: CEOs, Behavioral Complexity, and Firm Performance. *Human Relations*, 46, 543–574.

Harvard Business School Publishing. (2006). *Leadership Insights: Fifteen Unique Perspectives on Effective Leadership*. Boston: Author.

Hebb, D. O. (1961). The Mind's Eye. *Psychology Today*, 2(12), 54–68.

Hebb, D. O. (1969). Hebb on Hocus-Pocus: A Conversation with Elizabeth Hall. *Psychology Today*, 3(6), 20–28.

Helgesen, S. (1990). *The Female Advantage: Women's Ways of Leadership*. New York: Doubleday/Currency.

Helgesen, S. (1995). *The Web of Inclusion: A New Architecture for Building Great Organizations*. New York: Doubleday/Currency.

Hickson, D. J., & Pugh, D. S. (1995). *Management Worldwide: The Impact of Societal Culture on Organizations around the Globe*. London: Penguin.

Hill, L. A. (1992). *Becoming a Manager: Mastery of a New Identity*. Boston: Harvard Business School Press.

Hill, L. A. (2003). *Becoming a Manager: How New Managers Master the Challenges of Leadership* (2nd, expanded ed.). Boston: Harvard Business School Press.

Hill, L. A. (2007). Becoming the Boss. *Harvard Business Review*, 85 (January), 49–56.

Hodgson, R. C., Levinson, D. J., & Zaleznik, A. (1965) *The Executive Role Constellation*. Boston: Harvard Business School Press.

Hofstede, G. (1980). *Culture's Consequences International Differences in Work-Related Values*. Beverly Hills, CA: Sage.

Hofstede, G. (1993). Cultural Constraints in Management Theories. *Academy of Management Executive*, 7(1), 81–94.

Homans, G. C. (1950). *The Human Group*. New York: Harcourt Brace Jovanovich.

Homans, G. C. (1958). Social Behavior as Exchange. *American Journal of Sociology*, 62, 597–606.

Hopwood, B. (1981). *Whatever Happened to the British Motorcycle Industry?* San Leandro, CA: Haynes.

Horne J. H., & Lupton, T. (1965). The Work Activities of "Middle" Managers: An Exploratory Study. *Journal of Management Studies*, 7, 347–363.

Hurst, D. K. (1988). *Changing Management Metaphors: To Hell with the Helmsman*. Unpublished manuscript, Oakville, TN.

Huy, Q. N. (2001). In Praise of Middle Managers. *Harvard Business Review*, 79(8), 72–79.

Iacocca, L., Taylor, A., III, & Bellis, W. (1988). Iacocca in His Own Words. *Fortune*, August 29, pp. 38–43.

Inkson, K., Heising, A., & Rousseau, D. (2001). The Interim Manager: Prototype of the 21st-Century Worker? *Human Relations*, 54(3), 259–284.

Isenberg, D. J. (1984). How Senior Managers Think. *Harvard Business Review*, 62(6), 81–90.

Ives, B., & Olson, M. (1981). Manager or Technician? The Nature of the Information Systems Manager's Job. *MIS Quarterly*, 5(4), 49–63.

Kaplan, A. (1964). *The Conduct of Inquiry: Methodology for Behavioral Science*. San Francisco: Chandler.

Kaplan, R. E. (1983). Creativity in the Everyday Business of Managing. *Issues & Observations*, 3(2), 1ff.

Kaplan, R. E. (1984). Trade Routes: The Manager's Network of Relationships. *Organizational Dynamics*, 12(4), 37–52.

Kaplan, R. E. (1986). *The Warp and Woof of the General Manager's Job*. Center for Creative Leadership, Technical Report 27, August.

Keough, M., Doman, A., & Forrester, J. W. (1992). The CEO as Organization Designer: An Interview with Professor Jay W. Forrester, the Founder of System Dynamics. *McKinsey Quarterly*, 2, 3–30.

Khandwalla, P. N. (1977). *The Design of Organizations*. New York: Harcourt Brace Jovanovich.

Kiesler, S., Zubrow, D., Moses, A. M., & Geller, V. (1985). Affect in Computer-Meditated Communication: An Experiment in Synchronous Terminal-to-Terminal Discussion. *Human-Computer Interaction*, 1(1), 77–107.

Kotter, J. P. (1982a). *The General Managers*. New York: Free Press.

Kotter, J. P. (1982b). What Effective General Managers Really Do. *Harvard Business Review*, 60(6), 156–162.

Kotter, J. P. (1990). What Leaders Really Do. *Harvard Business Review*, 68(3), 103–111.

Kotter, J. P., & Lawrence, P. R. (1974). *Mayors in Action: Five Approaches to Urban Governance*. New York: Wiley.

Kraut, A. I., Pedigo, P. R., McKenna, D. D., & Dunnette, M. D. (2005). The Role of the Manager: What's Really Important in Different Management Jobs. *Academy of Management Executive*, 19(4), 122–129.

Kurke, L. B., & Aldrich, H. E. (1983). Mintzberg Was Right! A Replication and Extension of the Nature of Managerial Work. *Management Science*, 29(8), 975–984.

Lalonde, M. (1997). 6-Year Deal for City Boss. *Montreal Gazette*, September 22, pp. A1ff.

Lau, A. W., Newman, A. R., & Broedling, L. A. (1980). The Nature of Managerial Work in the Public Sector. *Public Administration Forum*, 19, 513–521.

Lebrecht, N. (1991). *The Maestro Myth: Great Conductors in Pursuit of Power*. Secaucus, NJ: Carol.

Lewin, D. (1979). On the Place of Design in Engineering. *Design Studies*, 1(2), 113–117.

Lewis, J. M., Beavers, W. R., Gossett, J. T., & Phillips, V. A. (1976). *No Single Thread: Psychological Health in Family Systems*. New York: Brunner/Mazel.

Lewis, R., & Stewart, R. (1958). *The Boss. The Life and Time of the British Businessman*. London: Phoenix House.

Likert, R. (1961). *New Patterns of Management*. New York: McGraw-Hill.

Lindblom, C. E. (1968). *The Policy-Making Process*. Englewood Cliffs, NJ: Prentice Hall.

Lindell, M., & Arvonen, J. (1996). The Nordic Management Style: An Investigation. In S. Jönsson (Ed.), *Perspectives of Scandinavian Management* (pp. 11–36). Gothenburg: Gothenburg Research Institute and Gothenburg School of Economics and Commercial Law.

Livingston, J. S. (1971). Myth of the Well-Educated Manager. *Harvard Business Review*, 49 (January–February), 79–89.

Lombardo, M., & McCall, M., Jr. (1982). Leaders on Line: Observations from a Simulation of Managerial Work. In J. G. Hunt, C. A. Schriesheim, & U. Sekaran (Eds.), *Leadership beyond Establishment Views* (pp. 50–67). Carbondale: Southern Illinois University Press.

Losada, C. (2004). *A Contribution to the Study of the Differences in Managerial Function: Political Managers' Function and Civil Service Managers' Function*. Unpublished PhD diss., Universitat Ramon Llull, Barcelona.

Lubatkin, M. H., Ndiaye, M., & Vengroff, R. (1997). The Nature of Managerial Work in Developing Countries: A Limited Test of the Universalist Hypothesis. *Journal of International Business Studies*, 28(4), 711–733.

Luthans, F., Hodgetts, R. M., & Rosenkrantz, S. A. (1988). *Real Managers*. Cambridge: Ballinger.

Luthans, F., Welsh, D. H. B., & Rosenkrantz, S. A. (1993). What Do Russian Managers Really Do? An Observational Study with Comparisons to US Managers. *Journal of International Business Studies*, 24(4), 741–761.

Maccoby, M. (1976). *The Gamesman*. New York: Simon and Schuster.

Maccoby, M. (2000). Narcissistic Leaders: The Incredible Pros, the Inevitable Cons. *Harvard Business Review*, 78(1), 68–77.

Maccoby, M. (2003). *The Productive Narcissist: The Promise and Peril of Visionary Leadership*. New York: Broadway Books.

Maeterlinck, M. (1901). *The Life of the Bee*. New York: Dodd, Mead.

Maital, S. (1988). Cooperation and Internal Efficiency. *Sloan Management Review* (Winter), 57–58.

Makridakis, S. (1990). *Forecasting, Planning and Strategy for the 21st Century*. New York: Free Press.

Maltz, M. D. (1997). *Bridging Gaps in Police Crime Data: Executive Summary*. Discussion Paper, BJS Fellow Program, Bureau of Justice Statistics. Washington, DC: U.S. Department of Justice, Office of Justice Programs.

Mangham, I. (1990). Managing as a Performing Art. *British Journal of Management*, 1(2), 105–115.

Marples, D. L. (1967). Studies of Managers: A Fresh Start? *Journal of Management Studies*, 4, 282–299.

Marshall, J., & Stewart, R. (1981). Managers Job Perceptions. Part II: Opportunities for, and Attitudes to Choice. *Journal of Management Studies*, 18(3), 263–275.

Martin, S. (1983). *Managing without Managers: Alternative Work Arrangements in Public Organizations*. Beverly Hills, CA: Sage.

Martinko, M. J., & Gardner, W. L. (1985). Beyond Structured Observation: Methodological Issues and New Directions. *Academy of Management Review*, 10(4), 676–695.

McCall, M. W., Jr. (1977). Leaders and Leadership: Of Substance and Shadow. In J. Hackman, E. Lawler, & L. Porter (Eds.), *Perspectives on Behavior in Organizations*. New York: McGraw-Hill.

McCall, M. W., Jr. (1988). Developing Executives through Work Experiences. *Human Resources Planning*, 11(1), 1–11.

McCall, M. W., Jr., Lombardo, M. M., & Morrison, A. M. (1988). *The Lessons of Experience: How Successful Executives Develop on the Job*. Lexington, MA: Lexington.

McCall, M. W., Jr., Morrison, A. M., & Hannan, R. L. (1978). *Studies of Managerial Work: Results and Methods* (Vol. 9, May). Greensboro, NC: Center for Creative Leadership.

McCall, M. W., Jr., & Segrist, C. A. (1980). *In Pursuit of the Manager's Job: Building on Mintzberg* (Vol. 14, March). Greensboro, NC: Center for Creative Leadership.

McCauley, C. D., Moxley, R. S., & Van Velsor, E. (Eds.). (1998). *The Center for Creative Leadership Handbook of Leadership Development*. San Francisco: Jossey-Bass.

McGregor, D. (1960). *The Human Side of Enterprise*. New York: McGraw-Hill.

McLuhan, H. M. (1962). *The Gutenberg Galaxy: The Making of Typographic Man*. Toronto: Toronto University Press.

Meindl, J. R., Ehrlich, S. B., & Dukerich, J. M. (1985). The Romance of Leadership. *Administrative Science Quarterly*, 30, 78–102.

Miles, R., & Snow, C. (1978). *Organizational Strategy, Structure and Process*. London: McGraw-Hill.

Miller, D. (1990). *The Icarus Paradox*. New York: HarperCollins.

Miller, G. A. (1956). The Magic Number Seven, Plus or Minus Two: Some Limits on Our Capacity for Processing Information. *Psychological Review*, 63, 81–97.

Mintzberg, H. (1970). Structured Observation as a Method to Study Managerial Work. *Journal of Management Studies*, February.

Mintzberg, H. (1973). *The Nature of Managerial Work*. New York: Harper & Row. Reprinted by Prentice-Hall (1980).

Mintzberg, H. (1975a). *Impediments to the Use of Management Information*. Monograph of the National Association of Accountants (U.S.) and Society of Industrial Accountants (Canada).

Mintzberg, H. (1975b). The Manager's Job: Folklore and Fact. *Harvard Business Review*, 53(2), 100–110.

Mintzberg, H. (1979). *The Structuring of Organizations: A Synthesis of the Research.* Englewood Cliffs, NJ: Prentice Hall.

Mintzberg, H. (1983a). *Power in and around Organizations*. Englewood Cliffs, NJ: Prentice Hall.

Mintzberg, H. (1983b). *Structure in Fives: Designing Effective Organizations*. Englewood Cliffs, NJ: Prentice Hall.

Mintzberg, H. (1987). Crafting Strategy. *Harvard Business Review*, 65(4), 66–75.

Mintzberg, H. (1989). *Mintzberg on Management: Inside Our Strange World of Organizations*. New York: Free Press.

Mintzberg, H. (1991). Managerial Work: Forty Years Later. In S. Carlson, *Executive Behaviour*. Uppsala: Uppsala University Press.

Mintzberg, H. (1994a). Managing as Blended Care. *Journal of Nursing Administration*, 24(9), 29–36.

Mintzberg, H. (1994b). *The Rise and Fall of Strategic Planning: Reconceiving Roles for Planning, Plans, Planners*. New York: Free Press.

Mintzberg, H. (1994c). Rounding Out the Manager's Job. *Sloan Management Review*, 36(1), 11–26.

Mintzberg, H. (1996a). Une journée avec un dirigeant. *Revue Française de Gestion*, 22(111), 106–114.

Mintzberg, H. (1996b). Managing Government, Governing Management. *Harvard Business Review*, 74(3), 75–83.

Mintzberg, H. (1997a). A Day in the Life of John Cleghorn. *Decision*, Fall.

Mintzberg, H. (1997b). Managing on the Edges. *International Journal of Public Sector Management*, 10(3), 131–153.

Mintzberg, H. (1997c). Toward Healthier Hospitals. *Health Care Manage Review*, 22(4), 9–18.

Mintzberg, H. (1998). Covert Leadership: Notes on Managing Professionals. *Harvard Business Review*, 76(6), 140–147.

Mintzberg, H. (2001a). Managing Exceptionally. *Organization Science*, 12(6), 759–771.

Mintzberg, H. (2001b). The Yin and the Yang of Managing. *Organizational Dynamics*, 29(4), 306–312.

Mintzberg, H. (2004a). Enough Leadership. *Harvard Business Review*, 82(11), 22.

Mintzberg, H. (2004b). *Managers Not MBAs: A Hard Look at the Soft Practice of Managing and Management Development*. San Francisco: Berrett-Koehler.

Mintzberg, H. (2005). Developing Theory about the Development of Theory. In K. G. Smith & M. A. Hitt (Eds.), *Great Minds in Management: The Process of Theory Development*. New York: Oxford University Press.

Mintzberg, H. (2007). *Tracking Strategies: Toward a General Theory*. New York: Oxford University Press.

Mintzberg, H. (2009a). America's Monumental Failure of Management. *Globe and Mail*, March 16, p. A13.

Mintzberg, H. (2009b). It's Time to Call the Bluff of those Highrolling CEOs. *Globe and Mail*, April 3.

Mintzberg, H. (2009c). Rebuilding Companies as Communities. *Harvard Business Review*, July–August.

Mintzberg, H., Ahlstrand, B., & Lampel, J. (2009). *Strategy Safari: A Guided Tour through the Wilds of Management*. New York: Free Press.

Mintzberg, H., & Bourgault, J. (2000). *Managing Publicly*. Toronto: IPAC.

Mintzberg, H., & Jørgensen, J. (1987). Emergent Strategy for Public Policy. *Canadian Public Administration*, 30(2), 214–229.

Mintzberg, H., & McHugh, A. (1985). Strategy Formation in an Adhocracy. *Administrative Science Quarterly*, 30, 160–197.

Mintzberg, H., & Moore, K. (2006). Global or Worldly? *World Business*, 1(1), 17.

Mintzberg, H., Simons, R., & Basu, K. (2002). Beyond Selfishness. *Sloan Management Review*, 44, 67–74.

Mintzberg, H., Taylor, W., & Waters, J. (1984). Tracking Strategies in the Birthplace of Canadian Tycoons: The Sherbrooke Record 1946–1976. *Canadian Journal of Administrative Sciences*, 1(1), 11–28.

Mintzberg, H., & Van der Heyden, L. (1999). Organigraphs: Drawing How Organizations Really Work. *Harvard Business Review*, September–October, pp. 87–94.

Mintzberg, H., & Van der Heyden, L. (2000). Re-viewing the Organization: Is It a Chain, a Hub or a Web? *Ivey Business Journal*, 65(1), 24–29.

Mintzberg, H., & Waters, J. A. (1985). Of Strategies, Deliberate and Emergent. *Strategic Management Journal*, 6(3), 257–272.

Mintzberg, H., & Westley, F. (2000). Sustaining the Institutional Environment. *Organization Studies*, 21, 71–94.

Moir, A., & Jessel, D. (1991). *Brain Sex: The Real Difference between Men and Women*. New York: Carol.

Moore, K. (2006). CAE's Robert Brown Has Hunger to Lead—and Win. *Globe and Mail*, July 17, p. B10.

Morris, V. C., Crowson, R. L., Hurwitz, E., Jr., & Porter-Gehrie, C. (1981). *The Urban Principal. Discretionary Decision-Making in a Large Educational Organization*. Chicago: University of Illinois, College of Education.

Morris, V. C., Crowson, R. L., Hurwitz, E., Jr., & Porter-Gehrie, C. (1982). The Urban Principal: Middle Manager in the Education Bureaucracy. *Phi Delta Kappan*, 64(10), 689–692.

Moskowitz, M. A. (1986). The Managerial Roles of Academic Library Directors: The Mintzberg Model. *College and Research Libraries*, 47(5), 452–459.

Neustadt, R. E. (1960). *Presidential Power: The Politics of Leadership*. New York: Wiley.

Noël, A. (1989). Strategic Cores and Magnificent Obsessions: Discovering Strategy Formation through Daily Activities of CEOs. *Strategic Management Journal*, 10(1), 33–49.

Nonaka, I. (1988). Towards Middle-Up-Down Management: Accelerating Information Creation. *Sloan Management Review*, Spring, 9–18.

Nonaka, I., & Takeuchi, H. (1995). *The Knowledge-Creating Company*. New York: Oxford University Press.

Noordegraaf, M. (1994). *Functioning of Male and Female Managers in the Public and*

Private Sector: Explorative Research Report. Rotterdam: Erasmus University, Department of Public Administration.

Noordegraaf, M. (2006). Professional Management of Professionals: Hybrid Organisations and Professional Management in Care and Welfare. In J. W. Duyvendak, T. Knijn, & M. Kremer (Eds.), *Policy, People, and the New Professional*. Amsterdam: Amsterdam University Press.

Noordegraaf, M., Meurs, P., & Montijn-Stoopendaal. (2005). Pushed Organizational Pulls Changing Responsibilities, Roles and Relations of Dutch Health Care Executives. *Public Management Review*, 7(1), 25–43.

Noordegraaf, M., & Stewart, R. (2000). Managerial Behaviour Research in Private and Public Sectors: Distinctiveness, Disputes and Directions. *Journal of Management Studies*, 37(3), 427–443.

Ohlott, P. J. (1998). Job Assignments. In C. D. McCauley, R. S. Moxley, & E. Van Velsor (Eds.), *The Center for Creative Leadership Handbook of Leadership Development* (pp. 127–159). San Francisco: Jossey-Bass.

Panko, R. R. (1992). Managerial Communication Patterns. *Journal of Organizational Computing*, 2(1), 95–122.

Paolillo, J. G. P. (1981). Role Profiles for Managers at Different Hierarchical Levels. *Proceedings of the Academy of Management*, pp. 91–94.

Paolillo, J. G. P. (1984). The Manager's Self Assessments of Managerial Roles: Small vs. Large Firms. *American Journal of Small Business*, 8(3), 58–64.

Papandreou, A. (1952). Some Basic Problems in the Theory of the Firm. In B. Haley (Ed.), *A Survey of Contemporary Economics* (pp. 183–222). Homewood, IL: Irwin.

Pascale, R. T. (1990). *Managing on the Edge: How Successful Companies Use Conflict to Stay Ahead*. London: Viking.

Pascale, R. T., & Athos, A. G. (1978). Zen and the Art of Management. *Harvard Business Review*, 56(2), 153–162.

Pascale, R. T., & Athos, A. G. (1981). *The Art of Japanese Management: Applications for American Executives*. New York: Simon and Schuster.

Pearce, C. L., & Conger, J. A. (2003). *Shared Leadership. Reframing the Hows and Whys of Leadership*. San Francisco: Sage.

Pearson, C. A. L., & Chatterjee, S. R. (2003). Managerial Work Roles in Asia: An Empirical Study of Mintzberg's Role Formulation in Four Asian Countries. *Journal of Management Development*, 22(8), 694–707.

Peter, L. J., & Hull, R. (1969). *The Peter Principle*. New York: Morrow.

Peters, T. J. (1979). Leadership: Sad Facts and Silver Linings. *Harvard Business Review*, November–December, pp. 164–172.

Peters, T. J. (1980). A Style for All Seasons. *Executive*, 6(3), 12–16.

Peters, T. J. (1990). *The Case for Experimentation: Or, You Can't Plan Your Way to Unplanning a Formerly Planned Economy*. Boston: TPG Communications.

Peters, T. J. (1994). *The Pursuit of Wow! Every Person's Guide to Topsy-turvy Times*. New York: Vintage Books.

Peters, T. J. (2003). *Re-imagine! Business Excellence in a Disruptive Age*. London: Dorling Kindersley.

Peters, T. J., & Waterman, R. H. (1982). *In Search of Excellence: Lessons from America's Best-Run Companies*. New York: Harper & Row.

Pettersen, I. J., Rotefoss, B., Jönsson, S., & Korneliussen, T. (2002). *Nordic Management & Business Administration Research—Quo Vadis?* (Vol. 5). Göteborg: Gothenburg Research Institute.

Pfeffer, J., & Salancik, G. R. (1978). *The External Control of Organizations: A Resource Dependence Perspective.* New York: Harper & Row.

Pfeffer, J., & Salancik, G. R. (2003). *The External Control of Organizations: A Resource Dependence Perspective.* Stanford, CA: Stanford University Press.

Pinsonneault, A., & Kraemer, K. L. (1997). Middle Management Downsizing: An Empirical Investigation of the Impact of Information Technology. *Management Science,* 43(5), 659–679.

Pinsonneault, A., & Rivard, S. (1998). Information Technology and the Nature of Managerial Work: From the Productivity Paradox to the Icarus Paradox? *MIS Quarterly,* September, pp. 287–311.

Pitcher, P. C. (1995). *Artists, Craftsmen and Technocrats: The Dreams, Realities and Illusions of Leadership.* Toronto: Stoddart.

Pitcher, P. C. (1997). *The Drama of Leadership.* New York: Wiley.

Pitner, N. J. (1982). *The Mintzberg Method: What Have We Really Learned?* Paper presented at the Annual Meeting of the American Educational Research Association, New York.

Pitner, N. J., & Ogawa, R. T. (1981). Organizational Leadership: The Case of the School Superintendent. *Educational Administration Quarterly,* 17(2), 45–65.

Porter, M. E. (1987). Corporate Strategy: The State of Strategic Thinking. *The Economist,* May 23, pp. 17–22.

Quinn, J. B. (1980). *Strategies for Change: Logical Incrementalism.* Homewood, IL: Irwin.

Quinn, R. E. (1988). *Beyond Rational Management: Mastering the Paradoxes and Competing Demands of High Performance.* San Francisco: Jossey-Bass.

Quinn, R. E., Faernan, S. R., Thompson, M. P., & McGrath, M. (1990). *Becoming a Master Manager: A Competency Framework.* New York: Wiley.

Raelin, J. A. (2000). *Work Based Learning: The New Frontier of Management Development.* Upper Saddle River, NJ: Prentice Hall.

Raelin, J. A. (2003). *Creating Leaderful Organizations: How to Bring Out Leadership in Everyone.* San Francisco: Berrett-Koehler.

Raphael, R. (1976). *Edges: Backcountry Lives in America Today on the Borderlands between Old Ways and the New.* New York: Knopf.

Robinson, W. (1925). Functionalizing a Business Organization. *Harvard Business Review,* pp. 321–338.

Roethlisberger, F., & Dickson, W. (1939). *Management and the Worker: An Account of a Research Program Conducted by the Western Electric Company, Chicago.* Cambridge, MA: Harvard University Press.

Rotman School of Management. (ca. 2005). *The Origin of Leaders.* Pamphlet, University of Toronto .

Rubin, S. E. (1974). What Is a Maestro? *New York Times Magazine,* September 29, pp. 32ff.

Sayles, L. R. (1964). *Managerial Behavior: Administration in Complex Organizations.* New York: McGraw-Hill.

Sayles, L. R. (1979). *Leadership:What Effective Managers Really Do . . . and How They Do It*. New York: McGraw-Hill.

Sayles, L. R. (1980). Managing on the Run. *Executive*, 6(3), 25–26.

Scase R., & Goffee R. (1989). *Reluctant Managers*. London: Unwin Hyman.

Selznick, P. (1957). *Leadership in Administration: A Sociological Interpretation*. Evanston, IL: Peterson.

Senge, P. M. (1990a). *The Fifth Discipline*. New York: Doubleday.

Senge, P. M. (1990b). The Leader's New Work: Building Learning Organizations. *Sloan Management Review*, Fall, pp. 7–23.

Senger, J. (1971). The Co-Manager Concept. *California Management Review*, 13, 71–83.

Service, E. R. (1962). *Primitive Social Organization:An Evolutionary Perspective*. New York: Random House.

Shartle, C. L. (1956). *Executive Performance and Leadership*. Englewood Cliffs, NJ: Prentice Hall.

Shimizu, R. (1980). The Growth of Firms in Japan. In *Empirical Study of Chief Executives* (pp. 173–194). Tokyo: Keio Tsushin Shuppan Sha.

Simon, H. A. (1969). *The Sciences of the Artificial*. Cambridge, MA: MIT Press.

Simons, R. (1995). *Levers of Control: How Managers Use Innovative Control Systems to Drive Strategic Renewal*. Boston: Harvard Business School Press.

Singer, E., & Wooton, L. M. (1976). The Triumph and Failure of Albert Speer's Administrative Genius. *Journal of Applied Behavioral Science*, 12(1), 79–103.

Skinner, W., & Sasser, W. E. (1977). Managers with Impact: Versatile and Inconsistent. *Harvard Business Review*, 55(6), 140–148.

Skolnick, A. S., & Skolnick, J. H. (1986). *Family in Transition: Rethinking Marriage, Sexuality, Child Rearing, and Family Organization* (5th ed.). Boston: Little, Brown.

Snyder, N., & Glueck, W. F. (1980). How Managers Plan: The Analysis of Managers' Activities. *Long Range Planning*, 13(1), 70–76.

Sproull, L., & Keisler, S. (1986). Reducing Social Context Cues: Electronic Mail in Organizational Communications. *Management Science*, 32(11), 1492–1512.

Stewart, R. (1967). *Managers and Their Jobs*. London: Macmillan.

Stewart, R. (1976). *Contrast in Management: A Study of Different Types of Managers' Jobs, Their Demands and Choices*. London: McGraw-Hill.

Stewart, R. (1979a). Managerial Agendas: Reactive or Proactive? *Organizational Dynamics*, 8(2), 34–47.

Stewart, R. (1979b). *The Reality of Management*. London: Pan Books.

Stewart, R. (1982a). *Choices for the Manager*. Englewood Cliffs, NJ: Prentice Hall.

Stewart, R. (1982b). A Model for Understanding Managerial Jobs and Behavior. *Academy of Management Review*, 7(1), 7–13.

Stewart, R. (1982c). The Relevance of Some Studies of Managerial Work and Behavior to Leadership Research. In J. G. Hunt, U. Sakaran, & C. A. Schriesheim (Eds.), *Leadership: Beyond Establishment Views* (pp. 11–30). Carbondale: Southern Illinois University Press.

Stewart, R. (1987). Middle Managers: Their Jobs and Behavior. In J. W. Lorsch (Ed.), *Handbook of Organizational Behavior* (pp. 385–403). Englewood Cliffs, NJ: Prentice Hall.

Stewart, R., Barsoux, J.-L., Kieser, A., Ganter, H.-D., & Walgenbach, P. (1994). *Managing in Britain and Germany.* New York: St. Martin's Press.

Stieglitz, H. (1970). The Chief Executive's Job—and the Size of the Company. *Conference Board Record*, 7 (September), 38–40.

Surowiecki, J. (2004). *The Wisdom of Crowds.* New York: Random House/Anchor Books.

Sussman, S. W., & Sproull, L. (1999). Straight Talk: Delivering Bad News through Electronic Communication. *Information Systems Research*, 10(2), 150–166.

Taylor, F. W. (1916). *The Principles of Scientific Management.* New York: Harper.

Teal, T. (1996). The Human Side of Management. *Harvard Business Review*, 74(6), 35–44.

Tengblad, S. (2000). *Continuity and Change in Managerial Work.* GUPEA, GRI Report, 2000:3. Göteborg University, School of Business, Economics, and Law.

Tengblad, S. (2002). Time and Space in Managerial Work. *Scandinavian Journal of Management*, 18(4), 543–565.

Tengblad, S. (2003). Classic, but Not Seminal: Revisiting the Pioneering Study of Managerial Work. *Scandinavian Journal of Management*, 19(1), 85–101.

Tengblad, S. (2004). Expectations of Alignment: Examining the Link between Financial Markets and Managerial Work. *Organization Studies*, 25(4), 583–606.

Tengblad, S. (2006). Is There a New Managerial Work? A Comparison with Henry Mintzberg's Classic Study 30 Years Later. *Journal of Management Studies*, 43(7), 1437–1461.

Terkel, S. (1974). *Working: People Talk about What They Do All Day and How They Feel about What They Do.* New York: Pantheon.

Thompson, J. D. (1967). *Organizations in Action: Social Science Bases of Administrative Theory.* New York: McGraw-Hill.

Trice, H. M., & Beyer, J. M. (1991). Cultural Leadership in Organizations. *Organization Science*, 2, 149–169.

Tsoukas, H. (2000). What Is Management? An Outline of a Metatheory. In S. Ackroyd & S. Fleetwood (Eds.), *Realist Perspectives on Management and Organization.* London: Routledge.

Tsui, A. S. (1984). A Role Set Analysis of Managerial Reputation. *Organizational Behavior and Human Performance*, 34, 64–96.

Vaill, P. B. (1989). *Managing as a Performing Art: New Ideas for a World of Chaotic Change.* San Francisco: Jossey-Bass.

Walgenbach, P., Ganter, H.-D., & Kieser, A. (1993). *Communication Problems of Cooperation across Different Business Systems: Lessons from a Cross-Cultural Study on Managerial Jobs and Behavior.* Paper presented at the European Business System Groups.

Wall, J. A. (1986). *Bosses.* Lexington: Lexington Books.

Watson, T. J. (1994). *In Search of Management: Culture, Chaos and Control in Managerial Work.* London: Routledge.

Watson, T. J. (1996). How Do Managers Think? *Management Learning*, 27(3), 323–341.

Weick, K. E. (1974a). Amendments to Organizational Theorizing. *Academy of Management Journal*, 17(3), 487–502.

Weick, K. E. (1974b). The Nature of Managerial Work (Book Review). *Administrative Science Quarterly*, 19(1), 111–118.

Weick, K. E. (1979). *The Social Psychology of Organizing* (2nd ed.). Reading, MA: Addison-Wesley.

Weick, K. E. (1980). The Management of Eloquence. *Executive*, 6(3), 18–21.

Weick, K. E. (1983). The Presumption of Logic in Executive Thought and Action. In S. Srivastva (Ed.), *The Executive Mind*. San Francisco: Jossey-Bass.

Weick, K. E. (1997). Book Review: The Challenger Launch Decision: Risky Technology, Culture, and Deviance at NASA. *Administrative Science Quarterly*, 42(2), 395–401.

Westley, F. R. (1990). Middle Managers and Strategy: Microdynamics of Inclusion. *Strategic Management Journal*, 11(5), 337–351.

Whitley, R. (1988). The Management Sciences and Managerial Skills. *Organization Studies*, 9(1), 47–68.

Whitley, R. (1989). On the Nature of Managerial Tasks: Their Distinguishing Characteristics and Organisation. *Journal of Management Studies* 26(3), 209–225.

Whitley, R. (1995). Academic Knowledge and Work Jurisdiction in Management *Organization Science*, 16(1), 81–105.

Whyte, W. F. (1955). *Street Corner Society*. Chicago. University of Chicago Press.

Wildavsky, Aaron. (1973). If Planning Is Everything, Maybe It's Nothing. *Policy Sciences*, 4(2), 127–153.

Willmott, H. (1984). Images and Ideals of Managerial Work: A Critical Examination of Conceptual and Empirical Accounts. *Journal of Management Studies*, 21(3), 349–368.

Wilson, E. O. (1971). *The Insect Societies*. Cambridge, MA: Belknap.

Winnicott, D. (1953). Transitional Objects and Transitional Phenomena. *International Journal of Psychoanalysis*, 34, 89–97.

Winnicott, D. W. (1955–1956). Clinical Varieties of Transference. *International Journal of Psycho-Analysis*, 37, 386.

Winnicott, D. W. (1967). Mirror-Role of the Mother and Family in Child Development. In P. Lomas (Ed.), *The Predicament of the Family: A Psycho-Analytical Symposium* (pp. 26–33). London: Hogarth.

Wolf, F. M. (1981). The Nature of Managerial Work: An Investigation of the Work of the Audit Manager. *Accounting Review*, 56(4), 861–881.

Wrapp, H. E. (1967). Good Managers Don't Make Police Decisions. *Harvard Business Review*, 45(5), 91–99.

Yu, K., Lu, Z., & Sun, Z. (1999). *A Comparative Study on Executives' Work Activities and Managerial Roles between China's Executives of State-Owned Enterprises and Their US Counterparts*. Paper presented at the Asian Academy of Management Conference, Kuala Terengganu, Malaysia, July 16–17.

Yukl, G. A. (1989). *Leadership in Organizations* (2nd ed.). Englewood Cliffs, NJ: Prentice Hall.

Zaleznik, A. (1977). Managers and Leaders: Are They Different? *Harvard Business Review*, May–June, pp. 67–78.

Zaleznik, A. (1989). *The Managerial Mystique: Restoring Leadership in Business*. New York: Harper & Row.

Zaleznik, A. (reprinted in 2004). Managers and Leaders: Are They Different? *Harvard Business Review*, 82(1), 74–81.

Index